MW00636303

I REFUSE TO QUIT!

I REFUSE TO QUIT!

The Autobiography of A Dreamer

Greg "Olskool Ice-Gre" Lewis

Library of Congress Cataloging-in-Publication Data is available.

ISBN 978-1-7352234-0-7 (Paperback)
ISBN 978-1-7352234-2-1 (Hardback)
ISBN 978-1-7352234-1-4 (ebook)

Scan the QR code to visit www.irefusetoquit.com for more information.

CONTENTS

PRAISE FOR GREG "OLSKOOL ICE-GRE" LEWIS

"Olskool Ice-Gre is the most upstanding human being that I know. He represents the pinnacle of good character. If everyone in the world had Greg's character, we would have world peace."

–Kanye West, Billionaire Christian Creative/Designer/Philanthropist

"Ice Gre has always brought something special to the table, from his artistry to the perspective use of his talents to elevate others. His influence is felt wherever he goes. I think his spirit shines through in all that he does and creates."

–Common, Grammy & Golden Globe Award Winning Rapper/Actor/Writer/Philanthropist/Activist

"There are certain types of people in the world that help it revolve: innovators, motivators and game changers. Olskool Ice-Gre has always been all of the above. You will never find a more generous, thoughtful, positive shaker than him. I've been blessed to witness his greatness and also learn from him throughout the years. And if you are ever blessed to get a moment with my brother you'll see and feel the energy I speak of."

-Deon Cole, Comedian/Actor/Comedy Writer

"Sometimes when you meet someone new you can't get a feel for them right away. When I met Chicago (Ice-Gre) in the gym, and spent time with him on our many weekend hiking trips, it was love at first sight— and I don't mean romantic. I mean his spirit and energy was so radiant you could not help but want to know more about him. He's a confident, caring, focused, enlighten, funny, bright and happy person who is always laughing. I knew we would get along."

**–Vanessa Bell-Calloway, NAACP Theater Award
Winning Actress/Director/Producer**

This book is about an amazing human being that helped to move a culture forward. One of my best friends. We call him Olskool Ice-Gre not just because he's old like me lol, but because his wisdom and loyalty stand the test of time.

–Coodie

Olskool Ice-Gre exemplifies what I consider the essence of a pure soul, embodying a persona of an individual whose heart is like a newborn yet to be jaded by life. Very few people are able to maintain this quality of innocence, but when you come across it you trust it because you know its intentions are good and like these pages, comes from a place of purity.

–Chike Ozah

**-Coodie & Chike, NAACP Award Winning Film Directors/
Screenwriters/Cinematographers/Producers**

"We live in a world where people often mistake activity for impact and confuse arrogance with accomplishment. In contrast to that, my brother Ice-Gre is someone who has had a tremendous impact on the culture but carried that power with humility that few in the entertainment business possess. The lessons contained within this book empower me and many others with a model for dreaming big and remaining focused that could be called "old school." But I look at it as simply the best way."

–Steve Pamon, Executive/Producer/Investor

"Ice-Gre and I share a similar story around the journey towards our personal success. We both know that the journey is not always a linear path. I Refuse to Quit! is a resilience story that reveals how Gre used his setbacks as building blocks towards his success. This book will serve as a guide for turning the roadblocks in your life into building blocks that can become highways to help navigate life's twists and turns."

**–David Banner,
Rapper/Producer/Actor/Activist/Philanthropist**

"I saw the trueness in Olskeezy (Ice-Gre)—the need to preserve the once forgotten art form and the need to keep it right rather than real. I felt almost obligated to lend myself to a true cause rather than some new cause. Ice-Gre is not here to appease the youth, but to teach the youth. I have not seen him without a smile on his face no matter what place in the race. That ability to smile in the face of adversity is remarkable. Olskool's positive attitude carried him all the way. There is something maybe only he knows that keeps him smiling."

–Special Ed, Hip Hop Legend/Rapper/Producer

"Ice-Gre is definitely a hustler. As long as I have known him, he has been on a constant grind. He was one of the first people I knew from Chicago who was making moves with legitimate record labels when the majority of us were just doing it locally."

–Don C, Designer/Licensed Brand Owner/Entrepreneur

"Greg 'Olskool Ice-Gre' Lewis is beyond a storyteller and a king MC. He is a curator of culture and an arranger of the soul's favorite theme songs. He is vital to art and music—its golden history and its promising future. During my own creative walk he has helped me make several benchmark moments happen. I'm forever grateful and will always have my ear close to the speaker."

–J.Ivy, Award Winning Poet/Author/Actor

"Positivity and empowerment is a word people are talking about more often these days. But a lot of people don't walk the talk. And, as a result, nothing gets accomplished. Ice-Gre walks every bit of the talk, all the while being an instrument of positivity and empowerment for himself and others. I admire his energy. Keep on energizing, my brother."

–Preston Glass, Multi-Platinum Award Winning Producer/Songwriter/Arranger

"Olskool Ice-Gre is one of the hardest working guys I've worked with, and it's been twenty plus years. He's always on top of his Game. If it wasn't for his grind, I wouldn't have become the top player that I've grown to be. They say you will be only as big as your teacher, and he taught a lot of us to be the best."

–Scrap Dirty, DJ/Radio Host/Entrepreneur

"Greg Lewis is the gold standard when it comes to excellence, integrity, and perseverance. He is encouraging and honest - both rare in the entertainment business. Solid!

–Garrard McClendon, Ph.D, Emmy Award Winning Media Host/Author/Professor (Chicago State University)

"I remember being a young woman and coming into a group of in-credibly fly gentlemen from the infamous strong city of Chicago and thinking, they carry the essence of their city on their backs. I remem-ber meeting Greg "Ice" and instantly feeling the most genuine family connection ever. His smile, his laughter and his way of telling a story would have you engaged in a conversation with him for hours with-out ever checking the time. One thing that I always recognized about him, which spoke to his character no matter what position in life he's in, is how he's always dedicated to taking care of the people around him and making sure they're at their best. They don't make 'em like G anymore; authentically connected, spiritually charged and dedicated to art in all its forms. A man whose sophistication supersedes the world around him. He can go back to his neighborhood in Chicago and be an example to the youth as well as come to Hollywood and inspire the best of them to be even greater. A true King in this generation and someone who will continue to carry our generation on his back."

–Miss Diddy, Brand Manager Entrepreneur/TV Personality/Lifestyle Specialist

"Olskool Ice-Gre brings his brilliant spirit as a performer, artist and humanitarian to everything he does. I am honored to call him a great collaborator and friend."

–Freddie Ravel, Motivational Maestro and Grammy-nominated Artist

This book is dedicated to my nephews Carson, Bryce and Walker. As I type this you are at the whimsical age of five, three and one years old respectively. My hope is that you guys are never more affected by the world around you than you are by the world you've created within you. What excites me most about your life is the fact that you have my sister as a mom. This alone puts a smile on my face because she's a woman who will leave room for you to explore whatever you conjure up in those beautiful minds. I want you guys to know you can talk to me about anything, especially your dreams because your uncle is an extremely optimistic, unapologetic dreamer. As you grow, you will meet people who will attempt to push their limitations on you, as well as sell you on their disbeliefs. But don't be fooled. Be respectful, be cordial and be attentive—but never be fooled! Your spirit can't afford to let the uncertainties of others affect your certainties.

This life is your video game, so play it well and become the best version of yourself. Trust me when I say no one can live the life the universe has designed specifically for you. So, follow your own path and heart even if it means traveling alone. When it comes to dreams most won't see what you see, but those who do will become allies. Collective energy produces amazing results, so don't be afraid of teamwork. But keep in mind, there's a thin line between selfishness and selflessness.

As you read the pages that follow, you will not only learn more about your uncle, but you'll also learn about the level of commitment it takes to make a dream reality. If there is any advice I could give, I'd simply say never be embarrassed or afraid to start over. And when you go, go all the way in! Love you nephews.

ACKNOWLEDGEMENTS

I want to start by giving thanks to God because I wouldn't have made it to this point without my belief and faith.

Next, I want to thank my mother who has stood by in support of me regardless of anyone's opinion or the decisions I've made; bad or good. Your prayers and belief mean the world to me.

To my extremely caring sister Angela "Mika" Taylor, aka Mosquito Bite. I'm so proud of you. Watching you juggle a full-time career and three boys like it's nothing exposed your superhero powers. I know where your heart is, and I know what you want. My prayer is that blessings flow continuously in your life. You deserve it all. I told you you'd be first lol.

To my aunt Sandra, you are one of a kind. There is no way to explain or express the level of love and respect I have for you in a few lines. You are above and beyond what most know an aunt to be. You bring understanding to the definition of family.

To my aunt Karen, I'll cherish what you and uncle Alvin did for me for the rest of my days. You believed and invested in me when my dreams seemed super farfetched to others. I've learned the meaning of true love watching you in life and in your marriage.

To my uncle Big Lee: I often say you and Sandra are the same person but, honestly, there is only one you. You have helped me through some of the most crucial times, and I want you to know I love you to life for it.

To my best friend since high school, Chill. Dude, you and I are so in tune that we go through the same things at the same time. It's scary. You are one of the most loyal, honest and supportive people in my life. Thank you, bro. Water is thicker than blood!

To my sis E.P, thank you for many years of love and lyrics. We made waves and touched people in ways I'm still learning about. Whether we pick up the phone one time or a hundred times to speak it doesn't weaken the relationship because, at this point, we're family.

To my very good friend and mentor Armers Moncure. Since we met, you have watered the seed of my entrepreneurial spirit. It's hard to find the correct words to express my appreciation, but I'll say this: I strive to be half as good as your presence has been in my life Q.

To my eternal spirit bro Kanye: wow, what a ride. The universe will not let our Libra and Gemini energy get too far apart for too long. Thank you for everything you've done and even more for the things you didn't do. To know you—like for real for real—is to love you. And brother, you have a lot of love in your heart. Let's continue to enjoy and create dope moments. You got a real one in me. Our brotherhood is in stone.

To my cousin-brother Kevin D. Burton. Your sudden and unexpected transition occurred during the final stages of the design and layout of this book. I wasn't prepared and honestly never would've been. You're part of the reason Olskool Ice-Gre exists, so your spirit will forever live inside my work. I love you, I miss you, rest well.

SPECIAL THANKS

I'd like to say thank you to the very concentrated team of individuals who put time, talent and energy into helping me complete this book. I'm relieved, overjoyed and grateful.

Lee Majors (Project Manager)
You liaised all of the business pertaining to this work, making sure all of my ideas and thoughts were properly realized and executed. Whether the required focus was offline or online the dedication you displayed during this process was recognized. We've teamed up to share good vibes with the world so many times it's only right that we let growth allow us to continue the process. I appreciate you cuzo, family first.

Cory Vicious (Graphic Design/Layout)
We've been creatively collaborating on projects together for a long time. Having you on the team again for the revised and refreshed version is even more special than the original. I say this because I'm aware you exercised a part of yourself one more time just for your boy. It was a lot of back and forth, as well as a few redo's but I know it'll all be worth it when the purpose of this effort is fully served. Gratitude brother.

Mike Quain (QUAINPHOTO)

Mike my man. We've been working a very long time. Since I made LA my residence you have been a go-to for all of my projects. I absolutely love the outcome of my cover shots. You are the man and someone I consider a very talented friend. One love.

One of the most important gifts bestowed upon humans is our ability to dream. I can still recall sitting in my grammar school classroom when the teacher asked, "What do you want to be when you grow up?" It was so exciting to see the expressions on the faces of my classmates, arms stretched to the skies frantically waiting to be called because everyone wanted to be the first to share their respective answer.

I always had a wildly creative answer: "the owner of the largest amusement park in the world" or "the owner of an extremely successful talent agency." Some of the other kids would say jobs like police officer, fireman, lawyer, doctor, nurse, astronaut, scientist or teacher. The most interesting answer to me was that one ambitious kid who would say, "I want to be the President of the United States." If you noticed I used the word "ambitious" because that's exactly how a child is viewed when they make a statement of that magnitude.

Fortunately, I was the imaginative kid who felt as if that kid's goal was actually attainable. As we grow, uncreative, pessimistic, negative people infiltrate our mental space in an effort to brainwash us into believing we have limits. As a child I never dreamed with limits. I believed the most unbelievable things were possible. And it's obvious this way of thinking is more forward, or we wouldn't have such remarkable advancements in the medical field and technology. So many industries are flourishing because of the overly ambitious kid who believes anything is possible. With the inception of social media, dreaming has almost become a lost practice. There was a time when socializing actually meant interacting with people you could touch. Don't get me wrong, I enjoy social media as much as the next person. But lately everyone—particularly our youth—has been living inside their cell phones literally hurting themselves to try and maintain a life they've created online. Fake has become the new real. It's unfortunate because there was a time when faking anything was unacceptable.

I grew up on the South Side of Chicago in the notorious Englewood community. As a child, I was told by statistics that my area had the highest crime rate in Chicago. I came up at a time when gangs ruled the street, not drugs. Although the two have been synonymous, the drug aspect didn't take precedence until later. I attended Charles S. Deneen Elementary and Chicago Vocational High School, both considered to be pretty rough public schools. I ran with some of the toughest guys on the South Side and didn't realize how "hood" my neighborhood was until I left to attend college. I call myself "a good guy from a bad block," which came from a joke my high school buddy Tommy used later in our adult life, about one of our boys named Sean. During one of our many "joke cracking" sessions, he said, "Sean lives on a good block in a bad neighborhood," and it was so funny we all fell to the floor laughing.

As I laughed, I began to think about how much that term really describes me—if the words were switched around. Being a creative, I found a way to breakdown and restructure that statement so I could use it as a moniker. The truth of the matter is, I've always been a good guy. I'd be lying if I said I never ended up in some of the scariest situations imaginable running with guys from the neighborhood but even they knew I was a good guy, which is why they were kind of overprotective when it came to me. I've always treated my close friends like brothers, probably because I grew up an only child. But what made them consider me a brother was my honesty and loyalty. Through the best and worst of times, they knew they could trust me, and I'd always tell them the truth, even if it temporarily interrupted our brotherhood.

More than anything, I pride myself on my friendships. Anyone who has connected with me, and gotten to know the person I really am, considers me one of their closest friends. In no way am I bragging, because it would be extremely corny and self-absorbed. I came to this conclusion based on observation, analyzing my real friendships as well as witnessing the results of my ways and actions. I've always been a loyal, honest, up front, no-nonsense, fun, respectful and real individual who is very comfortable being himself. I believe the easiest thing in the world to be is yourself. It sounds like a simple statement but in reality, it seems to be a very complex thing to execute. I've come in contact with countless individuals who refuse to be themselves. It's strange, but most believe we will like the person they create more than the person they are, which I feel is pretty asinine. As one of my animated childhood philosophers Popeye would say, "I yam what I yam and that's all that I yam."

I've never felt any pressure to live up to anyone else's standards, regardless of their financial status, influence or reputation. Peer pressure didn't exist to me. I can truly say I've been the most me I can be for the duration of my life, and others seem to respect, appreciate and even admire me for it. I definitely would have to credit my mother because she never fronted, or put on an act, as if we were better, doing better or living better than we were. So, I apparently adopted her style of being. I am my mother's only child, but she'll be the first to tell you that I wasn't the stereotypical only child. Although a few of my actions were typical of an only child, the majority of my ways were likened to that of a kid from a large, nuclear family. One of the traits that stood out most, and remains a constant in my life, is my willingness to step out on my own and take chances.

I believe I have taken more chances than the average person in my generation. Dreaming has been the catalyst for my desire to go wherever my beliefs take me. What's most intriguing about my travels is I've always done it alone, without the aid or influence of anyone or anything but my heart. A male only child is commonly labeled a "mama's boy" because he doesn't like to fly too far from the nest. My mother will tell you I broke that stereotype into a thousand pieces early on and continued the trend well into adulthood. Although, I will admit, the last ten to twelve years of my life have been great because I've come to appreciate the time spent in the same area as my mom. Change is good and should be welcomed.

Fortunately, I was blessed with a family who is very supportive and open, so adjusting to change has always come easy to me. Everything I've done, or currently doing is a direct result of accepting change. I'm stubborn in my beliefs but not in my realities. The biggest reality of all is that things will change, so adjust! I liken my approach as if I were a superhero. Superheroes refuse to be defeated and, if we are, it's temporary. A strategic plan is then devised in order to come back stronger. As we all know, the hero never loses! I've adopted this way of thinking as a lifestyle, and it keeps me motivated, as well as looking forward to another day. The secret to dreaming is looking forward to what's next. I refuse to believe that what happens next won't be better than what happened previously, because every moment is a fresh start. We can shape and mold each moment into whatever we want it to be. I've seen lives change in a matter of hours, so I'm convinced constant, forward motion is necessary if we want to receive our greatest reward.

Call me crazy but I believe dreamers are the all true and living. If you're living without a dream, you're walking dead! Achieving a dream gives us the ultimate satisfaction. If you doubt that statement, ask anyone who has accomplished anything based off of their passion, desire, persistence, hunger, focus or faith and listen to their response. I know from personal experience the level of satisfaction you feel from taking a thought to an idea, an idea to a plan, a plan to an action and an action to a desired result. It is truly the most euphoric feeling you can experience, outside of spiritual growth.

I find it amazing that dream killers still exist because the power of focus alone is so strong that it can cut through the thickest of doubt. I adopted several aliases as a Hip Hop artist but the one I embrace the most is "action." It took me several years to figure it out, but I am one of the few in my circle who have always put a plan into action. Whether the venture is successful or not, I always put forth the necessary action. As a matter of fact, I warn people who contact me for consulting services, or approach me with an idea that it may not be in their best interest to interact with me unless they're really ready to go all out.

Another thing I find amazing is how many people who want something for nothing! There are thousands of aspiring musicians, entertainers and athletes who are very talented that only want the end result. These individuals aren't willing to work part time, much less full time, on their craft. I've never been that guy. People have called me a lot of things, but the one thing they definitely can't call me is lazy!

If I had to express to you who I am in one sentence, I'd say: "I am a creative visionary who will inspire the world through music, art and entertainment, by being unafraid to take chances and go all-out for my dreams." The coolest part about this book is the original version was finished during one of the most pivotal and instrumental times in history. Barack Obama, a fellow Chicagoan from the South Side, became President of the United States. I'm sure several would like to believe the most exciting part about him securing a seat in the highest office was seeing a black man do it but that couldn't be further from the truth for me. Don't get me wrong, as a man of African descent, I was very happy to see a black man in office because it was a monumental accomplishment. In all honesty, I'd never exercised my right to vote until Barack Obama's run for office. I never believed politicians or fully understood politics and quite frankly I still don't. But I understood him when he spoke. For me, the most exciting part about Obama becoming President of the United States was seeing a fellow dreamer achieve the desired results against all odds. I felt his accomplishment would forever inspire the masses of children and adults who dream the impossible dream.

My goal, like most, is to be financially free. But my greatest desire is to touch you and free your thinking from the mental slavery forced on us by society since our youth. Hopefully, my personal experiences will motivate—as well as inspire and educate—you on your quest to becoming the greatest you. There are no tricks, lies or embellishments in the stories you're about to read. I assure you, all of the accounts shared in this book are God's honest truth. Those who know me will reminisce, recollect and, in several instances, be surprised and taken aback. To those who don't know me, let me introduce myself. My name is Greg "Olskool Ice-Gre" Lewis. I am a dreamer. And this is my autobiography.

CHAPTER 1

Music & I Meet

For as long as I can remember, I've been around music. As a child, I would sit next to my mother as she cracked open the latest album or twelve-inch record of whoever was hot at the moment. She would buy records at least two to three times a week but never listened to them until the weekend. Slim paper or plastic bags from a spot called Rose Records would be lying against the turntable, and I'd always slide them out and look at the cover art in amazement. I read what information I could and traced the font of the artists name with my finger. My mother stayed on top of all of the hits and she knew the words to every song. I vividly remember us sitting, legs folded on the shag carpet in the den of our apartment on 54th St and Ellis Ave in Hyde Park. We would sing songs together for hours. The coolest part was how she'd take my requests and play my favorite songs in between her own. To this day she says, "Remember when you were little how you used to ask me to play 'Strawberry Letter 22?'" It's funny because the title of the song is actually "Strawberry Letter 23," but as a kid all I knew was The Brothers Johnson were singing 22 so that was the title to me.

My biological father was a painter, carpenter and, most intriguing to me, a DJ. On several occasions he took me with him to the gigs or parties he would DJ. Most were during the day, but some were in the evening. I can recall sitting next to him in a smoky basement party where he would be spinning records. He was either really good or really good at playing what they wanted to hear, because people kept dancing and every now and then they'd high five or give a compliment on a record he played. It's funny, I had asthma and cigarette smoke drove me crazy as a child. But when I was around music, nothing bothered me. I would sit next to him the whole time while he worked the turntables, enjoying the reaction of the people when they heard their favorite song. The only time I would move was to get us some punch or whatever refreshment they had that I could drink. I know my mother is reading this in shock because I'm almost sure she doesn't know I used to be at parties with my old man. A few times he would say, "Don't tell yo mama I took you with me," and I'd keep it to myself to avoid an argument. Now that I look back on it, maybe I wasn't supposed to be there but for me those were good times.

The biggest and most significant musical influence in my life came from my own family. Almost all of the men on my mother's side of the family either play an instrument or can sing. My aunt Willisteen has five sons and all of them play an instrument. I spent the majority of my childhood, teenage and young adult years over at their house having jam sessions. One of the four upstairs bedrooms of the house was filled with instruments, amps, microphones, microphone stands, and a crate filled with all of the cords and adaptors necessary to make all of this stuff work. Whenever we talked about that particular bedroom, we referred to it as "the room." In the earlier jam sessions, I would sing backup and fake like I was playing guitar while my cousins really played.

As time progressed, I became interested in the drums, so my cousin Mane gave me a practice pad with an instruction book, and I practiced every day until I got my rhythm. Before I knew it, I'd graduated from faking the guitar, to playing the drums while singing backup. If you lived within earshot of the 5600 block of Shields, you knew where the music was coming from. We'd jam any day of the week for hours. But it really went down on the weekends. The people who lived or hung out on the block would gather outside the window, sit on the parked cars in the street, and just listen to us play for four hours straight.

We had all of the theatrics in "the room" to create that live concert feel. I'm talking colored bulbs, strobe lights, a smoke machine and lifts to give us that feeling of being on stage. Some of the best jam sessions were when we covered Prince and we'd go all out to look like The Revolution. My cousins had a closet right outside of "the room" that had several trench coats, blazers, scarves and hats. We'd pretty much play dress up whenever we portrayed Prince or The Time. We took those moments so serious that often times I thought I was in concert for real. It didn't help that the crowd outside would be interactive with us while staring up at the window, so it really felt like we were giving them a show. What was most exciting for me was the fact that my cousins were real musicians who not only played in church but also played weddings, graduations, receptions, cotillions and club gigs on the regular. I felt like I was a part of this family movement that was going to capture the music world like The Jacksons.

Seriously, "the room" was such an important part of my life that it even became the place to take girls when I started dating. If I met a young lady and wanted to show her a good time without worrying about money, I'd take her over to Kevin's and we'd go to "the room." Within an hour, Kevin would've taught the girl I was dating and her friends—when they tagged along—how to play simple melodies on the keyboard, synthesizer or tambourine. They would be so lost in the music they would forget we were upstairs in my aunt's crib. On more than one occasion, Kevin would call to tell me an ex-girlfriend stopped by just to say "hi," and often this would occur long after being involved with me. He would say, "She drove down the block, saw me on the porch, pulled over and talked and before you know it, she was up in 'the room' jamming." This became a regular thing for any male or female who spent time in "the room." The funniest situation of them all was when I came home for break after going away to college and saw one of my old flames had joined Kevin's band. We laugh about that to this day.

My aunt's house was also where I first got introduced to rap music and, odd as it may sound, not by any of my cousins who lived there. I was put on by my cousin Micah from Dayton Ohio, who came to Chicago and stayed with us for the summer. My biological father and mother never married, so through my stepfather I have an extended family that I was close with. Micah and I are either the same age or a year apart, so we had a lot in common. When he stayed with us for the summer, we hung tough, so wherever I went he was down to go. And most of the time that included a stop over my aunt's crib to hang out with my cousin Kevin in "the room." This one particular day Micah had a record with him that he said he was dying for me to hear, so he brought it with us to my aunt's. When we made it there, we went straight upstairs and he put the record on the turntable. What I heard changed my life. It was a 12" by Grandmaster Flash and the Furious Five. I was instantly drawn in by the voice of Melle Mel and the cuts from Grandmaster Flash. I wanted to learn more about this style of music. I was an instant fan; little did I know that two years later I would be creating the exact same thing.

Kevin was the youngest of the Burton brothers and closest to me in age, so we naturally gravitated towards one another. Although

I was tight with all of the Burton brothers, he was the one I hung with the most. We were together almost every day from my early childhood until I went away to school. It was "the room" where I learned everything from dance steps, the lyrics to the latest songs, timing, what to say to a girl, how to treat them, how and what to drink, drinking limits, different things about sex and just about anything that a young man needs to know. Kevin, his friends, his older brothers and their friends were all my big brothers. Now that I think about it, they were some very responsible guys because not one of them ever got in any trouble. And neither did I. I have to credit my big brothers for being a very positive influence in my life.

As my knowledge and understanding of music grew, so did my interest in rap music. This was about the same time the breakdance era hit Chicago. I was already poppin and interested in breakin' but my interest was piqued when my childhood best friend Corey, aka CoCo, pulled me into it.

Before he approached me, he'd already learned several breakdance moves from a guy named Pat who lived in our neighborhood. Pat would travel back and forth to New York City to learn new moves, practice and battle with his crew. CoCo started taking me with him to Pat's house regularly and he began teaching both of us all of the latest pop and break dance moves that he learned on the East Coast. He would also share stories about the various crews in New York and how seriously the artform was taken. Pat was one of the founding members of the Chicago chapter of a crew called The Floor Masters. He told us there were two crews from New York with Chicago chapters: Street Patrol and The Floor Masters.

We were pretty good by the time the breakdance era hit its peak and the movie *Breakin'* was released. We went to see the film and found ourselves in several victorious battles after it. I was a year or so into rapping at this point but still a bit apprehensive about letting it be known. My man CoCo heavily resembled one of the main characters in the movie named Turbo. So everyone kept calling him that. He and Turbo favored so much he even agreed that the dude could be his big brother, so he adopted the name Turbo Jr.

CoCo was poppin and breakin' all over the city wearing his trademark balloon baggies with Turbo Jr. on the back of all of his shirts. It wasn't long before everyone knew or heard about Turbo Jr. and his crew—which included me—who were known to smash crews downtown in Chicago, as well as in various parks around our neighborhood. We performed at block clubs, field house parties and our grammar school talent show, gaining more and more recognition.

Breakdancing was sweeping the nation and everyone we knew was into it but no one we knew was rapping. I was deep into rapping but kept it a secret. No one in my crew knew how serious or good I was until I decided to let it be known one day in the playground at Charles S. Deneen. Everyone circled around me as I freestyled about everything in the area. My friends and classmates went crazy. My nickname in grammar school was Gre-Gre, which was a play on the short version of my government name, Greg. So, as a rapper I decided to call myself Ice-Gre. I was a huge fan of Ice-T and back in the day "cold" or "ice" was a common prefix to use as a rapper, so I decided to call myself Ice-Gre. Since there weren't many people rapping at the time and breakdance was still the most popular element of the culture, I went with my heart and put all my energy into rap. I began working so hard on perfecting my freestyles that I stopped breakdancing.

By the time I reached the eighth grade, I was known as the premiere MC of my neighborhood. You could find me on the block and in the park freestyling for anyone who would listen. Everyone loved to hear me rap. They would always ask me to do it whenever there was a crowd and I always obliged. There were a few guys in my neighborhood who dabbled in rap but they hadn't quite mastered the flow, so they opted to play the back. I was confident. I was sure I was the best and no one in my neighborhood could touch me. I stood so strong in my belief that everyone else went along with it as well.

Summers in Chicago are great (extremely hot, but great!). Although gangs and gang violence were a huge problem during this era, it was a natural thing to learn how to maneuver through it. I grew up in the Englewood community on 72nd and Perry. Chicago is known for its park districts and the park was your connection to the hood.

I'll never forget Memorial Park, everything good and bad happened in that park. I literally lived across the street from the park, so it was nothing for me to spend half the day there. We had a fieldhouse with lots of activities, but there was no swimming pool. My friends and I loved to swim, so we were forced to walk four or five blocks west of Memorial Park to Hamilton Park. We always went six or seven friends deep because Hamilton Park could get rough and you wanted to have enough manpower if something went down. One day, my neighborhood buddy, Peanut, and I walked to Hamilton Park alone. I was rapping throughout the entire walk. Before entering Hamilton Park, you had to go under a viaduct. There was a guy walking ahead of us traveling in the same direction, who seemed to be moving slower as we approached.

I continued rapping, not worried or thinking at all, really. And before I knew it, this dude turned around, got right in my face and started rapping a verse with the ferocity of a lion, reminiscent of early LL Cool J. I was frozen in disbelief. This dude spit his best raps right in my face and I never said a word. My buddy Peanut, who was known to fight, realized what was going on and said, "What's up Gre, get him!" I said nothing. I just stood there, and the guy turned and walked away like nothing happened. All I could remember was he kept saying the names Top Dog and Double C in his rhyme, which clearly meant he was one of them and his partner or DJ was the other.

In that short second—which felt like an hour—I had just lost my first rap battle. I felt sick. I couldn't understand why I didn't say anything. My man Peanut laughed and joked about it all the way home. He and I lived around the corner from one another, so we pretty much walked each other home. I used to have a room that I fixed up in the basement of our apartment where I wrote my raps and listened to music. Later I learned that Top Dog and Double C were known names in the scene. So, I went to the basement after losing the battle and wrote like a maniac. I told myself I would never lose a battle again. I could've let the loss get to me. But **I REFUSE TO QUIT!**

The big Start

ONE day at home by my
self, didnt know what to
do just looking at the
shelf I look down I didnt want
to ep't then I said I can
Rap to the beat, the beat of
a drip the beat of a drop the
kind that makes your body
Rock so I thought of a team
a team of two we could
call our self the Awesome
2 crew, so I called my boy,
his Name was kid kool he
couldnt rap but wasent a
fool He said thats a good
Idea you what we can call our
friend mia we let her listen
to the beat she said you
know that beats to sweet
so my boy kid kool said
I can do this so he said it with
a little hiss. ⋯

I said man where did you
get that sound you know
that beat is all around
he said yea I know you
see we run the show
thats all I got to go. 6

big Start burrup   written
big big big Start   by ICE-Gre
                        & kid kool

Big Start: The actual manuscript of the very 1st rap I ever wrote ('83).
As you can see the beat box part was written in too...LOL

Me/

It was this girl here
name was Mel she made
me fill like I was in jail,
I ask her something she said no then
I said well I got to go
she got around her friends
she said I was crying all
I could say is thats she's
lieing I felt real bad I
dont wont to be sad so
I went to kid Kool like
I was glad, He said I know you
to long I know something wrong
Just listen to my beats to
go with your song, m! Smith

After the beats I felt
alright so we kept the
Rythm the Rythm all night.

me/ me/ me/ me/
MELENIe
Dont mess me!/

written
by Ice-Gre

The real manuscript of the 2nd rap I ever wrote. It was about a girl named Melanie who
turned me down when I asked her to be my girlfriend (written on back of Big Start)

10

My biological father Greg Lewis Sr. Djing one of the
many basement parties I attended with him as a kid.

My mom at the turntable

With Turbo Jr. during the
break dance era 83-84

CHAPTER 2

Music Follows Me to High School

The summer passed and school started again. It was 1985, my freshman year at Chicago Vocational High School, and I'll never forget it. I came to school looking like a hardcore B-boy. I wore a grey hooded Puma jogging suit with black and grey suede Pumas with grey fat laces. I was super comfortable my freshman year. CoCo, my best friend from the hood, was a sophomore, so I was solid with the upperclassmen. He told everybody I was his cousin, so I never experienced the stereotypical freshman antics. I may have forgotten to mention that CoCo was one of the roughest dudes I knew on the South Side. He would fight anybody, anytime, anywhere! What's funny about him was that he never started anything. But he wasn't the guy you wanted to start it with, because he always finished it.

I breezed through my freshman year like a seasoned veteran. During that year I tried my hand at graffiti but couldn't pull it off, so I stuck to rapping. It's funny because my biological father, my aunts and several of my cousins can draw but I've always been terrible. Hip Hop culture was really starting to develop, and rap music was becoming more of the focus. There were a few kids who rapped but none of them were outstanding.

One day I heard beats and rhymes coming out of the boy's locker room after gym class. As I sped up my walk to hurry and get in the locker room to see what was going on, I saw this guy banging a beat on the locker and another guy rapping. When the guy who was rapping stopped, the other guy started, and the first guy continued the beat. I was in awe but refused to let this opportunity pass. I slid in and got me a quick freestyle while the beat was still going. The locker room went crazy because they didn't expect me to rhyme but I did my thing, and received handshakes and high-fives from everybody.

As we were walking out of the gym one of the guys introduced himself as Anthony, shook my hand and said I was dope. I told him he was nice too, and we went about our way.

By the time I got to my six-period drafting class, everyone was already seated. As I scanned the room, I noticed a hand in the air motioning for me to come over. It was Anthony. It was in drafting where he and I learned how much we had in common. We quickly learned our biggest commonality was our love for rap music. Between gym and drafting class, Anthony and I forged a friendship that grew into a brotherhood by our junior year. We were both huge fans of a rapper named Just-Ice, who would always end his songs by screaming "peace," so that became the way we'd end all of our conversations. At this point I'd decided I wanted to pursue a career in the music industry and Anthony was on the same page, so we became a group. The only problem was we didn't have a name.

One of our classmates named Jason Garrett was the guy who ultimately gave us our name. We were all in the same English class and he used to listen to us rap in the back of the classroom. He said "y'all are always screaming peace so why don't you call yourself Peace Posse?" We thought it was perfect, so we rolled with it. Anthony didn't have a stage name, so I dubbed him Ant-Chill. Since my stage name plays off my real name, I did the same with his, except I added Chill because that was what I heard the dude that rapped with him in the locker room call him. I thought it had a nice ring to it, and everybody else agreed, so he went with it even though he didn't like it at first.

Chill and I became the most known rappers in school. We would rock rhymes before and after class, for our teachers, in the halls, at lunch, in the bathrooms, outside and in gym class. We started sharing a locker that happened to be in the center of the hall on the second floor which was the most active area in our high school. We had everything in our locker; mirrors, cologne, gum, hairbrushes, lotion and, most importantly, a speaker.

One of my buddies spliced the wires to a pair of headphones and connected it to the speaker wire, which allowed us to plug it into a Walkman cassette and play instrumentals through the speaker for us to rap over. In between classes, or before our lunch period, we'd give mini concerts. We didn't eat lunch often because we spent most of our lunch periods in the library reading the thesaurus and dictionary, learning new words. Rap was all about being intelligent and witty with your word usage or wordplay and we wanted to be the best that ever did it. I'll never forget the two librarians who were fond of us. They would keep two dictionaries and two thesauruses to the side, just for us. We made use of those books like no other students in the school.

Our first talent competition was at a banquet hall called The Hummingbird on 86th and Ashland. We called ourselves casual Hip

Hop because Chill and I performed in slacks and a dress shirt. By this time, our group consisted of a DJ and a few dancers. The stage at the Hummingbird was big and we used every inch. We had four dancers and a DJ, so we were all over the place. The crowd loved our energy and gave it up to us. We took second place, but you would've thought we took first by our excitement. To us it wasn't really about placing, we just wanted to perform. The funny thing is, later, we found out that two of the judges were friends with the guys who took first place, so we kind of got cheated, but again we didn't care.

The special guest performer was a female rapper by the name of Lady Jane. After she performed, she approached us and said she thought we were really talented and gave us an invitation to sit in on her upcoming studio session. We had never been to a studio, so we couldn't wait to experience it. My cousin Lazy Lee, who was a dancer and part of the crew, always had access to a vehicle so we all jumped in his father's minivan and headed to a studio, which was located on the North Side of Chicago. Lady Jane was recording a song where she had someone re-sing New Edition's "she got it going on" vocals from their single "N.E. Heart Break." She asked us to record the ad-libs, so we were extremely excited. That experience let us know we had to get in the studio and record.

The day we met Lady Jane, we also met a guy who founded a talent production company called T.O.M.A Productions, which was an acronym for Temple of Music Association. We later joined the company. Chill and I were down to do whatever it took to make our dreams come true and we weren't afraid to work. T.O.M.A would have weekly or bi-weekly meetings above a storefront on 79th & Halsted. Me, Chill, and our DJ, D-Trayne, would attend every single meeting. The guy talked to us about the basics of recording and music production. They also had a rehearsal area for artists to practice their live shows that was open for us to use.

The biggest thing they did was put us in a talent showcase on the Southside that was being held at a Masonic lodge on Ashland. At the showcase, there was another special guest performer named Rappin Tate the Great who was a big name locally. After our performance, Tate told us he liked our style and wanted to take us on tour overseas. Our eyes opened as big as saucers, and we smiled like we had won the championship. I told him we never been overseas and would love to go. But, of course, nothing ever came of this. But the idea of it all seemed so exciting at the time.

There were several local acts in T.O.M.A Productions but we were the standout act. We didn't stay with the organization long because they were an upstart and couldn't do much more than we were already doing for ourselves. I enjoyed all of the exciting moments and really believed all of the promises made to us. But even early on I was extremely determined, so even though T.O.M.A, Tate and several others did nothing to advance my career **I REFUSE TO QUIT!**

One of the best relationships we built as Peace Posse was with a radio personality by the name of Pink House, who had a college radio show called *Rap House* on WKKC 89.3FM. Pink House thought our group's music was great so he gave us an invitation to hang out with him at the station on a weekly basis. There were several of Chicago's most notable artists and crews there during this period, such as Ill State Assassins, Ten Tray Posse, Proper Posse, DA Smart, Sundance and more. Pink House wanted us to get in the mix and meet the movers and shakers of the city, and that's exactly what we did. We talked, freestyled, kicked verses, exchanged numbers and talked about each other's music. I would always thank Pink House when I'd run into him at Harold's Chicken Shack on 71st and Wabash.

A radio personality named Ramonski Luv gave us a lot of love and support on his show called the *Rap Down* on WGCI as well. Often times he would give Peace Posse a shout out in the middle of his show, which really helped make us a known name in the city.

One of my buddies from the neighborhood, who also had serious dreams of a rap career, plugged me with a situation. It was just another day in the hood, and I was playing basketball in Memorial Park when my man walked up to the fence and called me over. He told me he had a situation for me, if I were interested. He said Farley "Jackmaster" Funk was putting together a Hip House compilation and needed more artists, so he told him about my group. It was 1989 and Hip House music was huge. He said if I'm serious about the opportunity, call Farley and say, "I'm a member of the group MC Zone told you about" and he'll take it from there. I almost didn't believe Zone because Farley was a superstar House DJ and some-one I never imagined being able to just call. Well, of course I didn't hesitate to run home and call the number and, just like, he said Farley answered. I told him what I was supposed to tell him, and he gave me an address, date, time and said he's looking forward to meeting us.

I couldn't wait to tell Chill the good news. I called him and gave him the play-by-play of how it all went down. The first thing he said was "dude you're lying" in his signature I-can't-believe-it tone. I think we were scheduled to go to Farley's studio on a Friday because I don't recall going to school the morning after. We didn't have access to a car that day, so D-Trayne dropped us off but couldn't stay because he had something to do for his grandmother. Farley's studio was in the basement of his parents' house on 95th St, in a very nice neighborhood called Evergreen Park. We could tell his parents had money based on the location and size of the house. I grew up in the Englewood community and Chill in Jeffery Manor, so this neighborhood was 180 degrees from our normal surroundings. Anyway, we stepped on the porch, rang the bell and an older gentleman answered the door. We let him know who we were, who we came to see, and he politely introduced himself as Farley's Dad and directed us to the basement.

When we made it downstairs, we were amazed at the set up. His studio had just as much equipment as the one we visited with Lady Jane on the North Side of Chicago. We couldn't believe how state-of-the-art this facility was. Again, this was only our second time experiencing a real recording studio, outside of the makeshift set-up D-Trayne had in the basement of his grandmother's apartment. We looked through the glass that separated us from the control room and saw a tall, dark figure motioning us to come over. When we walked into the area, we couldn't help but smile. Farley stood up, reached out to shake our hand and said, "Peace Posse." Together we said "what's up" like two excited kids who just met their first superstar.

You gotta understand, this was Farley "Jackmaster" Funk! During this period, the man was a well-known celebrity in Chicago. Today, he is respected and heralded as a legendary DJ, producer and godfather of house music. We didn't know what to expect but we knew whatever it was, we were ready. The meet-and greet-quickly came to a close. Our excitement subsided, and Farley got right down to business.

The first thing he asked us was if we were familiar with Hip House music. We replied, "yes, but we've never made anything but Hip Hop." He said, "that's cool as long as you have rhythm and good timing—the recording process is all the same." He played the track he wanted us to write and record to as well as explained that it will be remixed, so the final version wouldn't sound anything like what we just heard. He said he had a surprise for us that we were going to love. We said "cool" and got a cassette copy of the track. He asked how long we needed to write, and we told him we'd be finish with it in a couple of hours. He laughed, then told us to come back next Saturday to record. Of course, we left Farley's studio extremely excited, reliving the whole thing as we walked to 95th St. where D-Trayne was picking us up at the bus stop.

Chill and I got back to the crib and start working on the song immediately. Although we'd never wrote a Hip House song, House music is our foundation and just like Farley said, it was easy. The reference track he gave us had a nice bounce to it. It was one of those minimalistic beat-driven House tracks producers made for their tapes that circulated around the city. It had a really nice rolling bassline which made it very easy for us to rap to. I came up with the hook "It's time to party," which naturally became the title of the song. I believe we practiced the song five hundred times or more. When we returned to Farley's studio the following weekend, I knocked my verse out in one take and Chill in two. Farley was blown away by our efficiency. He was so impressed and happy with our delivery and energy, he told us he got what he needed and that we were done.

It was our senior year of high school and my school was holding auditions for the senior talent show. Mrs. Richardson, who every upperclassman loved, was the teacher who organized the talent show every year. But this year she had other obligations, so the duties were passed on to Mr. Lynn. We viewed this as an opportunity to finally showcase our music for our classmates in an organized setting, so Peace Posse entering the talent show was a no brainer. Everybody expected to see us, and we really wanted to be a part of the show. Auditions were held in a classroom on the third floor after ninth period, which was before the last period of the day. Seniors didn't really have a tenth period class, so the schedule was perfect.

Chill and I entered the room and all of our peers who were considered "the talented seniors" were laughing and talking so the atmosphere was extremely comfortable. We signed the list and waited for Mr. Lynn to call our name. Some six or seven acts down the line we heard "Peace Posse" and took our position in the middle of the room. He asked what we will be doing, and we said "rapping." The room filled with cheers and wisecracks because everybody except Mr. Lynn knew who we were. He asked what song we will perform, and we told him one of our own and gave him a cassette with our music. We were in rare form, so much so that Mr. Lynn stopped the tape on the second verse and said, "Peace Posse is in!" He couldn't believe how good we were and felt that we deserved to be a part of the show on originality alone. We left the room receiving hugs and high-fives.

I went home, got on the phone and shared the info with the rest of the fellas. By this time, Peace Posse was more than just a group, we were a crew. Peace Posse the group consisted of Ant-Chill, DJ D-Trayne and me. Peace Posse the crew consisted of Virgil K-ool, who was my best friend from seventh grade; Chill's cousin Hasson; a female rapper I grew up with named Destiny; and my cousin Lazy Lee. Peace Posse the crew was a musical family with members who were friends and actual family, so it was easy to keep each other in the know of everything that took place involving the crew. A few days later a list of names that made the cut to perform in the senior talent show was posted. Chill and I—along with several other seniors—crowded around the list looking for our name. As I slid my finger down the piece of paper, I noticed Peace Posse was not on the list. We were confused and didn't understand what was going on being that we received automatic entry just a few days ago. As the school day came to an end we hustled quickly to the auditorium where practice was being held, took a seat and waited to speak with Mr. Lynn.

When we finally saw him, he seemed to be in disarray and very upset about how unorganized practice was going. He grabbed the mic and started shouting, "this is no time to play, you are supposed to be practicing your performance for the show, not running around acting a fool like you're not upperclassmen. If you hear me call Peace Posse, I need Peace Posse to come to the stage!" Now I'm sitting there in disbelief because he just used my group as an example which meant he doesn't remember cutting us out the show. We approached the stage and asked if we could speak to him for a moment. He said, "OK" and asked us, "What's up?" We told him we were the Peace Posse, the only group he decided was in the show because we did an original song and that we were not on the list. He said, "Yes, there were too many acts and we had to make cuts, but I don't think you guys were cut." He then looked at the roster, ran his finger down the page then looked back at us and simply said, "Wow, I guess you were cut." We asked: "Is that it? Are we really out of the show just like that?" And he said, "Yes." At that moment, I felt like things couldn't get any worse.

The next day word had gotten around the school that Peace Posse was unfairly cut from the senior talent show. Several students from the junior and senior class decided they were going to boycott the show in our honor. Although we were flattered by the support of our fellow Cavaliers, we told them not to do it because all of the students in the show were our friends. Plus, we were still going to go. Once they saw we were cool with it, everything went back to normal. I can't recall how it happened, but we were approached by a few of the seniors who were in the show who said there was room for us to get in the finale performance of Stop the Violence Movement's "Self-Destruction." But we kindly turned down the offer. In no way were we being stubborn, we just couldn't break the MC code and perform another rapper's lyrics on stage. Chill and I were true to the game and saying someone else's rhymes wasn't our style. We did attend the senior talent show and, needless to say, it was great. But I'd be lying if I said I was happy with how we were handled. That was a hard blow and I could've let it kill my drive or lower my self-esteem, but I **REFUSE TO QUIT!**

Peace Posse recording session 88-89
(In DJ D-Trayne's basement)

Peace Posse 88-89

Peace Posse Crew L to R:
Me, DJ D-Trayne, Virgil K-ool & Kenya

Peace Posse (The Group) 88-89

Peace Posse 89: We called our style Casual Hip Hop

Peace Posse 89: Casual Hip Hop

TOMA Productions Flier

CHAPTER 3

The Dream Gets a Higher Learning

I graduated high school in May and got accepted to Jackson State University and Southern Illinois University, the school Chill and I planned to attend together. I had to make a quick decision; I was starting college in the fall of 1989. I had been saying I was going to go to Jackson State University ever since I was a sophomore in high school because my cousin Lazy Lee was already a student at the university and kept pushing for me to attend. I used to wear JSU buttons and shirts before I ever really saw a college campus.

Now it's my senior year, and my mind was made up. SIU was the smart choice being that Chill and I are Peace Posse and we were planning to do big things. The only problem was I couldn't shake the visions of the black college experience that I witnessed the few visits I made to JSU's campus. Everything seemed so exciting. All I could think of was Lee introducing me to people, telling everyone I was his cousin and how I would be attending JSU. Everybody was super cool saying things like, "We're going to hold you down" and "Lee's family is my family." I'd never been to SIU but something inside told me I was the HBCU type, so I chose Jackson State University when it was all said and done.

I can remember my first day on the yard like it was yesterday. Every one of Lee's friends knew I was a rapper and heard stories about how good I was. I was immediately accepted like family and my skills were quickly put to the test. One of Lee's buddies Troy, who later became a close friend of mine, stood on a hill in front of Steward Hall dormitory and said, "If anybody can out flow my man Ice-Gre, I'll pay them." All of a sudden, a short, dark skinned guy walked past wearing a jogging suit and headphones. He was rapping to himself. He then stopped and said, "I can take him." Everybody started making a bunch of noise, causing a scene. Before I knew it, there was a huge crowd around us waiting to see a battle.

We introduced ourselves: he said his name was Tricky Snake, and I told him I was Ice-Gre. All I could think about was the time Top Dog let me have it under the viaduct entering Hamilton Park, so I was ready. He said his verse—which was pretty nice. Then I said my verse which had several wittier lines and much more wordplay than his, so the crowd went crazy. He tried to come again but I said an even better rhyme and the reaction of the crowd was so exaggerated this time he accepted defeat. He put his head down, smiled, shook my hand and told me I was dope. He said, "I'm from Chicago, too. So at least I lost to somebody from the crib." He and I became friends after that. It was my first day on campus and the word spread quickly. In a few short minutes, I had established myself as an MC from Chicago that you didn't want to battle.

Later that semester I entered the freshman talent show that was being held in the school's auditorium. I had become very tight with Troy's younger brother, Aaron, who was a freshman as well. His brother and my cousin were already boys, so he and I bonded quickly. It wasn't long before I found out he could dance and needed to utilize his skills.

I made up a routine to go with my song that he and Lee learned. They were the dancers for my first official performance at JSU. Remember, I was the new kid with the buzz, so everyone was looking forward to seeing me get down, especially the freshman class who that year had the largest enrollment in the school's history. Lee was already a dancer with Peace Posse, so he was used to learning routines. But Aaron, surprisingly, didn't take long catching on and memorizing the steps. We decided on a name for the dancers: The Shake Yo Ass Posse. We were being funny, but we knew we couldn't use profanity in the show so I decided it would be best to refer to them as S.Y.A.P on stage to avoid any problems. I had several quality instrumentals to choose from so I knew our sound would be great. When we hit the stage, the bass was hitting hard, the mic was clear and S.Y.A.P was in rare form. Since I made up the routine it was nothing for me to jump in and out of the dance moves between my verses which made the crowd go crazy. We were doing moves similar to how Big Daddy Kane or Heavy D would do with their dancers. I can't recall if there was a winner, or if the show was just for the freshman class to get to know each other, but either way I made my presence felt.

In the spring semester I changed my major from computer science to mass communications. The only reason I was a computer science major to begin with was because it had been drilled into my head since high school that computers was where the money was. So, I picked it as a major. However, I quickly found out just how much I disliked programming when I hit campus.

I spent most of my time focusing on school that semester, but an interesting thing happened when I went home for summer break.

My cousin Lee picked up a summer job through a security company that had him stationed at the Chicago convention center, McCormick Place. Summers in Chicago are a very active time for festivals and conventions, and for this particular summer, the sporting expo was being held. The event lasted a few days, and Lee kept telling me I should come up there and check it out. He figured I'd love it because they were showcasing all of the upcoming lines from several of our favorite brands. One day, Lee happened to be perusing the booth of a sporting apparel company called The Game and made a few comments about the graphic design on one of their t-shirts. A marketing executive by the name of Jill was so intrigued by what he had to say, she asked if he'd be interested in sitting on a creative panel where he could share some of those ideas with the executives of the company. Jill then told him he was welcomed to bring a friend, and everyone would receive free clothes for their time. At that point Lee was sold.

The first and only person he presented the opportunity to was me. All I could think of was getting a fresh hat or t-shirt to wear when I perform. The panel was held at one of the really nice hotels downtown. When we arrived, there were already a few people there socializing, so we spoke and shook a few hands. Once Jill saw Lee she immediately walked over, and he introduced me. She was a kind, spirited woman with a lot of energy. She seemed very happy that Lee and I showed up. Things began to tone down, and Jill opened up by introducing herself and explaining to everyone our purpose for being there. The vibe was very loose and no-nonsense, so they immediately began pulling out products and asking how we felt about particular pieces.

Some people had a few things to say while others were quiet. But Lee and I had a lot to say. This was our world and we wore this style of clothing, so we gave our input on just about every piece Jill and the guys put in front of us. It was to the point where the other people on the panel waited to hear what Lee and I had to say before they spoke. Before we knew it, the entire room was more into our ideas than their own. They seemed to enjoy listening to us breakdown how a design should be or what should be removed from a graphic. When the panel was over, they told us we could pick out any hat and shirt we wanted. My initial pick was a Georgetown Hoyas bucket cap that turned out to be a one of a kind demo, so I couldn't take that one. When I found my pick, I looked at Lee and said, "I'm going to rock this at our next show." At that point Jill became very interested in my comment and asked, "What do you do?" I told her I was a rap artist and I'm always performing so the hat and t-shirt will come in handy. She asked if she can hear me rap. I was always ready to rhyme so I switched into Ice-Gre mode and kicked a verse. The entire room applauded. I saw the look of amazement in Jill's eyes as her head turned back and forth between me and the faces of her business associates. She immediately pulled Lee and I in another room and said, "I want you guys to come to the Sporting Expo in Atlanta. Do you think you can make it? There are a few people I'd like you to meet." We told her we were students at Jackson State University in Mississippi so coming to Atlanta wouldn't be a problem at all. She then asked me to write down all of my information including my birthday. She said she would be in touch. I had no idea what was in store, but Lee and I enjoyed being involved.

Summer break was cool and my first year went by pretty smoothly. I made a bunch of new friends, and I was living the black college experience to the fullest. Now it's fall semester of my sophomore year, and I felt it was time to get actively involved with the events going on in Jackson. So, I started out on my quest to meet the tastemakers of the city.

The first thing I noticed before I ever entered the campus was a radio station on the corner before you hit the grounds of JSU. The name of this station was WJMI, and it was the number one station in Jackson. Everyone in the city listened to the station, including me. I heard a commercial run about a talent show they were sponsoring, so I took it upon myself to walk in and find out more information. Mind you, I am down south so the people were extremely polite and cordial. I'm laughing as I write this because I walked inside of the station like I was supposed to be there. I asked about the talent show. I was told I needed to speak to a guy named Alton Palmore. So, I waited as they called him. He came to the front and shook my hand as he introduced himself. I told him I was Ice-Gre, a rapper from Chicago attending Jackson State, and I wanted to know what I had to do to enter the talent contest. He asked if I had a demo, and I said, "Yes, but not on me now." He advised me to come back to the station with my demo and drop it off to him.

The next day, around the same time, I went to the station as instructed and dropped off a Peace Posse demo with my contact information. Less than a week later, I received a message on my answering machine saying they liked the demo and we were in the contest. I was so excited, I barely finished listening to the message before I called Chill. Unfortunately, he couldn't make it down south, so I was forced to perform solo.

A week passed and it was now the weekend of the contest. I had on my Chicago Bulls t-shirt, red Gap shorts, gold-framed glasses and a pair of all red Ellesse. I thought I was fresh to death. To top it all off, I had my hair in locs, but only on one side of my head. The contest was being held at Lake Hico Park on the North Side of Jackson. It was an extremely hot day, but I was ready to do my thing. A few of the acts were well known in the area. Two in particular were an R&B group named M.I.S.S and a rap group called Wildliffe Society, but I wasn't sweating either. I watched each group ahead of me attentively, mentally critiquing everything from their performance, to their crowd control, to their delivery. I was the last act. I felt confident that I could win and didn't feel any pressure from my competition. So, when the host Alton Palmore introduced me, I grabbed the mic with LL Cool J-confidence. I put on a pretty good performance, despite not having my partner, dancers or DJ. The audience showed me love but, in the end, it was a runoff for first place between M.I.S.S and a duo comprised of a singer and a rapper named Total Chaos—with Total Chaos winning the tie-breaking performance.

I felt as if there was no way I could win being that I was from out of town. All of the groups were either from Jackson, or had members in their group from Jackson, except me. Plus, it didn't help that the host cracked a joke about me possibly lying about being from Chicago when he introduced me, which brought more attention to the fact that I wasn't from Jackson. I have to admit, Total Chaos had a complete show with singing, rapping and dancing, so I could see how the crowd favored them. But to this day I wonder what made them turn "Mary Had a Little Lamb" into a rap song. The show ended peaceful, with all of the acts showing each other respect.

Later, I was approached by a guy named Vinnie G, saying he had a record label called Ocean Blue Records and that he was interested in signing Peace Posse. We exchanged numbers, and my crew and I went about our business. I had a little communication with the Ocean Blue Records guy after that day and we planned to get together, but it never happened. After a few unsuccessful attempts on my end I stopped reaching out. Plus, it was time for us to go home for one of the many breaks we get as college students.

For the Chicago students, the most convenient, and regular, means of transportation was Amtrak. Those fifteen-hour train rides created some of the most interesting stories of my college experience. On this particular ride home, Lee and I had a bag full of snacks and libations for the trip. As we waited for the train, this woman expressed out loud how she forgot to pick up something to sip for the train ride. We told her, "Don't sweat it, we have enough to go around." She smiled and said, "I'm hanging with y'all." For those of you who've never ridden the Amtrak as a college student, or with college students aboard, you wouldn't understand. The way it works is, once the train gets moving, they open the bar car which is like a cafeteria, and all of the students traveling hang out there for the majority of their ride. In the bar car you'll see tables stuffed four deep with serious games of spade, dominoes, checkers, chess and siggin.'

At our table, I pulled out the radio and popped in a beat tape and started freestyling. Students from other tables came over to get closer to the action. We had a nice crowd around our table, and I was the center of it all. But there were a few others who kicked a verse or two. The surprise of the night happened when, out of the blue, the woman who we gave an invitation to drink with us jumped in the cipher and kicked a serious verse. The entire bar car went crazy because she had an incredible flow. I immediately asked her name and she said Daphne. I said, "Wait a minute, you're the girl that everybody on campus has been telling me about." She then asked my name. And when I told her she said, "This is wild because everybody's been telling me I got to meet Ice-Gre."

We instantly clicked, and the drinks and rhymes flowed for the next five or six hours. She shared with me that she was trying to decide between two stage names: Ebony Poetress and The Female Messiah. She asked which one I thought was best. I suggested she use both. I told her she could call herself Ebony Poetress the Female Messiah. She loved it and said, "That's my new name." When the libations finally came to an end and the talk and laughter decreased, we began to head to our seats to get some much-needed rest. Later that morning, as we exited the train, I told Ebony Poetress to call me so we could speak more about what we had spoken about the night before, which was her becoming a member of Peace Posse. She promised she would. We said our goodbyes and headed for our bags. Over the break E.P—the name we gave her for short—and I became really cool, so I introduced her to the entire crew. I told them my intentions about putting her down with Peace Posse and, after hearing her skills, they all agreed that she would be a great addition to the crew. My position at that point was to give E.P direction and help groom her as an artist. I was able to do this because I was exposed to a lot more than her in regard to live performance, the proper structure for writing a verse and studio recording.

One of the coolest moments for Peace Posse happened during our first visit home as college students. The Hip House record we recorded with Farley came out and it was getting heavy rotation on our main radio station WGCI and the number one college station, WKKC. At this point, we were made aware of the surprise Farley spoke about. Being that our name was Peace Posse, he put our rap vocals over a very popular House record called "Smoking on a Peace Pipe." We thought it was a pretty creative idea and felt really good about being on the record. We called Farley and told him we keep hearing the record on the radio. He advised us to go to a record store on the West Side because they have a couple of copies of the record waiting for us. We felt like stars and couldn't believe someone actually had records waiting for us to pick up.

The record store he sent us to turned out to be the world-famous George's Music Room. Back then it wasn't in the location that made it famous. But, as always, George was there, and he knew exactly who we were when we said Farley sent us. At that moment we didn't realize we were in the presence of a soon-to-be legendary independent retailer.

Remember, we were college students, which meant we were out of school before high school students, so we went back to Chicago Vocational High School with our records in hand. We had just graduated a few shorts months earlier so the majority of faculty, staff and students were excited to see us and were very proud of our accomplishments. We walked through the halls showing the record to all of the junior and senior class because most of them knew or remembered us. Of course, Chill and I went to the library to show our favorite librarians the results of them holding those thesaurus and dictionaries for us. We also showed our English teacher that we actually did something with our talent, besides drive her crazy rapping in the back of class. We also had to drop in on Mrs. Richardson's class. She introduced us to her class and explained what we did and our accomplishments. The person we wanted to see the most was Mr. Lynn because we were still sore about him cutting us from the senior talent show. We wanted to rub our record in his face so he could know the mistake he made in being so careless and nonchalant in the cutting process for the talent show. I guess our vindictive thoughts worked against us; Mr. Lynn wasn't at work that day. We spent a couple of hours at our old school then headed back to the hood to catch up with our DJ.

The funny thing about the Farley situation was we never made any money because we never signed any paperwork. Although we had a popular song that got heavy rotation in our city, and became a hit overseas, it did nothing for our career. To this day, some remember the Hip House song where the guys rapped over "Smoking on a Peace Pipe," but they have no idea that one of the guys rapping is me. It was a letdown to make it to a point of actually having a real record released, but not experiencing a positive shift in our career or financial status. Situations like these make some of the most talented artists and musicians hate the music business and give up on their dreams. But **I REFUSE TO QUIT!**

Things really started to pick up when I returned to JSU for the spring semester. I began performing in various talent shows and contests as a solo artist representing Peace Posse. I would always lose to a local act, regardless of how good I was. Rapping wasn't as respected as singing at the time, so really good singers could easily beat a really good rapper. I always lost to this local singer by the name of Eddie Seawood.

Seawood had a great voice and he'd always cover the hottest R&B song of the moment and win over the crowd. He and I became friends through the competition, and we would both laugh, smile or point whenever we saw each other at shows. We both had this "not you again" thing going on, but in a respectful way. We both knew the only competition we had was each other. I must've lost to Eddie Seawood a thousand times, or at least it felt that way. The moment of truth finally came for me and it was much more than I expected. Jackson State University held a talent show in the music building called the JSU Apollo. The rules and theme of the show were exactly like the Apollo Theater in Harlem New York. Auditions were open to the public, not just to the students of Jackson State University, so there were a variety of talents in the mix.

As expected, Eddie Seawood was in the competition. As I walked through the backstage halls, I saw him look at me with his signature smile and cool demeanor as we simultaneously gave each other the "I see you" finger point. What was different about this competition, is that I was also going up against a few of my very good friends. There was one group that I felt would give me a run for my money in the rap category. They called themselves The Phunky Bumpkins. This group was a hometown favorite and pretty much local celebrities. They were also students of Jackson State University a year before I enrolled, so they had a solid campus fanbase as well. Waiting backstage for the announcer to introduce the next act was like being in a boxing match because each artist or group had its own support system hyping them up.

I'd learned that I had to have dancers to add to the dynamic of my performance. So, I used Lazy Lee and our temporary roommate Shaquan. As usual, I made up the routine for the guys to learn and we worked it out, so I could jump in and out of the action just like before. I came up with a new name for the dancers. Lazy Lee and Shaquan became Total Eclipse, because Lee has a light complexion and Shaquan is very dark.

We'd come up with these names joking and being funny, but we really used them. I always took myself lightly and all of my friends have a ridiculous sense of humor so ideas like these were the norm. Anyway, we finally heard them introduce Peace Posse and we ran out, rubbed the log and I told the crowd what we were about to do. As I looked out at all of the faces, I felt a rush and the music started. I ripped through my verses with no mistakes, stutters or stumbles and Total Eclipse were in perfect sync with every step. When it came time for me to join in the routine, we were flawless. Every detail we'd rehearsed came off effortlessly and the crowd obviously recognized, judging from the feedback we were receiving.

When the performance was over, they lined us up and the hostess waived her hand over the head of each contestant and the crowd response determined the winner. It came down to three contestants: Eddie Seawood, The Phunky Bumpkins and Peace Posse. We all had similar crowd responses and, unlike the rest of the shows, it was clear that it was rap's night to take center stage because the second series of "over the head" hand waves didn't lean in Eddie Seawood's favor. So now it was Peace Posse vs. The Phunky Bumpkins. I thought to myself, "If I lose at least I finally beat Eddie Seawood." At that moment the hand went above The Phunky Bumpkins and the crowd responded so loud I bowed my head, smiled at them and accepted defeat like a good sport. The pressure was gone. I figured, *"Hey, I gave it a good shot."* Then the hand went above me and my dancers and, to my surprise, the crowd was equally as loud except they included screams and a standing ovation. It was over, Peace Posse was announced the winner by the hostess and chosen by the people. I couldn't believe it! That was the most amazing feeling I'd had in a long time. The Phunky Bumpkins looked at me with the same smirk Eddie Seawood and I would give one another when we crossed paths. Like seasoned pros, they congratulated me and peacefully exited stage right. I would have never made it to that moment if I would've let the previous losses get to me. The easy way out would've been for me to believe I could never win against an artist in his hometown, but **I REFUSE TO QUIT!**

In the midst of several weekly performances, as well as a fulltime class schedule, I continuously took out of town road trips on the weekend. The majority of my travels were music- related. However, there were several that were "just for fun," where I visited other colleges and universities. One year I even went to Freaknic. (Freaknic is a book in itself, so I won't touch on the things that took place at that event.) Remember I talked about Jill and the guys at The Game? Well, it was time to reconnect with them over the weekend at the Sporting Expo in Atlanta.

We rented a car, got up really early and timed our trip so that we would make it to Atlanta in the afternoon. When we made it to the Convention Center, we immediately got excited because there was so much movement. It kind of reminded me of the McCormick Place, without the big city attitude. Jill gave us specific instructions on how to get in, and we followed them to the letter. Our names and badges were waiting for us at will call, so we got our credentials and headed to the main hall to find The Game's booth. When we reached the area, we saw Jill and she introduced us to a few names we had heard her mention. Jill took me around to meet several people, and all of them were already familiar with who I was and what I was there for. It was incredible! A few representatives from other companies—such as American Needle—said they'd love to work with me when The Game finished their business. I didn't quite understand the magnitude of the opportunity being presented, but I knew I wanted to be a part of it.

After a full day of hanging out with high level executives, interacting with representatives from various sporting goods companies and meeting most of The Game's top players, Jill got down to business. She said if we were interested, The Game wanted to endorse Peace Posse. We were told we would be clothed by the company; put in several commercials representing the brand and we'd have a promotional video that will run in all of the Foot Lockers across the nation. She said they would even finance the cost of our own music videos. She explained to us that new technology was about to be introduced, where all of the sporting goods stores, such as Foot Locker, were going to have television monitors in the store running promotional commercials for various brands. Peace Posse would represent The Game. She said there were a lot of intricate details to the deal, but we would get into that later. The conversation ended with her saying we'll see it all in the paperwork that's being drafted as we speak. I couldn't believe it. We were offered an endorsement deal and didn't have a record deal. This was truly a dream come true. The only thing they asked is that we send them pictures of us performing in the clothes. I thought, *"Pictures? Is that all they want? We can do pictures."* The next morning, we packed and hit the road to head back to Jackson.

The following week was a proud moment for me because everyone who attended JSU's Apollo walked up to me, gave their congratulations and said I had a dope performance. Even the students who weren't there told me they heard we killed it! I was in a zone as I walked into the student union feeling like I'd won an election. Then one of the most Hip Hop moments of my life happened.

Humdinga, one half of The Phunky Bumpkins, walked up to me and said, "You're trying to take over my town, we run this." I was shocked and, for a second, frozen in amazement. I couldn't believe this MC had the nerve to approach me like this. For some reason I didn't feel disrespected, I felt honored. This was his hometown and I was becoming the man, so for him to defend his territory was very Hip Hop of him. I normally would have said something slick and sparked up a battle, but his words somehow became the ice breaker to a very long conversation, and an even longer friendship. Instead of taking it to the cipher, we end up laughing and talking about the show. Needless to say, Humdinga and I began hanging out regularly and kept each other in the mix in regard to everything we were doing musically.

We found out we had several friends in common, which made our friendship grow even faster. Humdinga expressed to me that there weren't many straight up Hip Hop heads in Jackson because most of the rappers were hood, so they rhymed about the streets. He and his partner Fat Daddy felt they didn't really fit into that style, even though most of the guys were cats they grew up around or went to high school with.

A short time after building a friendship with Humdinga I was also approached by Mello T, the rapper of the group Wildliffe Society. Mello T told me he and his crew hosted regular events in the city and invited me to one that was being held in a ballroom of a hotel in downtown Jackson. He and his two DJ's had an organization called *Shake Em Up Sounds* and they would DJ or provide sound to various types of functions, while Mello T would MC.

I came to the event and before I knew it, I was on the mic rocking the crowd. The event was a high school luncheon or prom, because the kids were younger than us and they were pretty dressed up. I stayed until the night was over and his DJs were packing up the equipment. That's when Mello told me he liked my style and let me know he hosted a weekly event at the Elks Lodge down the street from the campus and I was welcome to come and perform. He said it was strictly rap performances, and it would be nice to bring some new flavor to the joint since they have a packed house every week. I told him I appreciate it and will take him up on the offer. He then gave me the information for the next event and told me he wanted to introduce me to a few people, so come check out the spot and hang out with him.

I shared the information with my man Humdinga and he, along with a few of our buddies, went to the Elks Lodge to check it out. Just like Mello said, the place was packed. We were impressed because we had no idea this was taking place in the city—much less down the street from campus. Once we saw the crowd, I found Mello and told him I was definitely down to rock. I introduced him to my crew and let him know they were MCs as well, and he said they could rock too. He and Humdinga were already friends because they were both names in the local scene.

We came back the next week prepared to get down but when we performed, we realized the energy wasn't the same for us as it was for Mello and the other groups who performed ahead of us. This was because the crowd was more into street rhymes and me and my guys were a bunch of Hip Hop heads. But Mello loved it, so he would let us perform every week regardless. After several performances with semi crowd participation Humdinga and I came up with a plan. We realized we weren't exactly what the crowd was used to hearing, so we came up with an idea that would allow us to continue getting our live performance on but not bore the natives.

We noticed we kept their attention for a total of four or five songs, but we were performing one group after the other, doing three songs a piece. This led to us losing the audience's attention two acts into our full set. We decided it would be better if we performed as a collective, since we were a different flavor than they were accustomed to. That way, we could do three or four songs as a group and get off stage before they got restless. We thought the idea was brilliant, so Humdinga and I came up with a name to go with the concept and that is how the musical collective later known as The Stewpot Stowaways was born.

Our ideology was: a pot of stew has variety and since we were using our music as a vessel to reach our destination, we considered ourselves stowaways for Hip Hop. At the next show, we told Mello to introduce us as The Stewpot Stowaways and we would take it from there. It was always five or six MCs, but we mixed it up, so everybody had a chance to perform within a three-song set. The idea worked! The people warmed up to us faster than we expected, plus we were off the stage before they could get bored with our intricate display of wordplay and metaphors. The Stewpot Stowaways started performing regularly as a unit. We began to make as much noise as a crew as we did individually. We even got permission from the university's president to perform on campus in a Hip Hop event we created called, "Madness on the Yard."

Our event on campus was captured in a photo and highlighted in Jackson State University's yearbook that year. Everything was going beautifully. We were the hot crew around town and were loved on campus, so we were ready to take our dream to the next level. We all got together and decided that the East Coast was for us because that's where we needed to be to get signed. We felt as though New York City was crowded, so we were going to get close to New York but not quite there. We decided we would all move to Philadelphia. Before we could get the plan in motion, financial hardship struck and several of our Stewpot Stowaway brothers were forced to go back home, taking our seven MC, eleven-member crew down to four; three MCs and one DJ. There was no way we could pull off our master plan with only four of our eleven members, so the dream died as well as The Stewpot Stowaways. It would have been easy at this point for me to accept defeat and gracefully bow out, but it's simply not a part of my character. At that moment, **I REFUSE TO QUIT!**

I neglected to mention that I lived off campus in an apartment complex that never had a Jackson State University student resident on its premises until Lee and I rented a two-bedroom there. The funny thing about the South O section of our apartment complex was we were the only guys in our unit. The remaining seven apartments were all occupied by single women. Some had kids, some didn't. But none of them were married. I naturally became friends with all of them and they loved us.

One of the women in the building, Beverly, was originally from New York but moved to Mississippi to raise her son. Once she found out how deep I was into pursuing a career in the music business, she told me she wanted me to meet her child's father because he was deep into the music business as well, and may be able to help me. She said, "You probably heard of him, his name is Lee, like your brother, and he used to DJ for Kool Moe Dee" (everyone in school called Lee and I brothers because of how close we were; but we are actually first cousins and it didn't help that we have the same last name, so when people said it, we just rolled with it). I replied, "are you talking about Easy Lee?" She said, "Yeah, that's him." I was floored. Out of all the neighbors in the world, I moved next door to the woman who has a child by a Hip Hop legend's DJ. This was great!

Beverly and I were extra cool, so there was no need to sweat her. I felt she would do what she said, when she told me she'll be sure to let me know the next time he's in town to see his son, Theo.

One day, while playing music in the house extremely loud, I heard a hard knock on the door. I knew it wasn't management or my neighbors, because they never said anything about our loud music. They all knew we were music industry guys, so they left us alone. When I got up and opened the door, I couldn't believe my eyes. It was DJ Easy Lee. He said, "I was wondering if you were going to hear me knocking. Are you Greg?" I said, "Yes, I am. It's an honor to meet you." I stepped out on the balcony and we talked for about twenty minutes. He told me he was impressed by my knowledge about Hip Hop. He said, "We should stay in touch. I'm living in Atlanta. Get my number from Beverly." Every time DJ Easy Lee came to see his son, he would stop by so he and I could talk. One particular visit he told me he was having a grand opening celebration for his production company and that I should come. He told me it would be a great networking opportunity and my roommates were welcome to come, too. He also said we could stay at his home, if we liked. I was blown away. I told him we would be there without a doubt!

A high school buddy of mine named Randal was staying with us that semester, so he, Lee and myself rented a car, made hotel reservations and drove to Atlanta. We knew we could've stayed with DJ Easy Lee, but we didn't want to invade his space, so we got a room at the LaQuinta Inn next to Six Flags, where we planned to spend our Friday. The next day, we made it to his place. We were amazed at how big the houses were in his neighborhood. All of the houses were sitting atop huge hills with really nice lawns. The scene was the extreme opposite of where we all lived in Chicago. I approached the house first and located Easy Lee. He welcomed me with open arms, introduced me to his wife and explained to her who I was and how we met. He then gave us a tour of the studio and told me his plans to put out records through the new deal he signed. He introduced me to his in-house producer and engineer Majesty. I was already familiar with him because his group, The King and I, had videos on MTV and BET. As time passed, more celebrities showed up. I met Jermaine Dupri, who was unknown nationally at the time; Silk Times Leather; a then-unknown Kris Kross; the little girl who played Aisha in a music video by the group ABC; East Point Chain Gang, whose members included future Goodie Mob members Big Gipp and Khujo; and a female VJ from MTV whose name I can't remember.

In my eyes, Easy Lee had it all. I was inspired by what was taking place, and I wanted to be a part of the movement. The showcase part of his celebration was about to start so he introduced himself and his family to all who were present. He even took the time to recognize me as his personal guest from Mississippi, which made me look important. Now it was time for the performances to begin.

Jermaine Dupri introduced a four-member all-girl group who kept their faces behind veils. They were called Atlanta's Best Kept Secret. I believe they later became the group Xscape. All of the performers did their thing. Afterwards, there was a lot of networking, mixing and mingling. I was in super network mode, so I worked the room like a champ, and everyone showed us love and respect. That was a special day for me, because Easy Lee made me feel as important as everyone who attended his celebration. Its moments like this you wish would never end. That day let me know I was going to be in the entertainment business for the rest of my life. We hung out until the last person left. Then, out of the blue, Easy Lee invited us inside to hang out with his friends and family.

I ate good food, cracked jokes, played with the kids and began to build a little camaraderie with this very cool brother. He invited us to join him, his family and friends for breakfast the next morning before we went back to Jackson. But as good as it sounded, we had to turn down the offer because we knew we had to get back. That was a very active time for me, but it was over before I knew it.

In Atlanta @ Dj Easy Lee's Entertainment Company kick off party

In Atlanta @ Dj Easy Lee's Entertainment Company kick off party
with Kriss Kross (just a couple of months before their multi-platinum success)

The original Stewpot Stowaways crew
@ The Elk's Lodge

CHAPTER 4

Growing Pains

It's now fall 1992, and I'm moving full-steam ahead. I'm a mass communication major with a concentration in broadcast production, so almost all of my class time is spent in the liberal arts building, where our school newspaper, *The Blue & White Flash*, was laid out and printed. Since the paper originated in my department, I was one of the first to see a write up on a group called Da Network. When I showed it to my crew, none of them were familiar with the group, so we assumed they were bad. Plus, we had never seen them in the live performance scene, so we figured they were one of those groups who hadn't put in any work but had an inside connection at the school newspaper.

Early in the semester, there was a talent showcase in the general-purpose room of the Student Union and, as expected, I was performing, representing the Peace Posse. At this juncture, my live performances were the highlight of our campus showcases but this time there was an unexpected surprise. The group we had labeled bad was sharing the bill with me. One of the members of the group, Kamikaze, knew who I was and approached me after the show and introduced himself. As he gave me the breakdown of his group, I heard him say his DJ was from Chicago. I then approached the DJ and gave him the Chicago test. Anyone who has attended an out of state college or university knows the test I'm referring to, because it's common practice when someone claims your city. Once his DJ and I spoke there was an instant connection between me and Da Network.

Kamikaze would approach me every couple of days telling me Vinnie G of Ocean Blue Records had been looking for me and wanted to sign us. Out of respect for him I would say, "OK." take Vinnie's number, but never call. I felt as if Ocean Blue Records wasn't serious about Peace Posse because Vinnie G approached me a year prior with the same talk but signed Total Chaos instead.

Kamikaze's persistence paid off; he eventually got me over to Ocean Blue Records. It was virtually impossible to avoid him because he and I were students at the same university, we were both mass communication majors, and we both were active in the music re-lated activities on campus, as well as Jackson's growing Hip Hop scene. And we were in the midst of a budding friendship, so it was only a matter of time before I had to give in to the pressure. When I arrived at Ocean Blue Records, I saw the Da Network, a female vocalist from Saint Louis named Erica and my man Humdinga of The Phunky Bumpkins (whose group once worked with the label under the name Point Blank.) It was explained to everyone that Ocean Blue Records' goal was to create a strong presence in the music industry, and we were the talent they needed to make this goal possible. Vinnie G spoke with the passion and seriousness of a man with a plan, and we were taken by the potential of his ideas. Don't forget, we were hungry young artists who knew we had what it took to be superstars but were smart enough to know we couldn't do it ourselves. This was it; the opportunity I'd been working so hard for. There was another guy there the entire time. He sat quietly as Vinnie G broke the plan down to us. I knew this guy served a purpose; I just didn't know what.

Just as my curiosity was reaching its highest point, Vinnie G introduced this mystery man and explained his role. He said, "This is X. He will handle all of the management duties for the company." He explained that anyone who signs with Ocean Blue Records will be managed by X. None of us had a manager, per se. But none of us felt comfortable being managed by this guy we didn't know. All of us must've made a weird expression at the same time, because X took it upon himself to speak at that moment. He explained that he was a businessman and he had a vested interest in Ocean Blue Records. He wanted to make sure the label, as well as all of its artists, were successful. He explained that he had solid connections with label executives, radio stations, clubs and multi-track recording studios—all of which will be used to the benefit of the artists. X stated his case very convincingly. By the time the meeting was over, we all felt a lot easier about the idea of X handling our career. A week or so later Peace Posse, Da Network and Erica all signed to Ocean Blue Records.

Vinnie and X decided that Peace Pose would be the group to kick off everything for the label. The first move was getting my partner in rhyme Chill to Mississippi. The plan was pretty simple: decide on a weekend to record and they would pay for a train ticket for him to come. Vinnie G had a pre-production recording studio set up in a small room in his garage. To save money and time, we would record vocals there and take the song to a big studio to mix. A few weekends later, he and I were recording what was supposed to be our potential first single. Everyone was excited and things seemed to be alright. I put on the headphones and knocked my verse out in one take. I passed the headphones to Chill and stepped out of the way so he could command the mic and a strange thing happened.

Chill began saying his verse and he didn't really know it. We had written the songs weeks before going into the studio, but it wasn't connecting. He had to start over more than he ever did in the past. After several bad takes, and a few strange looks from Lee and me, he decided to take a break and said he needed to talk to me. We walked outside the studio and leaned against a car. What he said next may have been the most unexpected thing I had ever heard from him.

Chill told me he wasn't interesting in rapping anymore. He said he still loved Hip Hop, but he no longer had an interest in pursuing a career as a recording artist. He began to break down how his situation was different from mine, starting with the fact that I attended a black college with an active Hip Hop environment. I knew he pledged Kappa a few months before I secured our deal, but I wasn't aware he hadn't been actively rapping the entire time. He said he signed the contract because he didn't want to let me down. He knew how much work I'd put in for the group, but his heart really wasn't in it anymore. He then said E.P and I sound great together, and I should consider being a group with her. I was shocked. We were the Peace Posse! This was our dream and we've been best friends since high school, so I didn't understand. In that moment it all became clear.

We are best friends, and this was the most honest thing anyone could ever do or ask of a real friend. I looked my brother in his eyes and said, "OK." I went back in the studio and told everyone it was a wrap for today. We went back to the house and enjoyed the rest of his stay in Jackson. Although we never made any music again, and Peace Posse as a group was officially over that day, he and I remain best friends. Respect goes a long way and Chill and I have a lot for each other. I would have loved to have seen Peace Posse become one of the greatest rap groups of all time, but that's not how the story ended. My best buddy made a conscious decision to stop pursuing his dream as an artist. But the hunger and passion to succeed in music and entertainment didn't leave me so **I REFUSE TO QUIT!**

The next day I explained to the label what took place and they understood. If they didn't—and just told me they did—it didn't matter because the reality was Peace Posse the group was no more. I continued to record a few solo records with Ocean Blue but nothing ever materialized in terms of a release. Actually, no one who signed to the label ever released any material, so I didn't feel cheated.

One of the best things that came out of the Ocean Blue Records situation was the relationship I built with X. We became very close friends. We hung out a lot and talked about everything from business ideas to personal goals. He thought I was very talented, so he would always utilize my business knowledge and artistic talent whenever he promoted a show in Jackson. X had a lot of industry contacts and he began to focus more on concert promotions. I did everything from stage managing his gospel shows to being the opening act at his rap shows. He and I stayed in touch even after I graduated and left Mississippi. Of course, his management duties faded along with the business dealings of the label. However, our friendship became stronger than any paperwork we had between us. The funny thing is X and I became better friends than I ever became with Vinnie G—who brought X into the fold.

I experienced more than my share of highs and lows during this period of my life. Nothing made me feel as low as when I received my grades for that semester. I had done so poor that my grade point average dropped below standard, so I received a letter saying I was being kicked out of JSU because of poor academic performance. I didn't realize what I had been doing until that moment.

I was in class, but my mind was somewhere else. I was doing my work, but not to the best of my ability. Physically I was at school but mentally I was out of town. It was my fault! I stopped caring about school because I thought I was about to be a rap superstar. Everything became clear to me, but it was too late. This was one of the scariest moments of my college life. All I kept thinking was, *"I'm almost eight hundred miles away from home, my family has been supporting me mentally and financially and I just got kicked out of the university. How could I have blown it like this?"*

I made a few calls and found out I could appeal the court's decision and try to get back in on academic probation. But that would take an entire semester which meant I would be out of school for months. I was too ashamed to tell my family, so I kept it a secret from everyone, except my mother and my cousin Lee. I started working odd jobs to hold myself down, but I would still hang on campus like I was there, so no one knew I was no longer enrolled in school. A buddy of mine hooked me up with a job working for a company called Frank Giles Painting Service. They were contracted to work on a newly built office complex, so I found myself hanging drywall, pressure washing, painting and cleaning. This wasn't what I traveled twelve hours out of state for, but it was what I had to do to hide my reality.

I started writing my letter of appeal to submit for consideration. Although my music-based dreams and endeavors were flourishing, my real life was in disarray. Several members of my family passed away that year, and I found myself at more funerals than I cared to attend. Between the deaths in my family, and the upswing in my music, I got lost in it all and my reality became twisted. When I asked what I am supposed to write, I was told "your story." I was instructed to explain what happened to get me to this point and why I should be given a second chance.

As easy as writing is for me, this assignment was very hard. I sat, staring at the paper for several minutes and couldn't think of what to write. As I drifted, contemplating the direction of the letter, it hit me. Just tell the truth. The only thing that could save me was the truth. I began telling my story, admitting how I stopped caring about school because I thought I was about to be a star. I wrote about how losing members of my family affected me more than I knew. I even admitted to almost dropping out to move to the East Coast to pursue my dream. Before I knew it, I had written five pages of nothing but the truth. I didn't even bother proofreading it. I just put it in an envelope and dropped it off at the appropriate building on campus. Just before the start of the new semester I received a letter stating that I had been accepted back into the university on academic probation. I was so excited and focused I earned a 3.0 grade point average for the semester and received a dean's list certificate. I can honestly say I was scared straight and never looked back after that.

I have seen several people give up when they were faced with a situation similar to mine. I have never carried myself as if I'm more special or more deserving of anything, but I am aware I'm blessed with a tolerance that is above normal so **I REFUSE TO QUIT!**

Me as the Easter Bunny at
Metro Center Mall. One of
the odd jobs I worked after
being kicked out of school.

CHAPTER 5

Crew Love & the Entrepreneur Spirit

In terms of my music, I had a lot to think about; a serious change was about to take place as far as the structure of my group. I knew the transition would be smooth because E.P and I had been working together for some time. Plus, she was featured on a song with Peace Posse, so we already knew how we would sound together. I took Chill's advice and started working with E.P in more of a group capacity rather than a management capacity. Before we could officially come together as a duo, Lee asked if I had ever thought about putting P-Dope in the group and becoming a three MC team.

P-Dope was a rapper I befriended who transferred to Jackson State from Morehouse College around the time Humdinga and I started the Stewpot Stowaways. He was already a part of the Stewpot crew, and he was one of the few left after things went bad. E.P and I both thought P Dope was an incredible lyricist, so I presented the idea to them both and they were with it. The outcome of this union was a group called Madd Skilz. The first thing we needed to do as a new group was get a demo done. The goal was to continue performing and make ourselves known as a collective. I reached out to a producer by the name of Andy C, who was one of my Stewpot Stowaway brothers, and let him know we wanted him to produce our demo. He came back to Jackson and we recorded a song called "All We Needed was a Chance." He could only stay for the weekend, but since we were all from Chicago arrangements were made for us to record a couple more songs at home during Christmas break.

Around the same time, I was approached by a brother on campus by the name of Armers Moncure. He was pursuing a degree in business management. He had been watching all of the things I was doing in regard to music and said he found it very interesting. He asked if I had a moment to talk. He and I took a walk up the campus and I listened to what he had to say. Armers, or "Q" as friends called him, was a very sharp and articulate brother with a cool demeanor who obviously thought about everything he was going to say before he approached me. He told me business management was his passion—as well as his major—and he wanted to know if he could lend his business expertise to the group.

Q was an entrepreneur at heart with several legitimate side hustles to boot but what attracted me most was his organization and structure. Every idea he articulated was carefully thought out with realistic goals. I'm a realist so he was truly relating to me. He asked me several questions, which I answered. He listened with an attentive ear, never interrupting or coming off as if he couldn't wait to speak. This brother was sure of himself and I was impressed by our conversation, so much so that it led to several more. It wasn't long before Q was introduced to the family, and we accepted his offer to become the personal manager for Madd Skilz. Outside of being the group's manager, he and I became very good friends because we both share that entrepreneur spirit.

By this time, there was a select group of talented individuals who would stop by my off-campus apartment for several music-related reasons. Some wanted direction, others wanted insight, and a few came by just to enjoy the music from my extensive cassette collection. Often, we would listen to each other's music, freestyle, watch videos and talk about Hip Hop. On many occasions, I would help groups get press in our school newspaper or help them perfect their live performance.

My girlfriend at the time used to get upset because artists or groups would often come by late at night and I always made time for them. She would say I was too nice, and they were interrupting our time together. One day, Humdinga and I were hanging out at my place and realized we had a bunch of hot talent amongst us, so we decided to rebuild The Stewpot Stowaways. We stuck with the same idea of bringing together Midwest and Southern flavor, but this time the crew was massive and a lot more balanced in terms of region, unlike the original Stewpot crew who were mostly from Chicago. The new Stewpot Stowaways consisted of Da Network (Kamikaze, Blaze and B Dazzle); Poetic Climax (Prizm, Coppatop, DJ Phingaprint and Twitch); Eclipse (Vice Versa and DJ Scrap); Native Soldiers (Esa and V Flava); Ego (PJ the id and Lil Bit the super); CT Da Decapitator; Satin and Wisdom X (David Banner, Abdullah and Tre').

We quickly became a force in the music scene in Jackson. The Stewpot Stowaways would perform at any and every event taking place in the city, including JSU's campus activities. We became one of the most known crews in the state and we made our presence known in surrounding states, like Tennessee, Arkansas, Alabama, Georgia and Texas. Before we knew it, the Stewpot Stowaways were local celebrities. The crowd showed us love at every show and kids even shouted our name in the malls when they recognized one of us.

It was an amazing time for Hip Hop and The Stewpot Stowaways were enjoying all of the benefits of having strength in numbers. Magazines and entertainment newspapers started sending writers to Jackson for the first time ever to find out more about the crew. At the time, Mississippi was the very last place in the world music industry insiders thought they would find such a talented group of individuals. My group went home for break and finished recording our demo so we could be prepared for any record deal possibilities.

After finishing our demo and returning to Jackson State, Q surprised us with a very unexpected, but welcomed, live performance. He told us he secured Madd Skilz a gig as the opening act for Grand Puba and Tupac at Tougaloo College. We couldn't believe it. We were all huge fans of Grand Puba from his Brand Nubian days and Tupac was on the rise, fresh out of the Digital Underground camp making waves as a new artist.

Q had a close buddy who was the president of the Student Government Association, so his business savvy, coupled with their relationship, got the group on the bill. I'll never forget how excited we were the day of the show. Q made sure we were there early; in case we ran into a problem. When we arrived, to our surprise, Grand Puba and Tupac were already there. Looking back on it, I laugh; nowadays it's rare for any artist to be on time for a show much less the headline act. We walked into the dressing room and introduced ourselves to Puba and his DJs Stud Doogie and Alamo. We let them know we were their opening act and told them how much we loved their music. They were all really cool, especially Alamo, who later asked if he could kick it with us to a few clubs after the show. We made our way around the room and introduced ourselves to Tupac and his crew who were just as cool. There were a lot of jokes and laughs going on.

We found out they were there so early because they were supposed to be doing a soundcheck, but the sound guy was running late. People were starting to fill up the bleacher seats of the gymnasium. We were in a cipher and our dancers were putting on a show, while everyone waited for the real show, so we didn't notice the sound-man made it but was having problems getting things working. We knew the guy from various shows we had done around town, so we were trying to help him figure out the problem. Before we knew it, Stud Doogie came over and started assisting the soundman. Then Alamo and eventually Tupac started to help out. We were all look-ing intensely at the soundboard, following wires trying to figure out why we weren't getting any sound. All of the artists and DJs were helping because they wanted to get their soundcheck out of the way so they could chill a bit before the show.

Everything was going positive until a drunk student in the bleach-ers screamed, "Why don't y'all get the fuck out of the way and let the sound man do his job." At that point, Tupac looked up in the stands and said, "Why don't you shut the fuck up and mind your business." The guy had to take it a step further and say, "Why don't you make me shut up." That's when all hell broke loose. Tupac took off running towards the guy and jumped up in the bleachers. He caught the bottom of his leg and tried pulling him down, but the stands were about five or six feet from the floor—with guard rails—which made it almost impossible to pull him down. Tupac eventually lost grip and let the guy's leg go. Security rushed in to get the guy out of the gym. At that point, Tupac started going out of control. He kept trying to attack the guy, but security wouldn't let him get close as they escorted him out. He was furious and pacing the floor as if he was looking for something to destroy. That's when I approached him.

I walked up to him and said, "'Pac, don't sweat that dude." He looked at me and said, with very animated hand gestures and an aggressive tone, "He must think I'm a punk or something." I calmly said, "No one thinks you're a punk, 'Pac. That dude is drunk. He doesn't even know what he's saying." He was looking me straight in the eyes, so I knew I had his attention. I continued and said, "I know this show doesn't mean anything to you, but if you tear this place up, the show will be canceled. It won't matter to you because you're already on but we're your opening act and this show means everything to us." Instantly he calmed down. He gave me a look as if I made a good point, shook his head and walked backstage. His crew was baffled and started asking, "What did you say to him?" The only thing they saw from us was exaggerated hand gestures and mouth movement. I noticed the guys with him had on Carhartt coats with Thug Life embroidered across the bottom, which lead me to believe they were a group. My thoughts were later proven correct because Thug Life eventually released a record. Anyway, I never told his Thug Life crew what I said. I just smiled and walked back over to my crew happy that the show was going to go on.

Needless to say, when the lights went low, and they introduced Madd Skilz, we rocked the show and we received a ridiculous amount of love. The highlight of our performance was the off-the-head freestyles we kicked at the end of our set. We all brought our A-game that night, but our newest member, P-Dope, was in rare form. He freestyled a verse that was so tight we knew it was the show closer. After he spit, we shut it down. You would've thought we were one of the main acts the way the crowd gave it up but that was the level of energy and precision that came with a Madd Skilz show. What we were most excited about was seeing Grand Puba, Tupac and both of their crews watching from backstage. When we walked off stage, they all gave us props, which meant everything to us.

Receiving a compliment or show of respect from an artist more established than you was the highest form of flattery. The sad reality is most new artists today are on an entirely different page. Veterans of the craft get little to no respect and more established artist are viewed as equals, even though they've put in three times more work. A hot single has up and comers believing they're superstars before they've made a real impact or solidified a career in music. I feel this is the number one sendoff of internet fame as it relates to the business of music, because things can change quickly and often do.

At the height of the Stewpot Stowaways reign, Q ran into a great business opportunity. An older couple opened a restaurant and bar directly across from Tougaloo College called The Shatto. He figured this could be the perfect platform to get Madd Skilz the regular exposure the group needed. He told me he already sat down with the couple and pitched the idea of a weekly live performance night. They were interested and he wanted me to help close the deal. I was super excited about this because there wasn't a club in Jackson that was dedicated to Hip Hop and this was the opportunity of a lifetime. Q felt that we should partner on the venture: his business knowledge and experience mixed with my music business knowledge and experience would make us a powerful team. It was the perfect idea and we felt confident we could make this a successful venture.

We sat down with the couple and explained the logistics from both sides. Our strongest selling point was bringing in the college crowd from both Tougaloo and Jackson State. The couple was very interested because business was moving pretty slow and they needed something that would draw a crowd. The older couple was already very fond of Q but after seeing our plan on paper, and hearing our idea broken down thoroughly, they were sold and agreed to let us open the club.

The Shatto was a two-story building with a nice sized parking lot that surrounded the structure. It had about as much square footage as a TGI Friday's but with a second level. When you entered the building, you came face to face with a staircase that led to an upstairs banquet hall. On the first level the restaurant occupied the entire left side and a sports bar took up space on the right. Our idea was to turn the upstairs area into a club because there was a substantial amount of square footage, a very nice bar, bathrooms and a large lobby. We figured we could bring in a small stage, rent sound equipment and provide live weekly entertainment courtesy of Madd Skilz. Since our objective was to cater to college students, we knew our cover charge had to be reasonable; we were going to ask for five dollars at the door. The purpose of acquiring the space was strictly a promotional vehicle for my group, so we wanted to call it something that went along with the theme of what we were trying to achieve. Q and I decided to call the club The Top Flow.

We thought the name was cool because "flow" is a term that refers to rapping which was what we were doing, and the venue was upstairs. As we were getting excited about the name and how creative it was Q's business sense kicked, "What if people don't get it? We don't want to put ourselves in position to have to explain. Plus, we could grow past just Hip Hop." I had to agree—my partner made a good point. I'm a Libra so I'm sold when something makes sense. So, we decided to alter the name slightly and call it The Top Floor. The new name didn't stray too far away from the concept of the original title, and it was just as witty, so we rolled with it.

The Top Floor became the first Hip Hop club in Jackson and the premiere spot for live Hip Hop. It wasn't long before we were show-casing every group or solo artist in The Stewpot Stowaways. The Top Floor unofficially became the entire crew's outlet for live per-formance, although it was created mostly for Madd Skilz.

Everyone had a great time, but Q and I had to keep in mind that we were responsible if any mishaps occurred. Attendance was great and rising week by week. We came up with a few cool promotional ideas such as selling cups of beer for one dollar. Q did the math and figured if we rented a keg, bought plastic cups and sold each cup for a buck we would triple the cost of what we paid for keg rental and cup purchases. We generated such a buzz that Q secured the first liquor sponsorship in the state of Mississippi, with Miller Genuine Draft. We were riding high. My group was one of the tightest acts in our crew. My crew was one of the tightest collectives in the state. My manager was the best business partner anyone could ask for. We were beginning to make a profit from our venture, and I was living the life of a local superstar rapper while I was still in college. All of my dreams seemed to be coming true. I felt as if nothing could screw up the momentum we had.

One day after school, Q called me and said we needed to talk. He was on his way to my place. When he arrived, he wasted no time: he said he had a sit down with the owners of The Shatto and he had bad news. I'm thinking to myself, did the place catch on fire? Did we leave a door unlocked and someone broke in? Are they upset with the crowd we were attracting? Did Tougaloo complain about the music? A thousand things raced through my head, but my thoughts were so far from the reality Q presented to me that I wouldn't have guessed correctly if he gave me a million tries. He told me the bank foreclosed on the property.

The owners were seriously behind on payments and our venture just wasn't enough to pull them out of debt. He told me the doors of The Shatto were closed for good. So, The Top Floor no longer existed. I was stunned. Having to write about it now takes me back to the emptiness and confusion I felt that day. We had only been open a few months—a few incredible months at that. I didn't understand how they could have let themselves get that far behind and how come we weren't told this well ahead of time. None of the questions mattered because the reality of the situation was that it was over. Once again, a dream was deferred, and it was for reasons beyond my control. It's moments like this that make the faint at heart throw in the towel and call the fight. But **I REFUSE TO QUIT!**

Greg "Olskool Ice-Gre" Lewis

Newspaper advertisement for performance @
Top Floor (Shatto Deluxe)

70

Madd Skilz 1st Demo

CHAPTER 6

Intro to Networking & Conventions

It's now the second semester of my junior year and all of the good, the bad and the ugly of the previous semester was left behind. I'm moving forward with a positive attitude. One day, while sitting in the lecture room in the liberal arts department an interesting thing took place. At the start of class, my professor stood front and center and told us he would not be teaching today, but he wanted us to meet a very important individual. He said that we should take notes on all of the information we were about to hear.

At that point, a very classy woman stood before us and introduced herself as the public relations person for a man by the name of Jack "The Rapper" Gibson. Now I had no idea who this guy was, but his name had "Rapper" in it, so I wanted to know. She kept her introduction short but did mention this guy was one of the pioneers of black radio. I'm thinking to myself, "Wow a pioneer in black radio with Rapper in his name? I really want to meet this guy." All of a sudden, the door of the lecture room flew open and a very fair skinned energetic man walked in. When I first saw him, I'm thinking, *"This guy isn't black."* Then he began to speak. He spoke with clarity and enthusiasm about his tenure in radio and how much he loved music. His charisma reminded me of a live show. He had all of the energy, mannerisms and eye contact that I have when performing on stage, and the impact he had on me was the same that I have on a crowd.

Mr. Gibson shared so much information with my class that day. He really got my attention when he started talking about his music convention, *Jack the Rapper's Family Affair*. He explained that it was an annual event held in Atlanta, where all of the industry's top artists and executive came to network and find new talent. I don't think anyone in that room was more excited than me at that moment. I looked around the room and a few students gave me the "this is for you" look and I smiled. I couldn't believe the names he said would be there. Several of my classmates were familiar with the artists he named, but I was familiar with the names of the executives, as well. Those were the people I dreamed of being in the same room with. Mr. Gibson ended the class by saying he would do something special for any student of Jackson State University's mass communications department who wanted to attend his music convention.

He then opened the floor for questions and told us if we wanted to reach him to contact his PR person, who began handing out cards. I was the first person to take a card and shake Mr. Gibson's hand. I told him my name, expressed how serious I was about my music career and let him know he would hear from me. I left class that day with a renewed spirit and focus. If I knew nothing else, I knew Madd Skilz had to attend Jack the Rapper's music convention.

The first person I shared the news with was our manager, Q. Of course, he thought attending the convention would be great for the group and even better in terms of him being able to network for us. He was as excited as I was, but we were faced with a serious problem: we were dead broke. Q invested so much of his own money into The Top Floor that all of his savings from other ventures were exhausted. I had no idea how we were going to pull off enough cash for seven of us to travel from Jackson to Atlanta. See, Madd Skilz consisted of myself; my two rhyme partners, E.P and P-Dope; two dancers, Flip Flop and Hot Sauce; my cousin Lazy Lee; and our manager Q.

We wanted the whole Madd Skilz crew to experience this moment. I felt as though this was going to be historic. A few days past and I reached out to Mr. Gibson's PR person and she agreed to meet with me the following week. She happened to be a resident of Jackson, so sitting down with her and talking face to face was not a problem. If I'm not mistaken, my guy Kamikaze attended the meeting with me. He was one of my closest friends in The Stewpot Stowaways and a resident of Jackson, so finding her office was easy with him tagging along.

When we entered her office, the first thing I noticed was how organized things were and that it was a decent size. She greeted us with the same professionalism and kindness she displayed in the lecture room. I've always been a straightforward guy so I got right to the point; I told her my group had to attend the convention, but we couldn't afford registration. I let her know that the per person rate was a little steep for a group of college students and asked if there was anyway a group rate could be worked out for us. Before she replied she looked me in the eyes with a smirk on her face as if she was impressed with my passion and straightforwardness. She asked, "How much can you afford?" and I replied, "How much can you take off?" Again, she smirked but this time she said, "Here's what I'm going to do: I'll contact Jack, speak to him about your situation and see what we can do for you guys." She then asked for the number of people in my organization, took my phone number and said she will contact us in a couple of days. That was good enough for me. We shook hands and I left her office feeling one step closer to my goal.

As Kamikaze and I were riding back to my crib, my mind was all over the place. I was thinking about ways to come up with money to satisfy whatever amount Mr. Gibson's PR person was going to say. I felt great vibes in the meeting and just believed everything was going to work out. Over the next couple of days, I continued my routine of full-time college student, full-time rapper—continuously thinking about where and how we were going to get the money to attend this convention. Lazy Lee and I shared an off-campus apartment and we had a routine we followed every time we came home. As soon as we walked through the door, we pushed play on the answering machine.

Well, this one particular day I pushed play and heard the voice I had been waiting to hear: Mr. Gibson's PR person. She said she had spoken to Jack and she had good news so call her back. I almost broke my fingers dialing this woman's phone number (I'm sure I broke a record for manual speed dial). When I spoke with her, she asked if I remembered when Jack said he would do something special for the students of the mass communications department who wanted to attend? She said his "something special" was a discounted registration fee. She informed me that I was the only student from my department who took advantage of the opportunity and he was impressed. Not only did we receive a discount on the registration fee, but Jack gave me an extremely reasonable group rate. When she told me the amount, I knew this was our come up. I thanked her profusely and told her I will get back to her before the deadline with a money order and our registration form.

I can't explain to you the excitement I felt at that moment. Again, the first person I told was Q and I reenacted the entire conversation verbatim. I said the rate they gave us at the very end. He was excited and impressed by my business savvy and told me I did a great job. Q has always been an extremely professional and polite guy but he's also extremely honest and straightforward. He gave me a few minutes to come down from my high then he calmly asked, "How are we going to pay for this new rate?" I was smashed by reality; I didn't have an answer for him.

Later that night I spoke with my best friend Chill and I shared the story with him. He was just as excited as he would have been if we were still a group. He told me he was proud of me, and he wanted to see me do my thing. It felt really good to hear that from Chill. Real friends are hard to come by and best friends are even harder, so I was blessed. Chill called me very early the next morning. I won't forget the words he said to me as long as I'm in my right mind and able to breathe. He said, "Man, you know I want to see you make it and this convention seems to be very important in helping you reach the dream so I'm going to give you two-thousand dollars to cover your registration fee, transportation, hotel cost and food for the weekend." He said, "Remember I told you I was going to receive money from the malpractice suit with my mom? Well I got it and I want to help you." I couldn't believe it. I almost didn't know what to say. I recall being quiet for a few seconds. Then I said thank you. He said, "Come on, man, this is me! You don't have to thank me, you're like my brother." When I hung up the phone I sat on the floor and silently cried tears of joy. That two-thousand dollars felt like twenty-two thousand dollars at the time. For a dreamer, that money meant everything. We were college students so the only time we had a large amount of money in bulk was when we'd receive our refund check.

I got in touch with Q, told him what Chill did for me and the amount of money we were working with. After a few positive words and verbal exchanges of excitement, he told me to give him a day or so to make a few calls and work on our budget. When Q came back with the budget, he said we were faced with a dilemma. There wasn't enough money to pay for a seven-passenger van, two to three hotel rooms, gas and food for everyone for the weekend. We went back and forth trying to make the two-thousand work for everyone, but it just wasn't going to happen. There was only one thing we could do that would make the money work for us and that was not take the entire squad. We let our two dancers know the situation and they understood and asked if we would bring back their badges so they could have them as keepsakes. P-Dope, the third MC in the group, was another story. We knew he would be upset so we let Q break the news to him, so he would understand the decision was business and not personal. He didn't take it as hard as we thought. In fact, he actually seemed very understanding. We told them if they could find a ride and a place to stay in Atlanta they could still come because registration was taken care of regardless.

We were on our way to what I knew would be a landmark event in the quest to become a Hip Hop superstar. Mind you, Atlanta is only six, sometimes five hours away from Jackson, depending on traffic and how you're driving so this wasn't a long ride. Before we knew it, we were at our hotel checking in, dropping our bags and heading out to the Marriott Marquis so we could register and pick up our credentials. When we arrived, we asked the hotel employees where to find registration and they pointed us in the right direction. There was so much going on and so much movement all around me. I had never seen anything like this before in my life, and I couldn't wait to get in the mix of it all. There were hundreds of people, you could feel the excitement and energy all throughout the hotel especially in the registration area. Once we received our credentials, we agreed on a rendezvous point in the hotel where we would meet in a few hours. Q went his way and we went ours.

The reason we split up was to allow Q to handle the business without any distractions. Everybody who was anybody in 1993 was at *Jack the Rapper's Family Affair*. You would run into your favorite artist on the escalator, the elevator or in the bathroom. It may sound crazy, but it made us feel like we were on the same level just being there. I'll never forget the atmosphere of that weekend and how Hip Hop was in full and total effect on a massive scale.

There were huge television monitors stacked on top of each other running the latest videos from artists. You couldn't help but stop and look because the images were so in your face. But the one video that commanded everyone's attention was the latest by Leaders of the New School. This video had to run about a million times, and I recall watching it every time it played. Leaders were super-hot, and this was the first single off of their second album. There were so many panel discussions and concerts that it was hard to choose just one. This music convention was similar to a cruise because the events were all inclusive. There was no extra fee to attend concerts or panels, only a time schedule for when and where each would start.

Before we could leave our rendezvous point, Treach from Naughty by Nature walked up to us and asked what was going on. I told him we just got here but we're about to get heavy in the mix. Our conversation with him lasted for about ten minutes but it felt like an hour. When he walked away, we excitedly talked about how down to earth he was and how no one is going to believe our story.

A couple of hours later E.P and I were walking down the street outside the hotel, and we saw Treach kicking a rhyme with a crowd of people around him. We walked up to the circle and watched for a minute and I told E.P to jump in and kick a rhyme. At first, she was reluctant, but I told her she will shock everybody with her skills because they've never heard a female with her flow. That had to be the magic words because she immediately jumped in and kicked a verse. In a matter of seconds Treach and the crowd was rocking out to E.P. She received cheers and praise, but nothing could beat the feeling I felt when I realized who was leaning on me with his hand on my shoulder bobbing his head.

It was none other than Q-Tip from A Tribe Called Quest. I thought I was going to explode with excitement because this was a super Hip Hop moment for me. After she finished her verse, I pulled her out of the cipher and hollered "Madd Skilz straight out of the Chi" and we walked away. We stepped out of the hotel to get some air to take in all that was going on, but there was just as much action on the streets. I loved every minute of it because this was how I dreamed of living my life on a daily basis.

An hour or so later, we met Q and Lee at the rendezvous spot. We then attended a few panels and showcases together. As we were waiting for an Arista Records showcase, we saw Madelyne Woods of the now defunct BET show Video LP shooting an episode live. I had a huge crush on Madelyne and my team knew so they start messing with me saying, "There goes your girl. What you gonna do now?" I used to always say how I would get her if I ever saw her in person. But I didn't expect to see her then. As I was taking in the beauty of Madelyne Woods, live and in color, Tupac and his crew passed by while she was taping, and she grabbed him for a quick interview. He started off regular, answering questions. Then out of the blue he started playfully cursing, talking junk and putting his middle finger up. She pushed him out of the view of the camera. At this point he and his crew were laughing profusely and kept walking right into the area I was standing.

I said, "What up, 'Pac" and he looked at me with a "I know you from somewhere" type of stare. I said, "Madd Skilz. We opened for you at Tougaloo College a month or two ago in Mississippi." He said, "Riiiiight. I remember. Did you see me blow her shit up?" He was referring to Madelyne Woods' set. I didn't reply. I just smiled. Then, 'Pac and about thirty guys walked on. I was kinda hurt by 'Pac's actions. Not because of my crush on Madelyne Woods, but because I dreamed of opportunities like the one he mistreated, and I didn't understand the logic behind his actions.

The Sony Records showcase was about to start and as I walked into the room I came face to face with Clive Davis, Jermaine Dupri, Fab 5 Freddy and a host of other notable individuals. I spoke, shook hands, introduced myself, my group and told them the city I represented. In the midst of my small talk with the industry bigwigs I felt someone hug me from behind. When I turned around to see who it was, I was shocked to find out it was Madelyne Woods. I was so caught off guard that I walked out of her hold, leaned on the wall and laid my head on my hands and playfully said, "Get away from me I can't take it." Based on their laughter, I knew all of the bigwigs got a kick out of my response.

From the way I was acting, they could tell I had a thing for her, and the closeness was more than I was prepared for. I asked her how she knows me and that's when I heard my team laughing. She said E.P told her how much I liked her and since she was on the way to the showcase, too, she wanted to meet me herself. I can honestly admit that was the first time I was kinda at a loss for words (the second was several years later when I ran into Janet Jackson in the hallway of a recording studio in Los Angeles; I'll save that story for another book).

The showcase was great. We got a chance to see and hear all of the talent on Sony Records' upcoming roster. The group that stood out the most was a female quartet Jermaine Dupri introduced called Xscape. They performed a few songs and really did their thing but the showcase that's forever etched in my memory was called "Rappin' to the A.M."

This event started at eight or nine o'clock at night and ended at six in the morning. Q and E.P opted to go back to our hotel and call it a night, but Lee and I stayed at the Marriott Marquis and attended the showcase. This had to be the longest non-stop rap showcase in history! I saw several of my favorite artists, a bunch I didn't know and quite a few I'd heard about. We left the showcase around five the next morning and it was still going strong. By the time I reached the hotel room, Q was awake and getting himself prepared to attend an eight o'clock panel. I had to lay down because I had been up and active for at least twenty-four hours straight.

The next day was the same as the day before: a series of showcases, panel discussions on various aspects of the music business and hardcore networking. I was having the time of my life! This was an environment I knew I could get used to. The only thing that could have taken this experience to the next level would have been being part of the new artist showcases. I didn't harp on it because Madd Skilz, along with a few groups and artists in my Stewpot Stowaways crew, had a show Sunday night at The Coliseum in downtown Jackson with Da Youngsta's and B Angie B. Although we were unsigned, we were as busy as any signed artist at the time. Jack the Rapper's convention was as exciting and informative as I believed it would be but it was time to hit the road so we could make it back in time for our performance.

When we arrived at The Coliseum, several members of the crew were there, and they had a thousand questions about the convention. I excitedly answered them all and shared a few hundred stories as well. Everybody was in good spirits and ready to rock the show. P-Dope asked a couple of questions and seemed to still be cool about not being able to attend. I shared a couple of stories with him but I didn't want to make him feel bad, so I kept it vague. It was about twenty minutes before show time, so we all headed back to the dressing room where Da Youngsta's were hanging.

I don't remember how it started, but suddenly I heard P-Dope and Da Youngsta's going at it, cracking jokes on one another. Da Youngsta's were getting the best of him. If this was anyone else it wouldn't be a problem, but P-Dope had a track record of not being able to take a joke, so I was wondering how long he was going to last. Before we made it to the stage, Da Youngsta's and P-Dope somehow engaged in a backstage water fight. When they ganged up on P-Dope and started getting the best of him, he got mad. For those who don't know, Da Youngsta's were one of rap music's first underground adolescent groups. They were three street kids who rapped about the hood from the perspective of a kid. Although they were much younger than us, they were much more successful than we were, so they had the attitudes and demeanor of artists much older. Well, P-Dope started arguing with the group and they didn't back down. Before we knew it the argument escalated and almost turned into a fight. P-Dope tried to rush the guys and some of the members of our crew had to hold him back. The entire crew was caught off guard by P's actions. Even worse the label representatives who were with Da Youngsta's—who we planned to politic with—were turned off because of how unprofessional our group member behaved.

Immediately I pulled P to the side and asked, "What is his problem?" He started screaming, "Those little niggas wet me up." The crazy part about it was that he was playing with them just as much as they were with him. I knew his attitude was coming from something bigger than just getting mad over water. It was the jokes coupled with not being able to attend the Jack the Rapper convention. He was harboring anger—Da Youngsta's simply gave him an excuse to let it out. He took full advantage of the opportunity.

The seriousness of this situation caused my group to get into a very heated argument. As it continued, P-Dope became more aggressive and even dished out a few threats to me. E.P and I were so infuriated by his threatening comments, coupled with him blowing our chance of being heard by Da Youngsta's label reps, that we kicked him out of the group. At that point we knew he didn't have any respect for himself, us or what we were trying to build as a collective. There was no talking sense to him at this point. P-Dope became so over the top and out of control he had to be restrained, forcing Q to have his own group member escorted out of the building by a security guard. This had to be one of the most embarrassing and shameful occurrences we experienced as a group. Not to mention all of this took place minutes before we were called on stage to perform. E.P and I were forced to quickly adjust our song and perform it as a duo, which we pulled off as if nothing changed.

A few days later, one of the members of the Stewpot Stowaways had a barbeque and I saw P for the first time since we had fallen out. To my surprise, he approached me and apologized for his actions and said, "We may not be a group anymore, but we're still Stew." and we instantly put our problems to rest. Unfortunately, like a day or two later P let his temper get him in a situation again. But this time the outcome was him being sentenced to forty-five years in prison so there were no hopes of us reconciling and becoming a trio again. I could've been mentally shaken and stirred by the back-to-back occurrences that took place, but I remained focused and kept it moving because **I REFUSE TO QUIT!**

CHAPTER 7

Taking Chances & Accepting Change

The spring semester of my junior year was the wildest of all my college years. But it didn't affect my grades, and I made it to senior year. The mass communications department opened their new television station which was run and operated by two individuals: a woman named Mrs. Alsobrooks and a gentleman named Mr. Wright. A variety of programming was created for the students to take part in, but in Mr. Wright's eyes, I was the perfect host for a show he created called *World Beat*. I would love to say it was my boyish good looks that influenced his decision but in reality, it was simply my hair.

I was the only person in my department and on campus at that time, wearing locs. *World Beat* highlighted videos, music and culture from around the world. So, in his producer mind my look fit the aesthetic. Mr. Wright wasn't aware that I performed regularly so I was very comfortable in front of a camera. I have to be honest; hosting was a completely different thing. Fortunately, I turned out to be a natural and he felt that my image resonated well on TV, so I secured the spot as the host of the show.

I started off with a female co-host who was actually from the islands. I loved her accent and we had great on-screen chemistry. Unfortunately, her image didn't resonate as well according to my producer. So, after a few episodes I began hosting the show alone. I found myself actively trying my hand in several things related to my major. My buddy Kamikaze and I approached a close mutual friend of ours by the name of Chris Carr, aka DJ Finesse, about starting an entertainment newspaper.

Outside of being a DJ, Chris was a radio personality and club owner as well as a former student at JSU, which is how we became friends. His outside endeavors became so demanding that he decided to leave school to become the entertainment mogul he was meant to be. There were no local entertainment publications that focused on the music we were listening to, so we decided to do something about it. Kamikaze and I had a solid relationship with Chris, so we felt comfortable approaching him with the idea. Fortunately, he felt the same way and agreed to publish the paper through his company Finesse Entertainment. But he made it clear that the writing and advertising duties were ours alone. Chris already had a functioning office for his company, so we operated the newspaper out of the same office.

I took on the position of Senior Editor as well as Head of Sales which meant I had to write and secure advertisement for the publication. Remember, I was a mass communications major, so newswriting was one of the many things I was taught. It was even easier for me to write about music and entertainment since it was what I loved. I've always been a natural salesman so convincing businesses to buy advertisement was no problem either. I was actually pretty good at it. We decided to call our publication *Da 411 Entertainment Newspaper*. Brad and I had big plans for the publication. But we didn't realize how much time and energy had to be put into operations and we were at our busiest in terms of performing so after the premiere issue it died.

Madd Skilz went through a transformation after P-Dope went to jail. E.P and I came to the realization that we were supposed to be a duo like Chill suggested a year earlier. With this change came a change in our rhymes as well as our thinking. We wanted a name that would represent where we were. The name we eventually decided on was Abstract Mindstate. I had a fire burning inside of me that wouldn't quit. I felt as if I had a lot to prove because of the various group changes I endured in such a short time. E.P and I went home once again to record new material but this time under a new name with a renewed vigor.

The outcome was a soulful display of lyrical dexterity. We created Hip Hop music that matched perfectly with who we were and what we wanted to express. This, coupled with consistent and solid showmanship, led to us becoming the standout group in the Stewpot Stowaways. Abstract Mindstate started doing several performances as a duo as well as various Stewpot Stowaway featured performances in places like Arkansas, Memphis and various parts of Mississippi.

One day while hanging out on campus, a guy was passing out flyers for an event that was taking place in Mobile, Alabama called *Breakout*. It was described to me as Freaknik mixed with a variety of live musical performances. The guy said it's going to be the next big thing. As I listened to him and read the flyer, I told him that he couldn't do an event like this without Abstract Mindstate and explained to him who we were. I really got his attention when I told him we were from Chicago; it turned out he was from there as well. I advised him to ask around as he promotes his event throughout the day and if he doesn't hear we're the ones, forget I asked to be on the show. I could tell he thought I was over promoting my group until he spent a day in the city and found out how much of a presence we really had. Later that evening the guy ran up to me with a look of amazement telling me everyone in the city knew about us and how he would love for us to perform but we would have to get to Mobile on our own. I told him we could, exchanged numbers and let him know he'll be seeing me again in a few weeks.

Since we were weeks ahead of the event, and E.P and I had a little cash from a refund check, we bought ourselves a plane ticket. The funny thing was the tickets cost little of nothing being that we were traveling from Mississippi to Alabama with almost a month grace period. To have a little extra spending cash, we decided against staying in the host hotel for the event. Instead, we booked a double room in a smaller, less expensive hotel not too far from the action. Kamikaze and a few of the other Stowaways drove to Mobile to give us support. As we traveled to various locations around the city where a variety of performances were supposed to take place, we began to get excited because the setup for each was on the level of a major event. All of the hottest rap acts and comedians were there and Abstract Mindstate was ready to rock.

Breakout seemed like something that should have taken place in one of the major markets but, for whatever reason, the organizers chose Mobile. Although everyone who was listed as a performer was there, we couldn't say the same for the crowd. My man told me heavy promotion was done for the event but from the looks of things the city didn't even show up because attendance was really low. The promoters asked comedian Eddie Griffen who was one of the performers, to try and get the people excited by telling a few jokes. But the few people who were there didn't seem to have any idea what was going on.

The good folks of Mobile were either unimpressed or not in tune with the roster of superstar Hip Hop acts and comedians who were in town for their enjoyment. Eddie Griffin tried his best to get a rise out of the people, but he only got a few chuckles. After realizing the first event was a bust, the promoter decided we should all head back to the host hotel and wait for the next event. The crew and I jumped in Kamikaze's car while Eddie Griffin and then up-and-coming comedian Freez Luv jumped into the promoter's vehicle.

As we were tailing them back to the hotel the promoter caught a flat, so we all pulled over. Eddie Griffin and Freez Luv started cracking jokes about the car that had us laughing beyond control. We were getting a free show on the side of the road. It had to be 100 degrees that day and every chance Eddie Griffin got he cracked a joke about it. As we stood sweating bullets, watching the promoter change his flat, we didn't notice Griffin and Luv had slipped into Kamikaze's Nissan Sentra and pulled off. Eddie was hanging out of the window screaming "so long suckers" as we laughed. After about ten minutes Kamikaze started to get a little nervous thinking it wasn't a joke anymore. But just as his worry started to reach its peak, Griffin and Luv pulled up laughing hysterically with refreshments in both hands. They joked about it being too damn hot to stand out there with nothing to drink and thanked Kamikaze for the ride. By this time the promoter was done fixing his flat. We got back in our cars and continued to the host hotel.

When we returned, all of the artists were hanging out in the lobby socializing with one another. Word was the event was a bust, so everybody wanted to find something to do. All of the major acts got paid for the show regardless but had to stay in Mobile for the night because their flights were scheduled for the next day. It was a letdown not to be able to perform, but several of my favorite artists were there so I went into network mode. Kamikaze and I were freestyle fanatics, so we started looking for our favorite rappers to spark up a battle. We searched for the Hieroglyphics camp, but we were told they paid the extra charge to change their tickets and left so we could forget sparking a cipher with them.

Next, we saw Jay-Z and Ski of Original Flavor and challenged them. This was one of our most historic battles that will never go down in history because no one was there to see it but us, Dame Dash and Tash of Tha Alkaholiks. Ski was more famous than Jay-Z at the time, but we were very aware of Jay's MC skills. Kamikaze went first, then Jay, then me, then Skee and we repeated the process for what seemed like an hour because neither of us would give up or run out of things to say. Those guys were incredible but Kamikaze and I were very sharp, so sharp that Skee finally called it a draw because it seemed as if none of us were going to stop. Jay and Skee gave us dap and said we were dope. I then asked if we could take a picture and they were with it. I still have the picture to this day.

After the battle we said we were going to get something to drink and Tash said he was riding with us. We were charged because Tha 'Liks were our favorite West Coast Hip Hop group but we didn't let on to how much we were fans. We played it cool. Tash made a call to his rap partner J-Ro to let him know he was making a run and he came downstairs and gave Tash a fifty-dollar bill and told him get whatever. We couldn't help but laugh because we considered ourselves big drinkers so to see one of Tha Alkaholiks say, "get whatever," in regard to liquor was classic.

As we rode to the liquor store with Tash in the backseat, we couldn't help but feel as if we were living our dreams. It got even better on the ride back when Tash suggested we come up to their room and have a few drinks with them. I couldn't believe it, an invitation to drink with my favorite West Coast Hip Hop group. This was what the trip was all about. As the drinks began to flow, the conversation increased, and the laughs began. It wasn't long before Kamikaze and I were going verse for verse with J-Ro and Tash, gaining more respect with each line we spit. After several verses and even more bottles of beer something strange happened. Tha Alkaholiks got sick! We thought this was a joke. I kept saying, "I know the Stewpot Stowaways didn't just outdrink Tha 'Liks. They kept saying it was something they ate, but we couldn't let them off that easy. We cracked jokes, rubbed it in and continued to drink. After we realized they were serious we laughed it off, exchanged numbers and left.

ABSTRACT MINDSTATE

the Misfitz of Dialogue

Contact
(601) 376-████ (pager)

Da 411 Entertainment Newspaper that I co-created with my man Brad aka Kamikaze

After free style battle with Jay Z & Skee @ the Clarion hotel at
Breakout (Mobile, AL)

With the Alkaholiks @ Clarion Hotel
at Breakout(Mobile, AL)

CHAPTER 8

Reality Bites

Unfortunately, Abstract Mindstate never got to perform but we didn't feel bad because none of the artists performed that weekend. I have never seen an event with such known names on the bill have a problem with attendance. The only thing the promoter kept saying was, "I guess Mobile wasn't ready for this event." I wasn't upset. I got the chance to battle Jay-Z and Skee and drink with Tha Alkaholiks. I also met almost every artist who was hot that year so it turned out to be a good trip. Kamikaze and the crew hopped in his car and left that day. E.P and I headed back to our hotel room and talked about all that took place as we prepared ourselves to jumped on a plane the next morning.

When we arrived in Jackson my man Chris Carr called and asked if I could come by his place because he wanted to talk to me about something. I made my way to his crib. When I got there, I sat down and I asked him, "What's up?" He began telling me how he wants to concentrate more on the record label side of his entertainment company but has yet to come across a group worth putting the time and money into. He said he had a few distribution opportunities on his hands but didn't want to use them unless he had a hot act. He went on to say how much he loved what Abstract Mindstate had been doing, how much he dug our sound and flow. He felt we were the type of group he could see putting on through his label. In essence, he offered my group a record deal.

This was a period when crews were ruling the game. The Stewpot Stowaways was a strong crew with several talented MCs and we were the talk of the town so as exciting as a deal for my group sounded, it seemed—in my mind—that it would be even bigger if we did a Stewpot Stowaway record. Chris wasn't too keen on the idea. In fact, he flat out said he didn't want to do it. He only wanted Abstract Mindstate. I was so persistence in my sales pitch he began to listen. Mind you, Chris was a young mogul in the making so he saw the potential in acquiring several talents for the price of one (although he felt we were the only ones with material that was ready to drop).

After a lengthy conversation, and a little help from Kamikaze, Chris finally decided to go against his initial wishes and do a Stewpot Stowaways album. He made it clear to me that he didn't feel as strong about a Stewpot Stowaway deal as he did about an Abstract Mindstate deal, but he admitted we made some strong points. From a business perspective our idea had greater value in the long run. Chris told me to give him a week or so to tie up a few loose ends as well as get the paperwork together and we can do a deal. Kamikaze and I shared the good news with the crew and let them know we would start working sometime after Freaknik.

Almost every student on campus was on their way to Atlanta for Freaknik '94. It was a very exciting time to be a black college student. David Banner, Kamikaze and I rented a car and drove down while the rest of the crew teamed up in several other vehicles and headed there as well. This was my second year straight attending Freaknik. However, this time it was totally out of control. There were so many fun but dangerous moments unlike the years before. The police were blocking off several streets which made it hard to travel smoothly to areas that were once frequented by the Freaknik crowd.

One of the standout moments for the Stewpot Stowaways was when David Banner jumped in a freestyle cipher with The Wu-Tang Clan in the backstage area of a concert at Morris Brown College. He blew the Clan away. They were thoroughly impressed with his flow and style. But before Kamikaze and I could show our skills, the massive crowd started running and broke down the barriers causing everyone to scatter to avoid being trampled. I actually fell down in the craziness but Kamikaze caught me by the arm and stopped me from hitting the ground so I wouldn't get trampled. I did get stepped on a few times and my brand-new Fila headband sun visor got knocked off my head and stomped into the dirt. It was moments like this that made Freaknik '94 so fun but dangerous.

In the midst of the chaos Kamikaze and I found David Banner and we headed to the car so we could go to the next spot. On our way to the car we saw a familiar face wandering around as if he was lost. It was J-Ro of Tha Alkaholiks. He said he got separated from his crew in the madness and believes he got left. We asked where he was headed, and he said to the Marriott Marquis on Peachtree. We told him he could ride with us because we were heading to Peachtree anyway, so J-Ro jumped in.

The day was extremely fun and filled with antics and public displays that would put Las Vegas to shame. Things didn't really get good until the sun set and we found ourselves in an unbelievable traffic jam on Peachtree. We were in the midst of half-naked women, loud music, laughing and a mix of celebrities and crazy college students. The scene looked like a block party on steroids. It was great! We were four or five blocks away from J-Ro's hotel, but traffic was moving so slow that David Banner, J-Ro and I got out of the car and walked, leaving Kamikaze behind the wheel in bumper to bumper traffic. We all took turns driving but unfortunately it was his turn, so he was forced to babysit the rental.

After a couple of hours in traffic, we finally made it to the Marriott Marquis and J-Ro invited us up for a few drinks. When we entered the room Tash, E-Swift and their road manager Anthony Andrews greeted us like old friends and showed us lots of love. Tha 'Liks immediately started passing out beers and said we were welcome to drink whatever we wanted. There was a table in the room with every kind of liquor you could imagine but the thing I'll never forget is how they had the bathtub filled with ice and bottles of beer as if the tub was a giant cooler. I received a page from another one of my Stewpot brothers, C.T. When I asked to use the phone, I mentioned the page was another member of our crew and Tha 'Liks told me to tell him to come hang out too. The night truly turned into a Stewpot Stowaway and Alkaholiks party.

I spent most of my time that night talking with Andrews. This brother was very laid back and cool. His demeanor reminded me a lot of our manager Q. Andrews told me that Tha 'Liks talked about us a lot after we met. He said they thought we were really good dudes and dope MCs. He expressed his fondness for us and said he respects our hustle. He asked that we stay in touch with him and gave me all of his contact information.

By this time everyone was feeling good, so the freestyle cipher kicked off. We spit rhymes and drank until the sun came up. We tried our best to hang with Tha 'Liks but we had to stop. These guys drank until we couldn't take another sip. When we told them, we couldn't drink another beer the tables turned in their favor.

They began to crack jokes saying, "Not the Stewpot Stowaways! We thought y'all were big drinkers." But we couldn't hang, it was time for us to throw in the towel. As we all said our peace and began to leave their room that's when I realized these guys had to really be sick in Alabama because they consumed more beer than the law allows. I must say Freaknik was an experience like no other and can only be understood by those who attended. Although it was only a weekend it felt like we were in Atlanta for a week, but it was time to head back to Jackson.

When I returned to JSU I had to really focus because I had dual tasks to complete that were equally important to me as a student and as an artist. The paperwork for the Stewpot Stowaways deal was done and we had to record a radio single right away so Chris could work his radio connects, in effort to build anticipation for the album. On the student side, I was a graduating senior and there were a number of signatures I had to acquire from various department heads before I could graduate. All of the performing stopped, so I spent my days on campus and my evenings in the studio writing and recording.

This was a very intense time for me because I was in the midst of accomplishing a dream and a goal at the same time. The production duties of the single were left in the hands of the two producers in the crew: Humdinga and David Banner. Once my vocals were laid for the single and B side I was done. Our single was called "Check it Out (Stewpot Flav)" and we recorded it at Fly Studios with our good friend Freddie Young. The B-side, "Verbal Shots," was recorded in the campus studio at Jackson State University which made it very convenient for me.

I eventually received all of the necessary signatures to graduate but when I sat down with my department head for review I heard the most shocking news a graduating senior could hear: she told me I was fine with my signatures but all mass communications majors have to have at least twenty-one hours of minor courses and from the looks of my transcripts I hadn't declared a minor. I was sick! How could this happen? Why didn't I know this information? Who is to blame? None of it really mattered because a minor was a requirement, so I had no time to point fingers.

As I sat with a blank expression, looking as if I was about to die, my department head told me not to worry we're going to figure it out. She began going through my transcripts like a detective and found that I had a few options. She explained that I had a few hours that could count towards a criminal justice or sociology minor. Either way I'd still be able to graduate but I'd have to go to summer school. Luckily for me JSU held two summer sessions (for the first time) so I was able to take a couple of classes per session which would give me the hours needed to satisfy the minor requirement for a mass communications degree. My plan was to graduate in May but it wasn't all bad because a ceremony was held in August as well, so I'd still get to walk.

I felt a thousand pounds lighter now that I was past what seemed like the ultimate roadblock to graduation. I was now able to focus on the Stewpot Stowaway business at hand. When our cassette singles came back from the pressing plant Chris quickly got them in stores throughout the state of Mississippi. He then set up everything for the release party, as well as promotion for the single. The advantage we had with Chris was he was a club owner so the drama and fees that come with renting a spot for a release party wasn't a problem.

Everything was in order. The deal was done, the commercials for the release party were running on the radio, the release date was solid and the fanbase we had created was excited and eager to show their support. The idea seemed like the most perfect thing that could have happened. I was proud of myself, my crew and looked forward to making an impact similar to that of the The WuTang Clan. They were the only other crew that could be compared to what we had created except the Stewpot Stowaways weren't just a crew of solo artists. We were a crew of solo artists and groups that also included female MCs so we were very original.

My emotions were filled with excitement and nervousness the day of the release party. This was the first time we were showcasing our material as a collective and it would be in stores for purchase the next day. We put together an even mix of songs that highlighted the best of our crew. As I approached the parking lot of the club, I was blown away by the amount of people that were hanging out waiting for the show to start. When I got out of the car a few people hanging around the entrance of the club hollered, "Stewpot" and threw up the peace sign. The feeling was unexplainable. We'd done what most thought was impossible and created a Hip Hop movement in the last place anyone would've expected: Jackson, Mississippi. As I entered the club, I saw Chris and he said, "Your folks are backstage." When I got back there everyone had smiles on their face, saying they couldn't believe the crowd we pulled. It seemed as if nothing could go wrong until Chris said, "Y'all are on in five minutes." That's when we realized that half of the crew wasn't there. Our crew was seventeen deep, so we didn't notice that some of the main MCs featured on the single wasn't present. This is when panic started to set in because there was nothing we could do but wait and hope the crew members who weren't there were going to show up in the next few minutes.

Chris came backstage handing out microphones saying, "It's show time," unaware that we were missing a few key members who were on the single. When I told him what was going on, he gave me a look of disgust and said, "How can you be late for your own release party and you're not a star yet?" I knew that this was a rhetorical question, but I didn't have an answer for him. He was right. I was feeling the pressure and started to get a little upset because I sacrificed my group deal for my crew, and it was obvious to me that everyone wasn't on the same page in terms of seriousness.

The crowd started getting restless and chanting "Stewpot", but we never came out. Kamikaze stepped on stage and explained to the crowd what was going on and the DJ started the music to kill time. Thirty minutes later the members we'd been waiting for showed up so we hurried and started the show. We still had a nice crowd, but lost a few over the thirty-minute wait. Regardless of all that took place we came out and rocked it like pros and the crowd got what they came to see. It wasn't until we left the stage and headed backstage that the real show began. There was a lot of anger between the crew members who were on time and the ones who were late. We got into a huge argument and almost fell out.

The topic of the argument was about being on time and taking your business seriously. We were in a heated debate for at least fifteen minutes, but it felt like forever. Chris came backstage and expressed his views about everything and said he refused to push the Stewpot Stowaway project any further until we got our stuff together as a crew. Needless to say, that was the end of the project. We never completed an album and Chris lost money pressing and promoting the single. Some members of the crew were more upset than others, but no one was more upset and disappointed than me. I put my own group's record deal on the line for my crew and everything went for bad. As expected, everyone began to go their separate ways, but I still had a very important task to complete.

I am proud to say that in August of 1994, I finished both sessions of summer school and graduated from Jackson State University's liberal arts department with a Bachelor of Science degree in mass communication. Earning my degree was equally as hard as accepting the fate of the Stewpot Stowaway deal. Plus, I was faced with one of those rare moments when making the wrong decision could affect the rest of my life. I could have pinched my nose and jumped feet first into that pool we call "the real world," exercising my hard-earned degree forgetting about the dream and all of the foul ups, bleeps and blunders that came with it. For some, going that route would be a safe and smart move. But, for me, "the real world" revolved around music. So even though a few of my family members thought I was crazy, and some in my crew either moved on or gave up, **I REFUSE TO QUIT!**

My College Diploma from Jackson State University

Debut release promo sticker

CHAPTER 9

The Sun Rises in the West

Instead of going back to Chicago after graduation, I decided to stay in Jackson a bit longer in order to try and turn all of the time and work I'd invested in my music into something. My partner E.P was still in school so Abstract Mindstate could continue to move forward. A few months into my stay, homecoming rolled around and an interesting occurrence took place.

I ran into this one brother from Detroit who I'd established a cool relationship with when he was on the yard. He remembered how active I was with music. He told me he lived in Los Angeles and worked for Relativity Records. That alone was interesting to me because my favorite solo MC, Common Sense, was signed to that label and he was from Chicago. Well, my guy went on to say he believed I would make it out there because I had the talent, hunger and persistence conducive for that environment and I should consider moving. He went as far to say he and I could grab a spot together if I was interested and he would show me how to get around the city. I was intrigued by his offer and flattered by his belief in my abilities. However, LA seemed like such a big jump so I told him, I would think about it.

Over the following weeks, I entertained the thought of moving to the West Coast while I worked on new concepts and song ideas for Abstract Mindstate. It must've been in the stars for me to experience LA because not even a full month after my buddy presented the idea, I received a call from Tha Alkaholiks' manager Anthony Andrews. By this time, he and I had established a solid friendship and he would check on me every once and a while to see what was moving in my world. I shared with him what was presented to me in terms of moving to LA and he told me if I decided to make a move, he could get me a job at Loud Records. He explained to me that a very good friend of his, Noa Ochi, is the head of publicity and is looking to hire an assistant. I had to ask him to repeat himself to make sure that I was hearing him correctly. He broke down the duties of the job and said the position needed to be filled in January. At this point I felt that Cali was calling me and maybe I needed to listen. But I didn't accept right then. I asked him to give me a couple of days to think about it and he said, "Cool, you have a couple of weeks, just don't take too long."

When I got off the phone with Andrews, I immediately called my good friend and producer Andy C to get his input. When I explained what was presented to me his exact words were, "Dude, if you don't go to LA, I'm going to come to Jackson and kick your ass." That was his way of saying I'm crazy if I don't take advantage of the opportunity. That was all I needed to hear. Although I knew at that moment, I was taking the job I still waited a few days before I called Andrews back because I wanted to marinate with my decision for a minute. I told E.P, my family, Chill and my man from Detroit who initially told me I should move to LA. I asked him if the roommate offer still stood. He said yes, but also added he needed about a month to work some things out on his end. That was cool. The position didn't start until January and it was November.

A few weeks passed and I called Andrews and told him I want the position, and he said he's going to pass my information on to Noa so expect a call. This had to be the most unexpected but welcomed position I had ever been in. Working for Loud Records was the last thing on my mind, but the expectations of the position were exactly what I'd been doing for years, just without pay. I've always been the type to take on a challenge and go for what I want, which is how I ended up attending a university that was almost eight hundred miles away from my home. I looked at this opportunity as graduate school. I'd already spent five years away from home as a college student so going to California was no different than going to Jackson State in my eyes.

A week or so later I received a called from a woman with an unfamiliar tone who asked to speak to Greg. I knew right away it had to be Noa's assistant, so I prepared myself to be transferred to my fate. When I told the woman it was me she said, "Hi this is Noa." In a very confused voice I replied, "Noa Ochi?" She said, "Yes, why did you say it like that?" I apologized and told her I was expecting a man. She laughed and said she gets that all the time. My confusion was sort of an ice breaker and it got really relaxed after that.

She began asking me a variety of questions about my experiences in the music business, my knowledge of Hip Hop and how much I knew about Loud Records. I was sure my man Andrews gave her the low down on me. But this was my time to show her how extensive my Hip Hop knowledge was in regard to the art and the business— especially Loud Records. I named all of the artists on their roster, gave her details about them and told her a little about the founder of the company. Noa was thoroughly impressed. The only thing she could say after I finished was, "Wow!" I took that as a good sign. The next thing she said was, "If I offer you the position are you willing to move to Los Angeles?" I replied, "Yes!" Noa didn't waste any more time. She told me she liked my vibe and I seemed to be everything she'd heard and would like to offer me the position. She told me to send her my resume, stay in touch and that she looked forward to meeting me in a few weeks. I was extremely excited and proud of myself because I'd sealed the deal over the phone. I had no idea how I was going to get to LA. I couldn't afford a plane ticket, but I remembered one of my good buddies from school named Groove worked for Southwest Airlines. When I told him about my opportunity and lack of funds, he hooked me up with a ticket.

December came and I called my man again to follow up on the roommate situation. I had to start solidifying a place to live because I was only a few weeks away from my move. When I reached him, he said he still wasn't ready but to give him a little more time and he'll be good. He told me that since he and I last spoke that he moved in with his girlfriend, but they broke up again and he was in the process of finding a place for us. This didn't sound good to me. I felt as if he wasn't telling me everything, but I trusted he would come through, so I let it ride.

At the end of the month my guy at Southwest Airlines contacted me and said I had to use the ticket he hooked me up with right away or it's going to be taken out of the system, so I had to leave. I called my guy in LA to check on the roommate situation and he started giving me a long story and I cut him off and said, "I'll call you later." I started throwing all of my clothes in a trunk, stuffed all of my music-related business in my backpack and headed for the airport that day. Yes, I left abruptly, but I didn't have a choice and I felt in my heart that everything would work out.

My plane had a connecting flight in Houston so I called my guy in LA to elaborate a little more on my plan and he said he would help me get situated and apologized for sending me off. After that, I called Chill to tell him I'd made the move and was waiting for my connecting flight to LA and he told me good luck and to call him when I landed because he has something for me. When I landed in LA my homey from Detroit picked me up from the airport and took me to the Days Inn on Sunset Boulevard. I had enough money to eat and stay in the room for a few days, so I was cool.

The next day I contacted Chill and he told me to go to Western Union because he put a little something in there for me. All I could say was, "OK" because I was caught so off guard. There was a Western Union within walking distance of the hotel. When I got there and submitted the paperwork and my ID, they gave me $500. I ran back to the hotel and called Chill, thanking him profusely. All he said was, "Come on, man. You're my brother. I got you. Now make it happen in big LA." Everything seemed to be falling in place and I was feeling really good about my decision to relocate. Chill and I spoke for a little while longer then I hung up with him to contact Noa to let her know I was in town and where I was staying. She told me she would come by, so I didn't leave my room much out of fear of missing her call.

It was the weekend of one of the award shows because a few rappers I was familiar with were staying in the same hotel. One in particular was this rapper from the Bay area, Dru Down. He and his entire crew were hanging out all over the hotel. I ended up in a conversation with one of the guys from his entourage and after I shared my story with him, he asked if I wanted to attend the award show with them. He said they have extra tickets and enough room for me to ride if I'm down.

I was blown away because I always dreamed of attending an awards show. But I couldn't because I was waiting to hear from Noa and missing her call was the last thing I wanted to do. I had to be a professional, plus I needed Noa to know I was serious about the opportunity. I kindly turned down the offer. I sat in my room watching television, occasionally walking out to the lobby but it was pretty quiet around the hotel because everyone was gone to the awards. I waited all day for Noa to call or show up, but she never did so I fell asleep.

The following afternoon I received a call from her saying she was on her way to my hotel. She apologized for not showing up the day before and told me she didn't make it because she went to the music awards. I said, "Cool, no problem. I'm here waiting for you." Deep down I felt a little sick because I could've gone myself. At that moment, I realized I had moved up to the big leagues because I never got faked out for a music awards show before. I had been on the outside looking in for so long, I didn't realize that I had made a transition to the inside.

I was staying in a hotel with several well-known artists who were nothing more than a music video to me days before. I was hours away from being an employee at the hottest independent Hip Hop label. I was in LA, of all places, and I was being invited to a music awards show by the very people I aspire to be. I had an epiphany; I was going to make it in the music business and LA was the place where all of my dreams would come true. When Noa made it to my room we sat and talked for about twenty minutes. The conversation went extremely well, and the vibe was just as pleasant in-person as it was on the phone weeks before. She gave me the address to the office and told me I start work the following Monday. I felt great! My Loud Records mission was accomplished.

I stayed in the Days Inn for a week but my man who was supposed to roommate with me found me a place to stay on a street called Cahuenga right off Santa Monica in Hollywood. When I got to the apartment, it looked a little strange but decent enough. We went inside and management took us to what would potentially be my place. When she opened the door to the apartment it turned out to be a furnished room with a sink, small refrigerator and a hot plate. She then explained that I would have to share two bathrooms with the entire floor. One bathroom had a shower and toilets and the other had a tub (as if I would use that!). This place was not what I was use to or expecting, plus the set up was the same as a college dormitory. My buddy stared at me with a puzzled look on his face. I don't think he expected it to be that way either, but I didn't have any time, so I had to settle for it until I got myself situated.

It was a month-to-month situation and I didn't see myself being there any longer than a month. I was determined to make LA work, so I accepted the room and looked forward to my destiny. I took the bus from my place to Loud Records, which at the time was located on Melrose Avenue. I would ride to the 8300 block of Santa Monica then walk several blocks over to Melrose. When I think back on it, that was a lot, but I had so much on my mind that walking from Santa Monica to Melrose was cool—plus I always wanted to get out of my apartment. I didn't make friends with anyone in my apartment building except one girl who I befriended towards the end of my stay. I forget her name, but she was an aspiring dancer and actress who moved to LA to make her dreams come true. She and I were close to the same age and on the same mission, so we became cool really quick.

Workdays at Loud Records were easy. My duties were things I enjoyed doing so it didn't feel like work to me. As the assistant to the head of publicity, I was responsible for contacting the editors of various music publications to advise them on the available interview times for our artists. This was great because it helped me build solid relationships with music editors and writers as well as Loud's artists because I was everyone's point of contact. Often, the artists would hold their phone interviews from my desk. Managing the record pool list was also a great thing because it put me in constant communication with several record pool heads and hundreds of DJs on a daily basis. They would mail in feedback sheets on the various singles we were pushing but sometimes I had to call and ask for feedback myself. Everyone loved talking about the records and/or the response the music was receiving.

Since I was the guy who also made sure they received the correct amount of records to service their DJs I became an important person to them. Whenever a music editor or head of a record pool would come to LA, they'd stop by the office to meet me. It was very cool and interesting to meet the individuals who were in control of exposing an artist to their fanbase from an image perspective as well as audio. The funny thing is I was already very familiar with various music editors and staff writers through my hustle as an artist. I always studied the editorial page of music publications, so my position allowed me to put a face with the names. Through this experience I learned how a star was created and the relationships I built worked for me in the years to come.

A short time into my new position Noa called me into our shared office space. I could tell from the expression on her face I wasn't going to like what I was about to hear. She told me she had a meeting with Steve Rifkind. Turned out the company went extremely over budget on one of its releases and, as a result, could not continue to pay me a "full time" salary for my position. She told me she was very sorry because she knew I relocated to LA and I was supposed to be on payroll as a full-fledged publicity assistant, but this was unexpected and out of her control. I sat speechless, like a deer caught in the headlights.

She then offered me an alternative. I could stay and become what was referred to as a "paid intern." This meant I'd need to hang in, continue my duties until the budget gets better, then I'll be put back on payroll. Or I could leave. She said she would totally understand if I left and would give me a good recommendation if needed. I asked how much do I make as a paid intern and she went on to explain that I'd be compensated for the cost of transportation and lunch. I would still receive a check on the day everyone else does but it will be considerably smaller. This was a hard pill for me to swallow. I was renting a room, I didn't have transportation, I didn't know anyone in LA besides my Detroit homey and my man Andrews who hooked me up with the job, and they were both living with their own families.

I didn't know what to think at that moment because I had so many immediate plans. But, in a blink of an eye, it all had to change. Noa told me to take my time to think about it and I continued my work for the day. I functioned as if nothing happened, but my mind was running non-stop trying to figure out a way around my dilemma. Throughout the day I questioned if I made the right move, and if I should take this as a sign to leave. The more I thought about it the stronger I felt. By the end of the day I sat down with Noa and flat out told her I was going to stay because there was something in LA for me, so **I REFUSE TO QUIT!**

CHAPTER 10

The Sun Sets in the West

My walk from Melrose to Santa Monica was filled with more thoughts than ever before. I normally used this time to think but I had to be strategic and figure out how to make this thing work for me. When I made it to my room, I called my Detroit homey and told him what happened. He told me I shouldn't leave and explained that it's like that with record labels, but things do turn around. He said he still believes I'm going to make it in LA, and he would help me out with my room rental if I chose to stay. I told him I already accepted the paid intern position because I didn't want to leave. I thanked him for looking out and accepted his offer of assistance. I didn't feel too bad because I was going to make a little money which would be enough to buy food, pay my phone, pager and bus fare which was just enough to continue my hustle.

I maintained a hardworking, professional demeanor at Loud, but my personal hustle went into full gear. I started using my resources to get the Stewpot Stowaways write ups in magazines as well as asking Noa if I could mail a few packages, which she didn't have a problem with. I also made copies of the record pool lists for myself and began telling DJ's about my crew. I started shopping deals for Kamikaze's group Da Network and David Banner. Funny enough,

David Banner would later sign to Steve Rifkind's label SRC. Little did Rifkind know he was introduced to Banner's music in '95 and was about to sign him through a subsidiary label deal he was working out with one of his artists named Coke from the group Mad Kap. I also set up a meeting for Andy C to come in and play tracks for a newly-signed Xzibit who was about to start working on his debut album.

I immediately started using my resources and over the months I found myself connecting my new people with my old people and creating situations. I was always on top of my Loud responsibilities so Noa never had any complaints. As a matter of fact, she seemed to appreciate, as well as respect, my knowledge and resourcefulness. This was proven when she came to me for advice on a promotional sticker for Tha Alkaholiks and actually used all of my ideas. In essence, I can say I created a promotional sticker for one of my favorite West Coast Hip Hop acts.

Things were going pretty smooth outside of the fact that I wasn't making the money I expected to be making. One day after a rooftop party at the office, a brother by the name of Fade gave me a ride home. We talked all the way to my crib, mostly about my plans in LA and my dreams as an artist. When we made it to my building everyone was hanging out sitting on the porch talking. It was a really calm and sunny day so I thought nothing of it. Fade and I may have sat in front of the building talking for another twenty to twenty-five minutes then I got out, thanked him for the ride and said peace. As I approached the building, I was met by the one chick I was cool with and she said, "You may want to check your room to see if it's still there." I was confused as to why she said that, so I asked, and she replied, "We had a fire and it started in the room next to yours."

At that moment everything made sense—that's why everyone was outside. The front of the building looked regular but once I stepped in, I could smell the smoke. There were firemen still working, water was everywhere, and half of the building was burned. The manager and a few firefighters walked me to my door explaining that my neighbor tried to dry a floor mat on her hot plate, fell asleep and set her room on fire killing her cat and almost herself. They were able to rescue her even though she burned our side of the building. The manager pulled out a key and handed it to the firefighter because my door was pad locked from being kicked in to extinguish the fire. As the doors swung open my heart was beating strong enough to give me a heart attack.

Surprisingly, the room was still intact, but the entire place was smoke damaged. All of my clothes hanging in the closet, my shoes, my toiletries, my telephone, answering machine and bedding were destroyed. The only thing I was able to salvage was my under-clothes and socks because I used a footlocker as a dresser, so they were protected from the water and smoke debris. I had only been in the place for three months, which was supposed to be three weeks, but circumstances forced me to stay.

I called my JSU buddy from Detroit, told him what happened and he came to pick me up. He told me I was welcome to stay with him, his girl and their two kids if I wanted. He said they had a house so there's plenty of room, I would just have to sleep on the daybed in the front room until I got on my feet. As he made his offer I kind of went into a daze, thinking about my life and the decisions I made up to that point. How did this happen? I was only following my heart and going after my dreams. It wasn't supposed to be this bad! I felt as if I'd just gone through an awful three hundred sixty-degree turn because the same guy offering me a place to sleep is the same guy who encouraged me to come to LA, assuring me we'd get an apartment from the start. Let me think back on all of this.

I was hired as a full-time salaried employee working under the Head of Publicity at Loud Records only to be demoted to "paid intern" a short time into the new position. Not to mention I abruptly relocated to Los Angeles, a place I had never been my entire life. Because of my Detroit homey's situation I had been forced to live in an apartment building in the Hollywood area, renting a room that cost almost the same amount as the three-bedroom apartment I had in Jackson, MS. Not only was I paying what I felt was an unfair price for a room with amenities similar to a dorm, but the building was filled with the most peculiar individuals. To make matters worse, the most peculiar of them all happen to be my next-door neighbor who somehow sets her room on fire and burns up our side of the building causing everything I own to be destroyed. When I came out of my daze my buddy was waiting for me to answer and I knew exactly what I had to do after that moment of clarity. I accepted his offer and continued my hustle in sunny Cali because I **REFUSE TO QUIT!**

The next day at the office was cool because everyone heard what happened and showed their support. I stocked up on the various promotional tees that were around the office and that got me through three or four weeks, until I was able to get some more clothes. I used my very small check and picked up a few pair of cool kicks from a place I'd never heard of in LA called Warehouse Shoes that had extremely reasonable prices. After three to four washes with a detergent and Pine Sol mixture, I was able to get the smoke smell out of my jeans, so they were wearable. Every now and again I could smell a faint stench of smoke when I wore them, but they got me through that rough period and were eventually replaced.

The entire time I was at Loud Records I never let anyone know I was an artist. Being on the inside of a record label can be a good and bad thing for an aspiring artist depending on how you carry it. It's great to be on the inside for obvious reasons. But if you begin to irritate your co-workers trying to push a demo—when that's not what you're there for—it can become a very bad thing. Bottom line: the insiders like to have control and when their control is compromised it doesn't work in an aspiring artist's favor. I wanted to prove myself as an employee before they found out anything about me as an artist, so I kept that side of myself a secret. Some five or six months into my position, I was playing an Abstract Mindstate demo at my desk, which was near the front of the office. No one was there except me and a very cool sister by the name of Tatia who was head of video promotions.

I didn't have the radio too loud, and I didn't think she was paying attention to my music anyway because she was in the back doing her thing. Suddenly, she stepped into my area and said the music I was listening to was dope. She asked, "Who is it?" I didn't want to tell her it was my group, but I also didn't want to lie. I smiled and thought *"What the hell, I'm six months into the job,"* and told her the truth. She didn't believe me at first because she had never heard me mention anything about being an artist. Once I convinced her that it was really me, she told me I needed to let Steve Rifkind hear my music and said she was going to set up a meeting for me. I didn't put any energy into it and kind of laughed it off and left it alone.

A day or so later, Tatia called me in the back and told me Steve wanted to see me. When I walked into his office, he greeted me and said, "Tatia told me you were dope and gave me your music and I've listened to it myself. You are good." He went on to explain the protocol of how a new artist gets signed to Loud Records. He said, although he likes my music, the final decision is up to his A&R's Matt

Life and Schott Free in the New York office. Schott was coming to LA in a few days so he arranged a meeting for me to sit with him and play my material.

At this point things started to seem as if a real situation could transpire but I played it cool so I wouldn't come off as frantic. I also didn't want to get too excited too quick because I had been here before and I knew how fast things can change. When I left his office Tatia was sitting with a look of excitement. She asked, "What happened?" I told her he liked it and set me up a meeting with Schott Free who will be in town in a few days. She gave me a high-five and said, "I told you." I walked back to my desk. On one hand I felt good but on the other hand I felt pressure because I heard about how critical New York A&Rs were in regard to artist outside of their city and my group was from Chicago. The only artist with a deal that had a sound close to ours was Common, so it wasn't like my city was a hotbed for talent at the time.

A few days later Schott showed up just as Steve promised. He then called me into his office, introduced us, asked if I had my demo, said he's letting us have his office so I can play my music and left. Schott had a really cool vibe so I didn't feel threatened or uncomfortable. He said, "So you work in the office," and I said, "Yes." then I explained how this meeting took place and he said, "That's cool." As I put the tape in Steve's system, I told him a little about the group and broke down the story behind the first song. As soon as the beat came on Free frowned and said, "This beat is banging," and asked who produced it. I told him my man Andy C and he said, "Nice, I like that joint." We continued on through about four or five songs. He told me the whole joint was dope, the beats, our flow and the hooks. He asked if the copy playing was his and I said, "Yes." Then he told me he wanted to vibe out to it a little more but he's about to connect with Tash and that he'll get back at me. We shook hands and I walked back to my desk.

I felt good about the listening session because Schott gave me nothing but positive feedback and, judging from the head nods, he was really digging it. I knew he was in town for a few days, so I didn't expect to hear anything from him for at least another week, so I went back to my regular grind.

About a week-and-a-half later I started to wonder why I hadn't heard anything, not to mention Tatia asked if he called a few times already. I let two weeks pass and gave him a call in the New York office to ask if he vibed out to it like he said. Normally, when I call the New York City office from the LA office I can get anybody on the phone. But this particular day all I got was a voicemail. I didn't sweat it. I left a message and waited a few days for a return call. A few days later I followed up with another call and got nothing but a voicemail again. This was odd. I could always reach someone in our sister office but strangely I couldn't get Schott Free on the line since we had our meeting. I waited a few more days and followed the same routine for at least a couple of weeks.

By the third week I decided I wouldn't call him anymore. I had left several messages on his voicemail days apart for two weeks straight. I was done! I felt like the person I told myself I would not become and that was the demo pusher who was on the inside. I admit I was a little confused because he seemed to really like the material, but I didn't let this slow me down. I went back to mailing David Banner and Da Network's demo everywhere, creating opportunities as I performed my duties.

Ten months and several rooftop parties later, Noa sat me down again to tell me I had been doing a great job but Loud was in even more of a budget crunch. Unfortunately, they had to let me and the receptionist who was hired just a few months after me go. I was devastated! I thought I was sitting down to hear her say everything is back in order and I'm being put back on salary, but I heard the extreme opposite. She said if there was any way to keep me on board she would, but the decision was not hers and I understood because Noa and I developed a solid working relationship during my time at the label. I felt she was telling me the truth. As unexpected and hard as this information was to digest, I didn't let it deter me or affect me negatively because I **REFUSE TO QUIT!**

Things weren't all that great staying with my buddy and his girl. It started off wonderfully because she went to Jackson State and I knew her before they were a couple, so she and I had a friendship separate from their relationship which made things very comfortable in the beginning. Later, as their relationship problems started to surface, I was put in the middle. Because I didn't have my own transportation and was living with them in Gardena—nowhere close to my job in Hollywood—I found myself in the house a lot. Unfortunately for my guy's girl, he was the industry type so he would hang out and go to after work sets and events that lasted well into the night. I didn't know his routine or where he was on a daily, unless I was with him or he came to one of Loud Records' events. He and I went to several industry events together, but we weren't on each other's clock, plus I didn't have a cell phone at the time. The problem was his girl believed I knew where he was at all times and began to get upset with me over his actions. This caused us to eventually have small disagreements that led to a few big arguments because she believed I was holding back information.

In the meantime, I was scouting out positions at other record labels in Hollywood. Especially since I knew my time at Loud was coming to an end. In a short time, with the help of a strong reference from

Noa, I secured an A&R administration position at Delicious Vinyl. I really wanted to be an A&R, but this was a start. The only drawback was the position wasn't going to be available for two months. It was a few weeks into October and my time was up at Loud at the end of the month; the position at Delicious Vinyl didn't start until January.

I wanted the A&R administration job even more than I wanted the publicity position at Loud because it was more in line with the A&R position, which I always saw myself in. I was faced with another dilemma because I was about to be out of a job with no source of income for two months. Unfortunately, my living situation was a bit chaotic, so I needed a miracle.

A few days later I received a call at the office from X, my very good friend and short-lived manager from the Ocean Blue Records days. We hadn't spoken in a while, so it was good to hear from him. I asked how he got my work number and he said he ran into Kamikaze and got it from him. He excitedly began telling me about his experience meeting Puff Daddy at a club in New Orleans. He said he told Puff he was starting a label and asked his advice on how to successfully get it kicked off. X said Diddy told him the same thing I told him years ago. He then said, "I need you Gre. I want you to come back to Jackson and help me run my label." His timing could not have been more perfect.

I told him about my situation at Loud ending in a few weeks, so I needed to make a move anyway. I let him know I had another label position at Delicious Vinyl that would be available in two months, but I didn't think I could last another day in my living situation. There was too much drama. He offered to buy me a plane ticket to Jackson, but I didn't need it; I still had a return flight from my initial move to LA that I had to use or lose by the end of the year. I was really excited about the prospect of running a record label. This was a better position than Loud Records or Delicious Vinyl because I would get to use all of my talents, make a lot of money and have total control of the situation.

With that in mind, I went home and told my guy I would be leaving at the end of the month. I explained my new situation to him, told him I feel good about it and said, "I gotta take a chance." He said he hated to see me go but he understood. The last call I made was to Mr. Wright, the creator and executive producer of *World Beat*. When I told him I was moving back to Jackson, he said my timing couldn't be better. They were shooting footage for an episode of *World Beat* in New Orleans so I should land there. That way I could host the show and ride back to Jackson with them. My last day at Loud Records was cool. Everybody showed me love and support on my decision and told me I'm always welcomed as long as they are with the company. Noa told me she had my back on whatever I needed. After that, I said peace to my Loud Records family and left the building.

THE STEW-TANG CLAN:
Not to be confused with the Wu, the
Stewpot Stowaways represent for Ol' Miss.

Hippa to the Hoppa Crooked Letter Style
MISSISSIPPI BLOWING

Mississippi. The word itself conjures up images of AmeriKKKa at its worst. Back in the day, the heart of Dixie was soaked with the blood of thousands of brothers and sisters whose only crime was the color of their skin. Burning crosses, WHITE ONLY signs and cotton plants littered the countryside, and, believe it or not, a brother was more likely to be hung from a tree than served in a restaurant.

Well, it's 1995 now, and Mississippi is still burning. The one thing that remains a constant source of upliftment from the scars of the past is that good ol' Mississippi music, but the brothas and sistas of today aren't using blues or gospel to express themselves. They use Hip-Hop.

It's backstage at the 21st Annual Jackson Mississippi Music Awards, and Kamikaze, the lead rapper of Da Network, is running his mouth as usual. His group is up for the Entertainer of the Year award, but they don't really expect to win. The award is probably going to go to a blues singer in a loud, blue polyester suit.

Wrong!

"It was a sense of accomplishment. Finally, me, B-Dazzle and Blaze had some recognition," says Kamikaze, looking back at the fateful night. "I was very proud, but the next day I still didn't have a record deal.

"There are plenty of brothers in Mississippi that have skills," he continues. "New York and Los Angeles are steadily dissing us. They are constantly knocking us down and believing the stereotypes—you know, being country and everything."

But these three lyricists are a far cry from the slow, dim-witted country yokels that most people envision when they think about the Magnolia State. At 8 a.m. Kamikaze turns into Brad Franklin, managing editor of the *Jackson Advocate*. B-Dazzle turns into Brandon Franklin, junior mass communications major at Jackson State University. And Blaze turns into John Cobb, the cable man.

"It's hard trying to juggle baseball, schoolwork and rap," says B-Dazzle. "But my one and only thing I wanna do is to break into this rap game. I feel like this is our year."

It was a Thursday night and everybody who was anybody in the Jack-town Hip-Hop scene was kickin' it over at Kamikaze's crib. EP of Abstract Mindstate is laid back on the couch cracking open her third can of Red Dog. DJ Phinga is in between some headphones looking for the perfect beat, and I'm sitting at the kitchen table interviewing the Wildlife Society.

"All the stories you hear about Mississippi are true," says Mellow T as he gently pours weed on some paper. "The first gang I was ever scared of was the Ku Klux Klan. Folks were trippin' about Vice Lords, but I was scared of the Klan." [tucked] in Mellow's waistline lets me know stories are fact, not fiction.

It was 1990 when Howie How, Sleepy [?] Mellow T hooked up and formed Wildlife. [?] later Rated-X joined the group, and the re[?] say, is history. In early '95 Wildlife inked a [?] Blunt Recordings.

As Mellow goes to the fridge for ano[ther] Dog, his partner in crime, Rated-X, walks [to] the door. Sportin' a fat black-leather skully, [?] everyone up, walks straight to the kitchen [?] commences rolling up a fat one.

"When we signed with Blunt I couldn't [?] nothing because I had just lost my pops," sa[ys] X. "My pops and I never had a close relation[ship,] the one thing I can say is, once I let him kno[w] was down for, he was really happy for me[.] Wildlife's album, *So Much Pain*, will be [?] latter part of the year.

"What's up? Don't nobody wanna intervie[w ?]

By this time she has taken down ab[out a] pack of Red Dog, but this is one sista who [?] her own. EP is the type of woman that w[?] your boy if she wasn't your girl. The 23-y[?]

not only the female half of the rap duo Abstract Mindstate, but she is also a senior physical education major at J-State. Meanwhile her rap partner, Kee Gee (Greg Lewis), is in Cali working at RCA/Loud and trying to get Mindstate a deal.

"It's not harder to make it being a female. It's just that when mother***kers hear it is a female rapping, they think she is gonna rap a certain way," says EP matter-of-factly of the gender conflict in the rap game. "What people don't understand is that females got as many skills as niggas, because I can fade niggas."

Let's see if she can: "I'm who they sent to test the

Rap Pages Article - Stewpot Stowaways

125

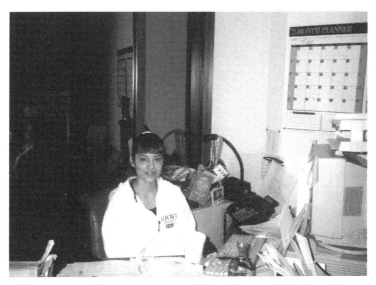

The woman who gave me my 1st real record label position:
Noa Ochi in her office @ Loud Records

With recording artist Xzibit at Loud Records

The guy who schooled me about street promotions on
a major label level: Bill "Bigga B" Operin (R.I.P)

Greg "Olskool Ice-Gre" Lewis

Rap Sheet Article - Stewpot Stowaways

128

CHAPTER 11

A New Beginning

That weekend my man took me to the airport. As strange as it may sound, it felt the same as it did when I landed in LA for the first time, except he was dropping me off instead of picking me up. In both instances I was preparing to take on a new challenge and continuing my quest to make dreams come true, so it was sort of déjà vu. I spoke with Mr. Wright from the airport and gave him the details of my flight. He said he would be there to pick me up.

When I landed in New Orleans, I could feel that good southern heat which has a much different feel from the heat in LA or Chicago. It was good to see Mr. Wright and he was happy to see me as well. As we were riding in his car, he had a smirk on his face that said something was up. He said he had a surprise for me and told me we would be shooting the show at the House of Blues. I thought that was cool, but the real surprise was that we were going to be taping a live performance of Ziggy Marley and the Melody Makers and I was going to be interviewing Ziggy. I thought that was the coolest situation ever, being that Ziggy Marley is the son of the legendary Bob Marley. I was excited and a little nervous, but this is what I do so I knew I could pull it off.

We made it to the House of Blues hours before the show so we could meet with the crew, set up our cameras and lighting, get our press credentials and plot out exactly how we want to approach the evening. After everything was in order we went into the restaurant and got something to eat. As it approached closer to show time the House of Blues filled to capacity. A section of the club was roped off specifically for us and the staff who treated us like celebrities. Everyone wanted to know who we were and what we were doing because a lot was going on in our area.

The people of New Orleans were very cordial, respectful and insanely excited to see Ziggy, who had a flawless set. Ziggy's people approached me and said, "Give us fifteen minutes and someone will come and get you guys so you can do the interview." About twenty-five minutes later, I was sitting next to Ziggy Marley laughing and talking about culture and music as if he and I were old friends. The interview was excellent, and Ziggy was a class act. After that interview I had a greater understanding of the Marley family, reggae music and Rastafarian culture.

The next morning, we headed to Jackson. The three-hour ride was fun because we talked about everything that happened the night before and I was able to share all of the amazing highs and lows of my California experience. Mr. Wright explained to me that he had to change the name of the show to *Rhythm of the World* because Jackson State owned *World Beat* and he wanted to take the show beyond the college. He told me he pitched the show to several cable networks, and a few were very interested. The only world music show on cable at the time was *Caribbean Rhythms* on BET, so our show was in high demand. My role became co-producer as well as host of the show because Mr. Wright loved my ideas and used a few for the New Orleans episode. This was great. I'm not even back in Jackson and I already have a possible nationwide gig and an executive position with an independent label owned by a very good friend and former manager. Things seemed to be falling in place without me exerting any energy towards it. I sat back in the passenger seat, took a deep breath and just took it all in. I can remember staring out the window, not saying a word, as we crossed that long bridge over a body of water that seemed to never end, thinking back on everything that happened to me. As strange as it may sound to some, I felt extremely blessed.

Although things didn't turn out the way I hoped or expected in any of my situations, pieces of my dream were constantly falling in my lap so who was I to complain? I made arrangements to stay with my partner in rhyme E.P, in her off-campus apartment until I got myself situated so I didn't have to worry about a place to stay right away. E.P was still in the same complex we used to live in—in a suburb of Jackson called Clinton. It was clean and quiet with only a couple of Jackson State students around because it wasn't very close to campus. E.P had a two-bedroom, so it was convenient and comfortable for us both. The first thing I did when I made it to E. P's was call X to let him know I made it. He asked if I had a minute because he wanted me to take a ride with him so we could talk.

That day X shared with me everything about his past—how he made his money, all of the various business ventures he was involved in and how so much has changed in his life since those days. We became even closer that day because he answered all of the questions I always wanted to know but never asked. He also clarified all of the rumors I had ever heard about him over the years (some were true while others were false). He said he wanted me to know everything about his past so we could move forward with our business in complete honesty. I was glad he went about things this way; I am an honest guy and I expect business partners and associates to be the same although that's hardly ever the case in the music business. Anyway, X and I were on another level, so we began plotting and planning our takeover with X Mark Records.

Over the next few weeks we made runs and talked about our strategies. We would hook up at least two to three times a week, grab something to eat and do everything from look at possible office locations to talk about what artists or groups will be the flagship acts for the label. X took me to places in Jackson I didn't know existed. He drove me through the areas and neighborhoods where the affluent lived, and I couldn't believe some of the houses that were in Mississippi. All of these beautiful areas were right in my backyard and I never knew about them. He also introduced me to his good friends at all of the big recording studios in and around Jackson as well as the executives at Malaco Records. X had a lot of relationships and everyone seemed to be in his corner, pushing him to start his label and ensuring him that they would provide whatever he needed to be successful. It was exciting because most of these were places I always wanted to get inside of while others were places I didn't know existed.

What made it great was he introduced me as his partner to the behind the scenes folks who played a key role in making sure our venture was a success, so respect was shown to me immediately. I learned there was so much more to Jackson than I thought, and I was now able to understand how The Stewpot Stowaways got so big in such an odd place. The city had a rich music history but the business was being run so white collar that it didn't resonate with the street, so it truly was about who you know. X and I ran around for weeks. Soon the weeks turned into a month.

Then one day, while doing our usual, a realization occurred. We'd been doing an excessive amount of talking, plotting, planning, strategizing, traveling around town, taking meetings and dreaming but no real execution. We hadn't moved forward on any of our ideas. One day I called him and said, "Lets connect, I need to talk to you." Once we were off and riding, I got right to the point and said, "X, why haven't we moved forward? I'm ready to do this—it's been a month." He looked at me and said, "Gre, I've been doing a lot of thinking and I'm worried. What if I lose all of my savings on this?" He said his savings was all of the money he had, and it was going to take most of it to get things going, and he's not sure if he wants to take a chance like that now.

I couldn't believe what I was hearing. Is this the same guy who called me at the office in LA frantic about making his move because of a conversation he had with Puff? Is this the same guy who wanted to buy me a plane ticket and told me I had to come help him run his label? My heart started beating as if I was about to have a heart attack. I didn't want these words to be true. I said, "X, I know you're not getting cold feet on me. I moved back to Jackson!" He said, "I know Gre. I'm sorry, but I can't do it." I knew X very well and I could tell from the expression on his face and the tone of his voice that he was serious.

At that moment everything seemed to magically stop. I had a moment of silence because I couldn't believe this was happening to me again. Just a few short months ago my man presented me with the ultimate idea, excitedly telling me how much I was needed in order for this transition to be successful and encouraging me to relocate once again. But now he has cold feet and decided he's not doing the label. As I'm writing this paragraph, I can feel the devastation all over again. The average person with a normal tolerance would have used this as an exit out of a life of painful ups and downs. But my way of thinking is far above average. And my tolerance level is way above normal so, **I REFUSE TO QUIT!**

Opening sequence of World Beat. The video show I hosted.

On location during an episode of World Beat.

Opening sequence of Rhythm of the World. The Video show I hosted and co-produced.

Interviewing Reggae music legend Ziggy Marley at House of Blues New Orleans

CHAPTER 12

Real Life Situations

I was in a weird position, and I didn't know what I was going to do. If you ask anyone who really knows me, they'll tell you I'm very organized. I always have a plan, but I'm not big on backup plans and this situation caused for a backup plan. And, honestly, I was stuck. I came home, broke the news to E.P and all she could say was, "Wow!" Well, I had a degree that was only a year old and it had never been exercised in my field, so I started submitting resumes to all of the local television stations in town. I had a few buddies from the mass communications department who were employed by some of the radio and television stations, so I figured why not go for it.

A few weeks later I received a call for an interview with channel 12 WJTV, a CBS affiliate. I didn't own a pair of dress shoes because nothing I did during that time required dress attire, so I wore my khakis, a denim shirt, Timberlands and a borrowed tie. This happened to be the one station that none of my college buddies were employed so I didn't have an inside connection. Fortunately, my interview went well and a week later I was hired as the cameraman for the morning and noon news. This was a cool position because I was comfortable working the camera. I'm a morning person so being there at 5am didn't faze me and it wasn't far from the apartment. I was able to help out around the house as well as take care of myself, so everything seemed OK—outside the fact that I didn't come back to Jackson to work at WJTV.

Around this time, I started dating a woman who was a co-worker to a buddy of mine. He said she overheard him talking about the Stewpot Stowaways and she asked if he knew the one guy with the long dreadlocks and he told her, "Yes. That's Greg. He's my boy." She began telling him how she attended several Stewpot shows and had a thing for me and asked if he would introduce us. Well that introduction happened, and we dated for several months. This woman was a few years older than me and she exposed me to several restaurants in Jackson I wasn't familiar with. Not only that, she also introduced me to red and white wine as well as encouraged me to stop eating red meat. It wasn't a talk about any negative effects to my body that got me off of the bull, it was her dating style. She was classy, very mature, more financially secure and loved going out to eat. We spent a significant amount of time wining and dining, so I didn't realize I hadn't eaten red meat in the course of a month, until she brought it to my attention. Once I realized I hadn't eaten red meat and didn't miss it; I gave it up instantly. This woman introduced me to several young successful lawyers and executives, people who weren't in my circle at the time.

It was as if I was being welcomed into another world, but really it was simply a level of life maturity I was reaching so my associates were changing. She and I had nothing but good times. She took me to her friend's socials, and I took her to the television station events such as the Christmas party that took place a few weeks after I was employed. We had a ball at the party. We danced, drank wine, ate pasta salad and I even freestyled with the band. Everyone noticed my date was a little older than me, but it made me look good because my male co-workers kept complimenting me about it all night. She didn't care, she was a free spirit and very into me. At this point things didn't seem that bad. I was in a new relationship; I was exercising my degree in my field (which isn't common) and I was eating healthier than I'd eaten my whole life.

This had to be the most non-music-related point in my life. Although I was still heavily into music and keeping up with who was hot as well as the ever-changing trends in Hip Hop, I wasn't playing an active role. As we continued on our courtship things were great, but a few strange occurrences took place. At one of her friend's house parties she somehow vanished into thin air. I found myself walking through the many twists and turns of this person's home trying to find her, but she was nowhere in sight. Out of the blue she reappeared smiling and laughing as if she was part of an inside joke asking me "am I cool." I wondered what was really going on. I told her I had been looking all over for her and she said she and her buddy were talking so I left it alone.

On another occasion she and I were chillin' at her place, having a movie day, and I went to the store to get some dip for the chips. When I returned, she started freaking out saying someone was in the house. She was so hysterical and convinced someone was there I had no choice but to walk upstairs and check things out. When I told her, no one was there she pointed to the top of the stairs saying, "They came through that window." I tried to show her they didn't, but she was too afraid to come up the stairs, so I balled a piece of paper up and threw it at the window to show her the screen was still there. When the paper bounced off the screen and hit the floor, she realized things were OK and calmed down.

If I wouldn't have been so passive, I would have realized the situations were getting weirder but they didn't seem that major, so I waved them off as no big deal. Weirdness hit its apex when she showed up at my place one day crying and bruised from what looked like a very bad fight. Her lip was busted and swollen, she had marks all over her face and a slight black eye. When I asked what happened she told me her ex-boyfriend beat her up. Retaliation was my first thought. I wanted to know where I could find him so I could handle him the way he handled her. She started begging me not to get involved and wouldn't tell me where to find him. That wasn't the reaction I was expecting from someone in her condition, so common sense told me there was more to the story.

At this point I started asking questions. "Why did he beat you up? How did he even get close to you? "Where were you when this happened?" She said, "Please don't get mad and call me stupid when I tell you this." I knew I was about to hear something crazy, so I just listened. She told me she was shopping for new furniture and ran into him in the store. He happened to be working at the place and said he could hook her up with a really good deal. He told her he could get her twelve hundred dollars' worth of furniture for five hundred dollars, but she would have to pick it up at one of the other locations where a friend of his works. She said it sounded like a deal, so she gave him the money. But when she went to the other location the friend didn't know anything about furniture being held or even a delivery scheduled in her name. At that point she realized she had been played. So, she got in touch with him and asked for her money back. He began avoiding her. After several failed attempts, she decided to go to his house and get her money. She said he started lying about it and they got into an argument that turned into a fight and that's when he beat her up. I asked how long had this been going on, and she said a little more than a week.

Things still weren't quite making sense, so I asked why did she go to his house instead of calling the police. I also wanted to know why she didn't tell his manager when she found out she got played. She didn't have an answer. My gut told me I wasn't getting the truth, so I told her just that. We were sitting in her car outside of my place and she saw in my eyes and heard in my voice that I was done and was about to break it off. After a moment of silence, she said, "I need to tell you something." She said it was something she had been hiding from me for a long time and that she hopes I didn't leave her when I heard it. What this woman told me was so far away from what I was thinking that I sat frozen for a moment trying to take in what was said.

She told me she was addicted to cocaine. All of the weird acts I witnessed were reactions from the drug. As she began to tell me about all of the times she was high around me everything started making sense. She said most of her late-night visits were because the drug keeps her awake. When I couldn't find her at the house party, she was in the bathroom doing it. The sudden nose bleeds I had witnessed a couple times was the cocaine. The time she got paranoid and thought someone broke in was the drug. And when she went to her ex boyfriend's house and tried to fight him for her money, she was high. That's why she didn't want the police involved; she didn't want this to come out.

I was in total shock. I couldn't believe I was so naïve. I asked if she had ever done it at my place. She said, "Yes, in the bathroom." Out of anger and confusion I cursed and then kicked her dashboard which caused her window to crack on my side. She grabbed me and begged me not to break it off with her. She promised she would stop doing drugs if I didn't leave her. She said I was the best guy she had ever dated and that she loved me more than her addiction. She said she would stop doing it to keep me. I was even more confused because I didn't know much about cocaine or the effects it has on the mind, body and spirit. I really liked this woman, but I was a little afraid of what I'd unknowingly gotten myself into. The one thing that worked in her favor was her honesty.

In that sitting she told me everything—all of the people in her life who do it with her and how she gets it. She told me she was afraid I was going to find out anyway because she and I had a few mutual friends, and she always thought one in particular was going to tell me. I told her this was a lot for me, and I needed a little time to think. I got out of the car and she drove off. I sat on the steps to my apartment staring at the door, wondering what I did to end up in this situation. Before I could really get deep in my thoughts, I received a call from my mother. As she and I were talking I sensed that she wanted to say more than what was being said. The strange thing was that my mother was calling more in the six months I had been back in Jackson than she did when I was a college student. I asked her, "Is everything OK?" She replied, "Everything is not OK, and I've wanted to tell you something for quite some time now."

She said she was getting a divorce from my stepfather, who she had been married to for twenty-three years. She said things hadn't been good for a while, but she was trying to find a way to tell me. This was a total blow. My stepfather raised me since I was three years old, but this wasn't about me. It was about her, so I asked if she needed me. My mother is a very strong, independent woman so when she simply replied, "It would help." I knew it was serious and time for me to leave Jackson.

It just so happened that my aunt Sandra and my cousin Joe—who was out of school for the summer—were in town from Chicago visiting family. I explained to my aunt what was happening and asked if I could ride home with them. The ride from Jackson to Chicago is a ten to twelve-hour trek so I had plenty of time to think. After a combination of blows, one in my love life and the other in my family life, you'd think I would be out for the count. But as hard as it was to accept the reality of both situations, I **REFUSE TO QUIT!**

CHAPTER 13

Behind the Scenes

As soon as I touched ground in Chicago, I called my guy Andy C and told him what was going on. He immediately pulled me into a situation he was developing with two very talented female MCs named Shawnna and Teefa who called themselves Syndicate. He told me he met the ladies at his brother's barbershop, and they were the truth! He said they had star potential but were a little rough around the edges, so he wanted me to groom them. The role I played consisted of me teaching them interview etiquette, writing their bio, getting them a photo shoot as well as creating a promotional campaign to introduce the group and their music to the public. He pretty much needed me to do for them what I'd done for my own group as well as several artists in the Stewpot Stowaways.

My personal experience coupled with the knowledge and experience I acquired at Loud Records made me the perfect person to help take the project to the next level according to Andy C. He created the tracks, engineered the sessions and schooled them on all aspects of vocal production and arrangement. We worked every day for weeks, getting more and more familiar with one another and I eventually developed a level of trust with them. As a result, I set up and executed what became their first photo shoot, wrote their first bio and created a campaign for their debut single titled "Jenny Jonez." After recording an album worth of material Andy C decided he wanted to mix it up a little by bringing in another producer to add flavor to the project. He called up his buddy No I.D who produced the only outside track on the demo, a song called "Sweet & Dangerous." At that point, I hit the streets passing out a bumper sticker Andy C and I created that said, "Did you hear about Jenny?" Chicago had its first all Hip Hop radio station called 106 Jamz which was ran by my old buddy Pink House. The main on-air DJ was my former Stewpot Stowaway brother Tone B. Nibble. So, Andy C and I both had solid relationships at the station.

The campaign had the streets buzzing. No one knew exactly what, "Did you hear about Jenny?" meant. Andy C used his own money to press vinyl and cassette singles and we spent tireless nights working the club scene making sure every DJ in the city had the wax. At that point he went to 106 Jamz and gave the record to Pink House and Tone B. Nibble. Before we knew it Syndicate's debut single, "Jenny Jonez," was receiving close to 50 spins a week outshining Dr. Dre's "Keep Their Heads Ringin'."

Now the streets were starting to connect the bumper sticker to the song and the movement took on a new life. Syndicate became the talk of the town and "Jenny Jonez" was one of the hottest songs on radio. The girls were extremely excited and very eager to sign a record deal. And because Andy C didn't have any official paperwork, they seized the opportunity when No I.D presented a situation that would allow them to be signed at the same record label he and his good friend Common Sense were signed. Andy C was sick because he put all he had into Syndicate and thought paperwork was unnecessary because they had a bond. Unfortunately, it didn't turn out like he expected. The sad part about it was Andy had a few deal situations set up for Syndicate, but they slipped away before anything could materialize. I was shocked and a little disappointed by what took place but not as broken up as Andy C. Overall, he had a lot more time invested than I did. The end result was him deciding that he was no longer interested in producing Hip Hop.

During the recording of Syndicate's album, we worked with a female vocalist named Val, who was dating my cousin. Andy promised to work with her when we finished Syndicate's project, so she approached him about recording. Just when I thought he had given up on the music, his interest switched from Hip Hop to R&B and we began working on Val's demo. My role was a little more hands-on this time because Andy C put my R&B song-writing abilities to use for this project. Since Val and I both worked a nine to five (I was employed at Triton College), we would record vocals on the weekends and Andy and I would make changes and corrections during the week. Although Val was a songwriter herself, I wrote and arranged the first few songs. We had a nice flow but three songs into her demo, Val decided she enjoyed the writing process more than being an artist and suggested that we work with a choir buddy of hers. She said she had an amazing voice. Andy and I were stumped for a moment, but we decided to give the vocalist a listen before we made any comments or challenged her decision. The vocalist turned out to be as amazing as she promised.

Her name was Angela and we immediately refocused our direction towards her and began working on her project as if nothing changed. Andy learned a big lesson from the Syndicate situation, so he suggested we form a production company and get paperwork done on Angela right away. There were four primary players involved in the forming of our production company and we all had our roles. Andy C was the music producer; Val and I were songwriter/arrangers; and Lee handled the business of it all. Since our company consisted of four souls coming together to create soulful music, we called the company 4 The Soul Productions. We felt we were on to something because the energy between us was great. We had all been a part of each other's lives for a very long time, so the business ran as smooth as we expected. Angela had an amazing jazz texture to her voice, reminiscent of Nancy Wilson. The thing that surprised me most was that she didn't have a jazz background nor was she a jazz enthusiast. This was her natural voice and simply the way she sang.

Angela was a very fast learner. She caught on to vocal arrangements quickly and corrected mistakes in a few short takes. As fast as Val and I would write a song and teach her the arrangement, she would record it. Three or four of my songs made it onto her five-song demo. We were extremely happy with the outcome and quality of her project. Our evolution was evident because Syndicate's project and Val's demo was recorded in Andy C's basement studio, but Angela's demo was cut in a very nice state-of-the-art twenty-four track recording facility. Andy C was head engineer and manager, so we had unlimited access to the studio. The only problem we were faced with in regard to Angela was her husband.

He was younger than she was and a little insecure so every now and then he would bring an uneven, slightly overprotective vibe to the environment. It was as if he was worried about one of the male figures in the company taking advantage of her. On a few occasions, he became so overbearing that we were forced to have a talk with him. We explained our intentions with her and expressed how we didn't want his energy to bring stress to the project. We had a respectful, open and honest conversation that lead to a clear understanding. As a result, he decided to stop coming to the recording sessions in order for us to work with her in a comfortable, stress-free environment. Angela connected very well with my songs. So much so she found it hard to believe I was a Hip Hop artist.

When the demo was complete, Andy C spent several days and nights mixing the project. I sat in on several of the mixes because he wanted to make sure the vocals were exactly how I envisioned them to sound. We were on a roll and everything seemed to be in perfect harmony until we got word from Val that Angela had gotten cold feet. She wasn't sure if she wanted to pursue a professional singing career. We quickly set up a meeting with her to get an understanding of what was going on. When Angela arrived, she seemed shaken and confident that the world would not accept her as a recording artist. She made every excuse in the book ranging from her age to her hair color. We talked and talked trying to convince her that she was super talented, and the world needed to hear her music. The more we talked the more excuses she made, and not once did it seem as if she was going to give in. After several hours of trying to get her to see what we saw, we finally told her there's nothing we can do if she really doesn't want to pursue her music. After a few days, and more conformation from Val that nothing would change Angela's mind, Andy C lost it!

He couldn't deal with the back-to-back letdowns and decided he needed a break from the music business altogether. If 4 The Soul Productions was a body, he was the heart. Being that he was the producer and engineer, when he stepped away, there were no tracks for Val and me to write to. With no music or lyrics being written, there was no business for Lee to handle so the company dissolved. Val and Lee re-focused their energy back on their nine to five and carried on with their lives as if nothing ever happened. But it wasn't that simple for me. I couldn't just walk away. **I REFUSE TO QUIT!**

4 the soul productions

June 5, 1997

Dear *Abstract* ;

We have received your material and would like to thank you for your submission.

However our roster here at Kedar Entertainment is presently full. We are concentrating

all our resources on our acts at hand but urge you to continue to work hard. Best wishes

in all of your musical endeavors.

Respectfully,

Kedar Entertainment

Kedar Entertainment Rejection Letter

January 9, 1998

Greg Lewis
Abstract Mindstate
█████ 111th Place
Chicago, IL 60643

    Re: Product Submission:

Dear Greg:

Thank you for submitting your material to Priority Records and we apologize for the delay in responding.

Regrettably, we decline the opportunity to be a home for your music. Your hard work and determination, however, do not go unnoticed, and we wish you luck in your future endeavors.

Best regards,

Garnett March
VP, Urban Music

GM/ds

Priority Records LLC
6430 Sunset Boulevard
Hollywood, California 90028
Telephone (213) 467 ███
Telecopier (213) 856 ███

Priority Records LLC
32 West 18th St.
New York, New York 10011
Telephone (212) 627 ███
Telecopier (212) 627 ███

Priority Records Rejection Letter

CHAPTER 14

Back on my Grind

The year was 1998 and my partner in rhyme, E.P, had moved back home in August of the following year. We were ready to pick up where we left off. While reading one of the many Hip Hop publications, I saw an advertisement for a company in New York City called A&R Online. At this point, online services like this were the new wave in music technology so not too many were aware. To be honest I wasn't online like that at the time, but I took a chance and mailed them music from one of our previous demos and they loved it. The goal of this company was to aid in securing record deals for talented unsigned artists. They had relationships with a database of music magazines, club and concert promoters and record labels. If they got you a record deal the company received a finder's fee. Their plan was to create a demand for an artist or group by getting them as much exposure as possible. Their biggest thing was securing live performance opportunities and that was right up our alley. We were known as a live performance group, so I felt this would work for us.

After carefully reading over their paperwork, as well as having it reviewed by an attorney, we signed an agreement with A&R Online and became one of their clients. In the beginning things were great.

They called us all the time and put us on the phone with various individuals in their organization who all spoke highly about us and expressed how they loved the quality of Hip Hop we created. They told us we were going to be their marquee group. We were going to be the ones that would become stars and make a name for the company. They said they were going to use all of their resources to secure us a much-deserved record deal. Before we knew it, we were in a few press releases and on the company site. They were sending our music to all of the industry publications and were working diligently to secure as many write-ups and reviews as possible. Our first trip to NYC happened because of A&R Online. They didn't pay for our travel, but they did secure two very important performances. They told us if we could get to NYC, we would be able to perform at the Lyricist Lounge and Kool DJ Red Alerts' ten-year anniversary. I had a job, so it was no problem paying for a couple of bus tickets to NYC to make dreams come true. We called Val's sister, Aria, who lived in Fort Greene at the time and asked if we could crash for the weekend. She said, "No problem."

When we arrived in New York it was the weirdest experience ever because it looked nothing like we imagined. It was crazy cluttered and very dirty, but I couldn't stop thinking, *"Wow, this is the place where Hip Hop was born."* E.P and I caught a cab from the bus station to Aria's place in Brooklyn. The neighborhoods were much more diverse than the neighborhoods in Chicago, so it was strange to see such a variety of ethnicities within areas that were supposed to be "the hood." Once we got to Brooklyn and settled down, I contacted our point person to let her know we were in town. She told me she wanted the group to come to the office the next day and everyone was looking forward to meeting us in person. We caught a cab everywhere we went. I don't think I had ever ridden in a cab as much as I did during our very first trip to New York.

The next day we went to A&R Online's office and met the whole crew. That night we were scheduled for two events, so I reached out to a few of my contacts and we made a few rounds. One of the places we visited that day was Frontline Promotions were Val's sister Aria worked. We were there to meet with a brother I'd befriended via phone named Screwdriver, who was on their street team. It was good to finally meet him in person because we had spoken several times prior to meeting. He showed us around the office and broke down what Frontline Promotions was all about. We kicked it with him for an hour or so and headed out. We made a few stops at some of the stores to check out the gym shoes because New York has a huge selection. After we did a little shopping, we headed back to Brooklyn to get ready for our debut performance in New York City.

That night we were instructed to go to a club in Manhattan—I forget the name—and let a guy named Anthony know who we were. When we arrived, there was a long line and a crowd of people outside. I can recall my first introduction to Dead Prez' crew The People's Army. They approached the door and introduced themselves in a military like fashion before they were let in. When we reached the front and told the guy with the list who we were, he found our name and told us we were cool, so I felt relieved and thought everything was all good. As I went further and further into this basement club the Hip Hop vibe got thicker and thicker. The music was extremely loud, and the energy was incredible. The DJ was playing all of the right records, so I was in heaven. I always wanted to see it like this, and it took coming all the way to New York to experience Hip Hop in a club the right way.

As I searched the spot for anyone who looked like they were running things I began asking around for Anthony. Everyone told me he was there, but it took me a minute to find him. When I finally found him, I introduced myself and told him who we were. He didn't seem to know what I was talking about until I explained who we were with. He then asked if our contact person was there. I told him, "No, she told us to find you and let you know we were here and you would let us know when we go on stage." He said he couldn't let us on until she came because they were overbooked and had to cut a few acts. I didn't understand so I explained that we traveled from Chicago for this performance and I was told everything was taken care of by A&R Online. He said he couldn't do anything until a representative from the company got there. Of course, our representative never showed up so we were forced to watch all of the other acts perform and freestyle, knowing we were supposed to be on stage as well.

I was very upset and confused as to why Anthony didn't know who we were and why our A&R Online rep had us out there like that. Since we were in New York and determined to make it work we left the spot and went to our next performance at Red Alert's anniversary celebration. When we arrived at the club we were met with a pleasant surprise. The club was covered with Abstract Mindstate flyers. Just as we were wondering how this happened, Screwdriver popped up out of nowhere telling us he had his street team lace the spot before we got there to make our presence known. We exchanged pounds, hugs and thanked him profusely. He simply said, "Don't sweat it, that's what I do." and let us know he had to stop by a few more spots so he had to go. I immediately started searching the room for the contact person our rep told us to find. I found him with no problem, introduced myself and the group and told him the company that put us on the show. Fortunately, he knew who we were. He then told me the show would be starting soon and let me know our position in the line-up. He said our performance couldn't be longer than five minutes which was cool because none of our songs were that long.

Our A&R Online rep told us she would meet us at the last spot and didn't show up, so we figured she'd make it to this spot without a doubt. We were early in the lineup, so after a couple of performances they introduced Abstract Mindstate. E.P and I were charged because we wanted to perform at Lyricist Lounge and got played so we were going to give the crowd at this venue everything we had. The song started and E.P kicked the first verse. We had the crowd in our zone. They were rocking with us. As we said the hook, we let them know we represented Chicago. But right as I started my verse the music faded and the host—who was also our point of contact—walked on stage with a mic and said give it up for Abstract Mindstate, not even two minutes into our show. I couldn't believe it! To this day I don't understand what happened or why our rep from A&R Online didn't show up again.

At this point we were super-heated, but we knew we had to keep our cool because we weren't at home and didn't know a single person in the club, so the odds were not in our favor. All we could do was give the host a few cold stares and watch the rest of the show. The only reason we stayed was to see Black Moon, who were the special guest performers. Right after they did their thing, we left. E.P and I complained about how bad everything went all the way home. We talked about the money it cost to get there, how important Lyricists Lounge was to our career and why A&R Online played us like they did. We didn't want to do anything else at that point but leave New York. Our trip didn't turn out to be anything like the brochure, so I knew we were going to cut all ties with A&R Online because they handled us very unprofessionally. We expected a lot more out of the company that spoke so highly of us, our music and all of the incredible plans they had in regard to our career. I couldn't wait to speak to our representative to find out what happened, so

I called as soon as we made it back to Aria's place. I kept getting a voicemail.

The next day the rep from A&R Online called back and told me a long story about the drama she had with her boyfriend, which was why she didn't make it to our shows. I told her everything went terribly, and we were very unhappy with how we were handled at both clubs. I then said we would speak later because we were on our way to the bus station to go back to Chicago. The following day I called A&R Online and spoke to the guy who ran the company. He apologized for his partner's actions and promised nothing like that would ever happen again. I knew it wasn't his fault we got so badly mishandled, but she represented the company, so it was the company's fault. I explained to him that we were very unhappy with everything that took place and lost a lot of time and money on the trip, so we decided we want to end our situation with A&R Online. He understood and we severed our ties with the company. That debacle was enough to make a grown man throw a tantrum and say, "To hell with it." But **I REFUSE TO QUIT!**

Around this time, Andy C was keeping himself busy doing a lot of engineering work and building studios for clients. Luckily for us, he got bitten by the production bug and began making Hip Hop tracks again. I told Andy C Abstract Mindstate wanted to record a new demo. He was happy to know E.P was home for good and agreed to jump back in the producer seat for a new demo. Andy knew with us he could be as creative and soulful as he wanted because we always pushed the envelope whenever we came together to create. This was exactly what he needed after the craziness, so it worked out for both of us.

When we sat down to discuss the direction of the demo, he told us he had an idea and needed us to trust him. He said he wanted to do things a little different than we did in the past in terms of the overall approach. Instead of us choosing from a bunch of tracks he created beforehand, he wanted to tailor the tracks to us. He wanted to give us a general idea of where to take the song and we write the lyrics from there. This was very different from our regular routine but the trust factor between us was so high that we accepted the challenge. We were very comfortable and familiar with his production, so we knew what to expect. Andy C is a very soulful guy. He keeps his production thick by incorporating lots of instrumentation and background vocals into the track. The first track he gave us was an extremely bass heavy, hard-hitting, stutter stepping, boom bap type of beat. We were a little confused because this was the exact opposite of a typical Andy C track. The production was minimal and pretty much driven by the beat. Upon first listen E.P and I felt as if it was kind of odd and unfinished, but as we sat and listened, the more we understood what he created. The track was very different, but at the same time very dope, so we were now all on the same page. E.P began writing her verse in the production room with him while I made a run to the store to get some snacks because I knew we were going to be working for a while.

When I returned, Andy C called me in the room and told me to listen. He pushed play on the track, and we all bobbed our heads in unison. Just as I began to wonder what I was listening for, E.P.'s verse appeared out of nowhere. She spit the hottest sixteen bars about the state of the music industry I'd ever heard from her. She had a smile on her face that let me know she knew she killed it! I couldn't believe she wrote and recorded that verse before I got back from the store. E.P normally takes a while to record her vocals, but she didn't this time, so I knew we had something special with this song. I was so charged from hearing E.P.'s verse, I asked Andy C to let the instrumental of the track play and I sat down and wrote my verse in fifteen or twenty minutes.

The concept of the song was about how rappers get in the game, get a big head after having one hit single, then fall off. Sounds like something we could've written yesterday, huh? I had a hook I wrote for another song I felt would work perfect for this song and my thoughts were confirmed from their reaction after hearing it with the track. The hook went: "Now every song that we make got that hook / And every picture that we take got that look/ And every time we roll up y'all looking shook / Mad at the world, didn't have what it took." We titled the song "Shook," and it later became the song that put Abstract Mindstate on the map. We continued our new process of Andy C tailoring the tracks just for us. We would write during the week and record on the weekend because I worked a nine to five. We recorded another song called "Misfitz In This" that had such strong radio potential we pressed it as a vinyl release, with the Cap D (All Natural)-produced "Hip Hop Manifesto" on the B-side. I shipped that record to DJ pools everywhere. The record began to create a buzz for the group, so we started performing all over Chicago. We performed any and everywhere, big or small. It didn't matter to us as long as they heard our songs, we were happy.

Abstract Mindstate performing @ The African Festival of the Arts '98 in Chicago

Abstract Mindstate performing @ The African Festival of the Arts '98 in Chicago

Abstract Mindstate performing @ The African Festival of the Arts '98 in Chicago

The Group **RAP PAGES.**
voted "About 2 Blow"
Dec. '98 issue

4 the SOUL Productions Inc.
in conjunction with

RAP PAGES.

PRESENTS:
An Exclusive Listening Party for
CHICAGO'S OWN

ABSTRACT MINDSTATE
the Misfitz of Dialogue

LIVE PERFORMANCE

WHERE: THE HOLLYWOOD
           ATHLETIC CLUB
           6525 W SUNSET BLVD
           LOS ANGELES, CA
WHEN: DEC. 14th, 1998
CLOCK: BETWEEN 7 to 11:00 PM

$10 at the Door
21 and older to witness the flav!

Listening Party Flier - Los Angeles

An Exclusive Listening Party for

ABSTRACT MINDSTATE The MISFITZ OF DIALOGUE

Introducing their Hot New Underground Single

MISTFITZ IN THIS

Monday, December 14th, 1998
7p.m. to 11p.m.
at
The Hollywood Athletic Club.
6525 West Sunset Blvd.
Los Angeles, CA.

MUSIC PROVIDED BY THE WORLD FAMOUS BEAT JUNKIES

Special Performance by Abstract Mindstate the Mistfitz of Dialogue

You Must Present This Invitation
To Enter the VIP Room Only
Invitation Entitles you to Complimentary
Drinks and Hors d' oeuvres

RSVP for Greater Los Angeles Area
Contact: Ronda Penrice at Rap Pages (213) 651-5400 Ext. 7300

RSVP for Chicago and Surrounding Areas
Contact: 773-445-7530

Brought to you by Reciprocity L.L.C.

Listen Party Invite for Single - Los Angeles

4 the SOUL Productions Inc.

in conjunction with

The African Festival of the Arts

PRESENTS:

CHICAGO'S OWN

ABSTRACT MINDSTATE

the Misfitz of Dialogue

LIVE IN CONCERT
LIVE IN CONCERT
LIVE IN CONCERT

WHERE: DUSABLE MUSEUM
WHEN: SEPT. 4, 1998
CLOCK: BETWEEN 4 - 7:00 PM

You Gotta Support the Home Team!

African Festival of the Arts Flier

Abstract Mindstate debut single.

CHAPTER 15

The Quest for an Investor

I worked for a collection agency called First Data Corporation in the south suburbs of Chicago. I don't know if you are familiar with the atmosphere of a collection agency, but it's normally a pretty large space of individuals separated by cubicles working tirelessly to collect payments on delinquent accounts. Morale sometimes gets low because we have to deal with so many personal issues and attitudes. At FDC, specifically, when this happened upper management would come up with ideas to boost morale. One idea in particular caused for the supervisors to rap so upper management put the word out that they needed to meet with anyone in the office who was a rapper. Out of a few hundred employees, three rappers were brought to the table. I was one of the three.

A woman introduced herself as LaTina Cunningham, director of operations for FDC. She asked our names and began to explain her plan and how she wanted to work rap into her morale boosting. She needed us to write raps for the supervisors as well as teach them how to say it. We were told this was a special project and no one on the floor knew what was going on outside of the supervisors. She explained that she would allow us to take paid time off the phones every day for the next few weeks to accomplish the goal.

Not being on the phones collecting was enough for me but getting paid to write raps made it that much sweeter. I agreed. Over the next few weeks we worked with the supervisors and they learned the raps we wrote for them. The whole thing was a surprise. One day, out of the blue, the entire office was treated to a performance by the supervisors that included costumes, lights, music, beads and candy. It was like Mardi Gras in the office for an hour. LaTina's plan worked great. All of the employees enjoyed the show and, just as she hoped, morale was boosted.

Out of the three MCs I was the only one who told LaTina that I wanted her to hear my music. She told me she would love to hear it and that I could bring it by her office anytime. The only thing I wanted was her opinion because I lived for feedback. A few days after I dropped the CD off to her office, a supervisor told me she requested to see me. Now, I'm not thinking about my CD because I dropped it off days ago—plus I was in work mode, thinking I had done something wrong—so I was a little confused. When I entered the office, she had a strange look on her face which confused me even more. She told me she had been listening to my CD for the past few days and it was "really, really good." I thanked her and told her I hoped she would dig it.

She went on to explain how she was far from an expert when it comes to Hip Hop, but she knows good music and my product was simply good music that happened to be Hip Hop. We talked for a minute about the importance of music and why Abstract Mindstate chose to create our style of Hip Hop. She then asked what it would take to get our music heard and I replied "money." I explained that it takes marketing and promotion to properly get the music to the people and that service costs. I told her we were having a listening party in a few weeks for our single "Misfitz In This" at a sports bar downtown called The Garage and that she was welcome to come to see how it all goes down. Once I let her know we would be performing she said she would definitely be there.

The turnout of the listening party was much more than we expected. This was clearly the breaking point for Abstract Mindstate because close to two hundred people showed up to a place that could only hold about one hundred fifty people comfortably. Our original Stewpot brother Tone B. Nibble—who is a very respected DJ in Chicago to this day—was on the ones and two's. A few radio personalities came out and Chicago's longest running and most notable video show, Channel Zero, was on site to interview us and capture the moment. Hometown Hip Hop favorite Common came to support as well as a Londoner named Fiona Bloom who was interested in signing us to her New York based label 321 Records/Zero Hour Ent. Abstract Mindstate was in rare form as we performed both our A and B side singles. The stars were aligned that night and we shined just as bright.

After the listening party a few interesting things happened. Fiona Met with Armers, who was co-managing us with Lee, and said they wanted to do a deal. She said we'll be receiving paperwork when she makes it back to the office in New York. LaTina approached me and let me know she was all in if I wanted an investor to get our product out. All of the DJs at the party were requesting copies of the single and just about everyone in the place wanted to buy our music but we didn't have anything to sell. At that point, Andy C pulled me to the side and told me it was time for us to put our music out ourselves because it was obvious, we had a fanbase. Several things were going on that night and each was positive.

The next day, we made a stop by Val's crib, where Lee was, to pick up something. Common owns the building she stayed in and he lived in the basement. I don't know if he heard us talking outside or what, but he came upstairs and started talking to us about the show. We were kinda in a rush because we had to get to my house to do a phone interview with Rap Pages, one of the leading Hip Hop publications at the time. He told us we had an excellent show and said he really liked our performance. He said it was tight how we only performed a couple of songs then mixed it up with the people. He called us "pros" and said we have his support. As I pulled off, I definitely felt honored because we were huge fans of Common's work and to know he respected us as much as we did him and his music made it that much more surreal. I didn't have time to enjoy the moment because I was more concerned with making it back to my place to do the phone interview.

The following Monday at work everyone was talking about our listening party. Those who were there spoke in excited, exaggerated tones which made our fellow co-workers feel as if they missed the event of the century, and they did. The thing that meant the most to me, surprisingly, wasn't the record deal offer—which turned out to be a single deal with terms we didn't care for, so we turned it down. Nor was it the various signed artists such as Common who showed up to support or all of the love the crowd showed us when we performed. The thing that meant the most to me was successfully pulling off the listening party itself. I thought I could do it and I did!

All of the music industry knowledge and experience I'd acquired from the business side, in terms of marketing and promoting, to the artistic side was put to the test and I passed. I must say I was very proud of myself and the relationships I had built that allowed me to do what I did. Over the next few days LaTina and I sat down and came up with a budget for our seven-song ep release, and I went to work. Her investment company was called RECIPROCITY LLC and she established it to invest in the arts. Until me, she had only invested in artists such as painters and sculptors. In her mind art was art so she felt as though she was carrying out her company's purpose. It was strange because LaTina and I had like-minds except she was a fortune 500 company type and I was a music industry type. But all of the same rules applied so we got along very well. Who would've thought the director of operations of my job would become my investor? On one hand being in business with the big boss at the gig was great. But on the other hand, it made for a few awkward moments. When you work in an office that has hundreds of employees in one space separated by cubicles the maturity level often times is equivalent to that of a high school.

There were so many rumors about LaTina and I having a secret love affair that I couldn't help but laugh. I was in her office more often than the other employees, so they fooled themselves into believing it was more than what it was. Those who came to the listening party saw "the big boss" there and made what they wanted out of our interaction. The funny thing about it is that I never let it bother me. I was too focused. I did wonder why the women at the job put so much energy into it. Once I figured out how much it was going to cost to press our seven-song ep, and five hundred pieces of vinyl, I presented the amount to LaTina and we moved forward.

The demand for Abstract Mindstate's music was pretty high so we took the songs we had completed at the time, mixed and mastered them and decided we'd release them as a CD titled The Last Demo: The EP. We called it the last demo because we knew we were done making demos at that point. The songs on the project were intended to be our new five song demo but we recorded two extra songs, added them to the collection and sent it to the CD press. An EP was common practice even back then. A lot of people still don't know the letters stand for "extended play," which means the release is longer than a single (one to two songs) but less than an album (nine or more). The lead single for The Last Demo: The EP was "Shook." The single became Abstract Mindstate's signature live performance song and went on to gain the group even more recognition than the first single, "Misfitz In This." When you mention Abstract Mindstate to most DJs they reference our records by color. Before the DJs became familiar with the group, I used bright colors on the label of the wax to make our vinyl stand out. I knew we needed something to separate our vinyl from the various signed artists. Plus, I was able to make them remember our wax by saying the colors and it worked like a charm. I also knew our wax would be easier to read in the dark when they're fingering through their records. DJs who have followed us from the beginning say they have the yellow label 12" referring to "Misfitz In This." While those who were introduced to us during our underground takeover say, "I have the orange label 12" referring to "Shook." Shook garnered the group more accolades than we ever could have imagined. Andy C had a vision when he created the track and it became very clear that he knew exactly what he was doing.

ABSTRACT MINDSTATE:

MISFITZ OF DIALOGUE

BY BILLY JOHNSON JR.

E.P. THE HELLCAT, THE FEMALE HALF OF CHICAGO'S ABSTRACT MINDSTATE, IS standing on the front porch of her family's modest home on the city's west side. She's not looking directly into the camera. Instead, she's gazing down the street with a serious expression, recounting her days growing up. This introductory clip from Abstract Mindstate's self-produced, 30-minute promotional video is professional enough to be aired on BET.

Despite its crispness, the video wasn't financed by a major record company, but by Olskool Ice-Gre, E.P.'s brotherlike rhyme partner from Chicago's Southside. Ice-Gre insists that his and E.P.'s seriousness about the music business is what separates them from other artists.

"We carry ourselves like signed artists—no level of arrogance at all," Ice-Gre explains. "You know how many shows we've done?" he asks. "We've rocked with Tupac. We actually rocked harder than 'Pac."

The proof of their powerful stage presence was evident the night before this interview at the Garage in Chicago as the duo unleashed the contents of their fifth demo, the definitively titled *The Last Demo*. The house was packed. Local notables Common and Gray were in attendance, as were a few out-of-town record company CEOs who were scouting the duo. This response gave Abstract Mindstate renewed hope that their numerous years of paying dues—15 for Ice-Gre and 12 for E.P.—would finally pay off.

Another promising sign is that they've seen friends from their college Hip-Hop collective—the Stowpot Stowaways—get their big break. Last year, the Stowaways group Crooked Lettaz signed with Penalty Records, home to Noreaga and Lord Finesse. This news encouraged Abstract Mindstate to push even harder.

Both Ice-Gre and E.P. can go toe-to-toe with members of Hip-Hop's elite—not only with freestyle lyrics but with substance. On "Real Life Situations," the best of *The Last Demo*'s five songs, Ice-Gre rhymes about helping his mom run the house after she and Ice-Gre's father divorced; they were together for 23 years.

Working part time/Having hard times/'Cause I can't kick in/Mom is nervous/The mortgage is due/What we gone do?/I need your help son/It what she be scream
helping me. In the
cerns. Shomari's m
keep it real for her.

Abstract Mind
oriented Hip-Hop
the years, but it h
tive of their lifest
enough to receiv

Ice-Gre says T
secure the group
the business. But
train back to Chi
State University i
plan. "How bad d
doing anything el

It's obvious th
Ice-Gre knowingly
"We're going t
ly pays off," E.P. d
motherf*ckers."

Rap Pages Article - Abstract Mindstate

172

INTRO.........1:20

THE CHICAGO FIRE..........5:06

MISFITZ IN THIS...........4:18

HIP HOP MANIFESTO..........3:24

REAL LIFE SITUATIONS.........3:52

GET YO GROOVE ON..........3:18

SHOOK.........3:54

Executive producers : Abstract Mindstate the M.O.D.
© 1999 4 the SOUL productions INC.
Warning All Rights Reserved. Unauthorized duplication is a violation of applicble laws.

Abstract Mindstate's very first CD

CHAPTER 16

I Want My MTV

Another amazing opportunity presented itself around this time. MTV ran an advertisement for a live talent showcase called *The Cut,* hosted by Lisa "Left Eye" Lopes of TLC. The only requirement was that you had to be an unsigned artist. The prize was an MTV produced music video with rotation of the video on the station. I would do anything to get my group in position for a record deal, so I mailed our demo to MTV. There was so much going on with the group at the time that I forgot about the contest until Armers called me with some exciting news. He said he received a call from the producers at MTV and they loved our demo. They wanted us to fly out and audition to be on the show. This was a little surreal for me, so I asked Armers if he was joking.

At that moment he put me on hold, did a three-way call, and got the producers on the phone. The producers said our music was incredible and if we were half as good as our demo, we would definitely make *The Cut.* I was charged! I told them our live show is so much better than our demo so get ready to let us on the show. They laughed and told me they would call our manager back with all of the details. They then asked if we could make it to Burbank, California to the MTV studios. I was floored! This was the opportunity of a lifetime and could not have happened at a better time. We were known for having a very strong live show, so this was right up our alley. Not to mention the demo we sent them was on its way to the press to become our first official CD.

The plane ride to LA was exciting. All I could think about was the possibilities. Although I had no clue about the level of competition, I knew we were the best! My Mom had recently moved from Chicago to Los Angeles, so she picked us up from the airport. We didn't have time to do anything but head to Burbank when we got off the plane. It was as if we were signed artists because we had so much going on in Chicago that we couldn't stay long in LA. Our return flight was scheduled for the same day. My Mother was very excited and proud that E.P and I were auditioning which got me even more excited. When we arrived at the MTV studios parking lot the guard pointed us to the correct entrance and showed us where to park. From the outside it looked like a big, plain, white, concrete facility until you entered. Once we were inside it was another world.

There was a lot of movement and soundstages set up for several of the shows that aired daily on the network. We checked in and were told to wait in a room with the rest of the contestants who were auditioning. There were artists from everywhere. We mixed and mingled with everyone as we filled out the various forms that were handed to us upon entering the room. It wasn't long before they began calling names from a list to come and audition. We were almost the last to audition. It was obvious they called contestants according to their position on the sign in sheet and since the room was almost full that put us close to the bottom. It felt as if we were waiting for five or more hours but, in actuality, we might have waited a little over an hour; the audition process was pretty fast. In the midst of a conversation with one of the remaining few con-testants, an MTV representative walked in, called our name, asked if we had our music handy and told us we were up next. E.P and I looked at each other with a "here we go" expression, said peace to the room, and followed the representative to our destiny.

The representative showed us the set where the show was going to be taped, then walked us through a narrow hall into an all-white room. The room had nothing but a table, a panel of judges, a small audio set-up and a few microphones. It was kind of a stiff situation, nothing like the room that was just shown to us where the show would actually be taped. That room had a vibe, like a small performance venue but this was an audition, so I was ready! The judges were very warm and inviting as they introduced themselves and asked us to tell them a little about Abstract Mindstate. As a performer, you get asked this question all the time, so the answer was articulated very well. After the initial introductions, one of the judges asked for our music, gave us the microphones and we got ready to show the panel why we were chosen to audition. When the music started, I did my usual pre-crowd hype before starting my verse and the panel was all smiles. I went into my verse with an exaggerated energy, similar to that of LL Cool J in Krush Groove, but a strange thing happened when I reached the halfway point of my verse.

The judges began looking weird, stopped the music and asked if "the young lady" could look at them while she was performing because her eyes were on her feet the whole time. I almost froze in shock! I couldn't believe the judge had to say that to E.P. We were seasoned performers who mastered the live show, so this caught me off-guard, but I quickly composed myself. When the music started again, I jumped right back into it but I didn't hear E.P filling in on my verses so I looked back a couple times but she wasn't looking so she didn't catch my expression. Since I couldn't make eye contact with her, I proceeded to perform trying to overcompensate by giving as much energy as I could. By the time we got to the hook of the song the judges stopped the music and said, "Thank you, that's all we need to see."

As we shook their hands on the way out, one of the judges advised E.P to always address the crowd when she's performing. I smiled as if this advice was welcomed but inside, I was furious! I couldn't believe what happened. I knew we just blew the audition. As soon as we got out the doors of the studio, I asked E.P why she wasn't filling in on my verse like we normally do in live shows. She said, "I was, I was just so on top of your words you couldn't hear it." I knew this wasn't true, so we got into a small back-and-forth argument and stopped talking to each other. The ride from Burbank to LAX airport was an hour or so because of traffic and we were silent the entire ride. I was very upset about our performance and she knew it. Even my mom chose not to say anything about it the whole ride, so the vibe in the car was very uncomfortable.

When we arrived at the airport, I hugged my mom and told her I would call when we landed in Chicago. We didn't have any luggage, and this was years before 9/11 so checking-in and making it to our gate was a breeze. E.P and I never had arguments, and if we ever disagreed, we talked it out before it could turn into anything serious. This time was very different. I didn't know what was going on in her head but in mine, I kept replaying the comment made by the judge. I was telling myself, "I know we're better performers." We'd spent our own money to travel all the way to Los Angeles for a once in a lifetime opportunity and we didn't show up! That's the thing about being in a group, everyone has to be on their A-game, or it will hurt the whole. In order to be successful in a group or on a team, you have to always think about the whole because it's never about you and you alone. It's amazing how much you can learn about yourself by being a part of an organized group.

Our flight began to board, and we still weren't speaking to one another. If you're a person who travels often, you know that sometimes you end up catching a flight that isn't really full and there's enough room for everyone to sit in a row by themselves. Well, this was the case on our return flight to Chicago. E.P. sat on one side of the plane in her own row and I sat on the opposite side a couple rows back. Once the plane reached its desired altitude, the stewardess announced they were dimming the lights in the cabin and, if we wanted, we could use the overhead lights for our personal convenience. I took off my seat belt, laid back across the length of the seats starred at the roof of the plane. Out of the darkness I heard, "I was nervous." I sat up and looked in E.P.'s direction and asked, "What did you say?" She repeated, "I was nervous." This was the breaking point for our silent treatment.

I asked her why she didn't tell me that from the beginning. I know how we perform and how it sounds when she fills in on my verse. It wasn't there. She then admitted to making excuses because she felt she let me down. I explained to her that I can understand a natural emotion like nervousness if she owns up to it. But my anger came from the excuses when I knew better. We had one of the best conversations we had in years. Because of this incident we grew as a group. We talked the entire four-hour ride, addressing everything surrounding the audition. She said everything was cool until she walked into the room and saw the judges. That's when she realized we were at MTV and this was a big deal. It was the cold atmosphere of the audition room that made her so nervous. I was there and I remember the coldness of the room, so I was able to understand how it was possible to feel the way she felt. But she had never shown any signs of nervousness until then, so my expectations were extremely high.

I can honestly say I learned another side of my partner on that flight. We'd been working on music for about seven or eight years and I thought I fully knew her. But it took that situation for her to open up and show me her vulnerable side. To know E.P. is to love her, but if you don't know her, she can be an intimidating individual so seeing her intimidated by anything was new to me. I felt better about the situation at this point and hoped the judges saw the potential in Abstract Mindstate past the mistakes. The only thing I dreaded was, having to tell our team we didn't give the performance they had come to expect from us, but it was pretty late when we landed so I knew I could sleep on it before having to relive the moment.

The next day was just as expected; I received a call from Armers asking how the audition went. Of course, Armers and the team were very surprised when they learned we didn't shine like the stars they felt we were. They were even more surprised to hear anything about E.P. being nervous. Armers was the only person that asked how I felt about it. I expressed my real feelings to him in that regard, but I also shared with him that E.P. and I had a growing moment on the plane. I told him I believed we would never have that problem again. Although I knew deep in his heart, he wanted to hear another classic Abstract Mindstate live performance story, he was happy to know I moved past it without any bitter feelings towards my partner. Unfortunately, we didn't receive a call back and we never heard from MTV again. Even worse, the artist that won the overall competition was a female who had a male counterpart kinda like us except they weren't a group. That's showbiz and we had our shot. I could have really let this situation take me off my square because it was a once in a lifetime opportunity and I put my all into it. As much as it killed me inside to watch it all slip away, I knew it was far from over, so **I REFUSE TO QUIT!**

CHAPTER 17

The Last Demo

Before going to California to audition for *The Cut,* I ordered five hundred CD copies of The Last Demo: The EP. Today that doesn't sound like much, but in 1998 it felt like we had a million copies. I sold one hundred fifty at my job alone. The rest were sold at our live shows and in mom and pop record stores throughout Chicago. This was a time when being original and on top of your game was a good thing, which is why I was so heavy into reading any and all publications that had to do with music—especially Hip Hop. During my reading I came across an advertisement for a talent competition being held by Salem cigarettes, sponsored by Def Jam called the Salem Orb-e Nationwide Talent competition. I took a chance and submitted a few Abstract Mindstate songs. The judges liked the material and entered us into the competition. This wasn't the normal talent show where the judges or crowd pick the best and that artist is crowned the winner.

There were three phases for each category—music, art, dance and comedy—that had to be won in order to be crowned the overall winner in your category. The first phase was local, which meant we had to win against contestants in our city. The event was held at a small club with seventeen local acts competing for the position.

The special guest performers were Carl Thomas, who's single "I Wish" would become huge, and Rahzel, the GodFather of Noise from The Roots.

After a very long list of performances, Abstract Mindstate walked away the winners of the local phase. The second phase was regional, and it was also held in Chicago but at The Park West which is a much larger venue. This time around, contestants from all over the Midwest were competing to go to the finals and we were representing Chicago. The special guest performer was Gang Starr and the house was packed with industry people from all over the world. We gave what we thought was one of our strongest performances to date and the judges obviously felt the same because we walked away winners for the Midwest, beating out five other performers. We were now set to go to the finals in New York City. We were excited about our victory, but we didn't have much time to celebrate because we were hitting the road in a few hours to head to Atlanta to the Rap Sheet convention.

This particular convention was special because the publication was folding soon, so I knew this would be a memorable moment in Hip Hop. All of the industry insiders were there so it was an amazing experience. One of the highlights of the day took place when Guru of Gang Starr approached the group in the lobby of the convention center and told us we were dope and we tore it down in Chicago. I felt honored to receive praise from a group we felt embodied the essence of Hip Hop. The second highlight came when our very own Chicago-born-and-raised, nationally respected music industry veteran George Daniels saw us and said, "Y'all are some hard-working motherfuckers." He had an expression on his face that spoke volumes, so he really said a whole lot more than his words. We thanked him and I felt equally honored by his comment. This was a very busy time for Abstract Mindstate and we were making our rounds by land, air or sea. I didn't care how we got to the next event, all I knew was we were going to be there representing ourselves and our city.

We made our presence felt at the Rap Sheet convention in more ways than one. We had so much promotional material you would have thought we were a signed act. We had t-shirts, flyers, stickers and press kits. At one of the demo listening sessions, we were the star attraction. I put together our press kits following industry standard all the way down to the correct sides the content should be placed within the pockets of the folder. We made sure we were at the session early enough to enter our product. The listening session took place in a huge ballroom with speakers in the ceiling so everyone could hear the demos all the way to the back of the room. The room was close to full and you could see the various expressions as they played the demos.

The panel included a host of music industry professionals who gave their critiques of each demo that was played. As you could imagine they had something to say about almost every demo and most of it wasn't good. Finally, we saw them pick up our package and one of the panelists looked at our content in amazement. We had no idea what was going on so we got a little nervous when the speaker leaned into his mic and said, "Where is Abstract Mindstate? Could Abstract Mindstate raise a hand so I can see who you are?" E.P and I stood up—wearing our personalized baseball jerseys with the group name on the front. The guy said, "Y'all need to pay attention to this group because this is how a press kit should look." He went on to talk about how we have included all of the necessary documents such as a professional promo shot, bio, press and the one thing everyone else forgot, contact information. He passed our kit down the panel and everyone gave us praise for our presentation. The guy put the CD in the radio and said, "If your music is as good as your presentation you guys are going to make it in this game."

They asked which song we would like them to play and we told them "Shook." After the song played the entire room stood up and started clapping. It was amazing, we became the focus of the demo listening session. Everyone on the panel said we were great and almost everyone in the room exchanged contact information with us. A then unknown Ludacris approached us and introduced himself as Chris Lova Lova of Atlanta's Hot 97.5. He said he wanted to play "Shook" on his Kiss it or Diss it segment on the radio. We gave him a copy of the vinyl and he gave us the number to the station and the time to call. We felt great after the demo listening, so we hung out in Atlanta for the rest of the day until it was time to get back to our hotel to call Chris Lova Lova.

That evening, at the time we were told, we picked up the phone and called Hot 97.5. Without a hitch, we got through to Chris Lova Lova and he put us on hold. After a few minutes he came back and introduced us live on the air, told the audience how he met us, let us say a few things and played the song. Seconds after "Shook" played he said the phones were lighting up and we got nothing but positive feedback. The people loved the song and Chris Lova Lova adamantly told us to stay in touch with him because he was working on a few things. Atlanta was very productive, and it was a privilege to attend what will always be remembered as the last Rap Sheet convention. Good thing I didn't quit.

A few weeks later, we were on a plane to New York City to perform in the finals of The Salem Orb-e Nationwide Talent Search. KBA Marketing (who had offices in Chicago) was the company that handled everything so our flight arrangements, hotel accommodations, ground transportation and credentials were all taken care of when we landed in New York City. We could tell by the level of professionalism and promptness that we were dealing with a huge corporation because they left no stone unturned. The company only paid for the group to come, but my cousin (our manager at the time) Lee bought himself a ticket as well as my good buddy and graphics guy, Jabari. Our investor LaTina flew in and my best friend from seventh grade, Primo, drove up from Virginia to show support. We were crew deep at the event and felt good about our chances of winning.

The event was being held at the Hammerstein Ballroom and the top prize in the music category was forty-eight hours of studio time at a major New York recording facility, a photoshoot with photographer Jonathan Mannion, press in major music publications and a first-place plaque. The categories were music, art, comedy and dance. There were four finalists in each category representing the Midwest, East Coast, West Coast and the South. Comedian Bill Bellamy was the host and Faith Evans and Pharoahe Monch were special guest performers. Since this was a Def Jam sponsored event, all of the finalists were taken to meet Russell Simmons and the celebrity panel of judges, which included Fat Joe and DJ Premier. I shook hands with them all and talked a bit, but I was in deep concentration. We were in the finals, representing the Midwest and in New York, the place where Hip Hop gets the red-carpet treatment but also the place where we had nothing but bad live performance experiences. The entire Chicago KBA Marketing office was there and all of them either knew us or were familiar with our name because we were the talk of Chi-town. I can say we had a nice amount of support in the house. Unfortunately, they had nothing to do with the decision-making process in regard to the competition.

An announcement was made that the show was about to begin, and you could see the packed house of five thousand patrons start to settle down and focus their attention toward the stage. This was our largest crowd to date. We had rocked a few hundred shows but never to a crowd of this magnitude. The host, Bill Bellamy, walked out and immediately got the crowd live. He gave a quick overview of the competition, explaining how they chose the best-of-the-best from each region in four different categories, ranging from music, art, dance and—his favorite—comedy. He then broke down the rules and details in a side-splitting fashion. As all of the contestants gathered backstage it was brought to our attention that the music category will kick off the show and we were the first act to perform. The pressure was on, but we were prepared. We knew we had the right song to get this New York crowd open.

E.P and I slide to a corner backstage and bowed our heads in our prerequisite prayer before we hit the stage. A few short moments later Bill Bellamy energetically introduced us, and we were handed our microphones and ran out on stage. E.P and I always took thirty to forty seconds to get the crowd hyped with a little call and response before performing. It worked like magic. The New York crowd was very receptive and gave us a lot of energy. We gave the soundman the cue and jumped right into the song that got us to New York: "Shook." E.P and I had a flawless performance. All of our movements were perfect, and we spit our verses with the confidence and swagger of seasoned vets. The New York crowd could tell we were the real deal, and this was evident from the sound level of the applause when we reached the end of the song. We had done it! We finally got to show a New York crowd that we were the truth. The cheers we received meant more to us than that crowd would ever know. But I could proudly say we earned it. When Bill Bellamy came back out, he said, "Wow, it's gonna be hard to come after them." (and I have the video footage to prove it).

When we walked offstage and out into the crowd to watch the rest of the show everyone gave us pounds and love saying we were hot. I couldn't stop smiling as I shook over a hundred hands and said "thank you" at least a thousand times. When the next performer

came out, he was nice, but his live performance and crowd response wasn't as good as ours. I remember E.P and I looking at each
other smiling saying "we got him." The next act to hit the stage was
a group from Brooklyn and everyone knows Brooklyn is always in
the house. When Bill Bellamy introduced them and he said where
they were from, the crowd went into a frenzy. At that moment E.P
and I got nervous because we felt the pressure of home court advantage working against us. There were five or six guys on stage
and at least four or five had a mic in hand. They told the soundman
to start their track, but they were all talking at the same time and
missed their cue. So, they told the soundman to start the track over.
E.P and I looked at each other and smiled again; we knew their
mishap would work in our favor.

When the track started, they were all talking at the same time again
and almost missed their cue again. The group's performance was
extremely unorganized and loud. Everyone was saying different
things and filling in at different times, so it made it hard for anyone to understand the rapper who was taking the lead. I believe
four of them rapped and the others were supposed to be hype
men. Every time the crowd got bored and stopped giving them
energy—which happened several times throughout their performance—they screamed "where Brooklyn at?" and the crowd would
go nuts. Then they introduced one of the guys who was on stage
with them and he turned out to be a known Brooklyn MC that we
were very familiar with because he was a signed artist. The crowd
cheered for that artist, but the group's chances of shining brighter
than Abstract Mindstate was pretty much over. Their track stopped
and they talked wildly for a couple of minutes and finally left the
stage. After the music segment of the contest was over, it was obvious that we were the best group. Unfortunately, we had to wait

until they judged the contestants in all of the categories before they announced any of the winners.

The event finally reached its end and it was time for Bill Bellamy to announce the winners. I don't remember the order in which he announced the categories, but I do remember when he got to music, we were all ears. He cracked a few jokes about the contest and the contestants then got right to it. "And the winner in the category of music is," and he said the group from Brooklyn and our mouths dropped. The group ran out on stage and grabbed the plaque, held it above their heads and jumped around in excitement. The odd thing was you could hear mixed reviews from the crowd because there were just as many boos as there were cheers. I was amazed by the judges' decision because the rules of the contest stated that an artist or group performance could not be longer than five minutes, the use of profanity was prohibited, and the act couldn't be signed or associated with a signed act. The group from Brooklyn did all of the above.

Their performance lasted close to ten minutes because of the mistakes at the beginning, they had a false start, they continuously used profanity throughout their show, and they had a signed artist on stage with them. For them to walk away the winners was ludicrous. I was very unhappy with the decision, but I maintained a good sportsman like demeanor and took it like a man. I knew we were cheated out of a well-deserved win but what could I say—we were cursed in New York. As I walked through the crowd to make my way to the VIP room several people in the audience stopped me and said, "You guys were really the winners. Y'all were the best group tonight." That made me feel good because the people are the real judges and it was clear we impressed them and the host that night. It was a sad plane ride back to Chicago because we were blatantly robbed and couldn't do a thing about it.

A week or so later we received a call from the executives at RJ Reynolds—the company that owned Salem cigarettes—saying that the board had a meeting in regard to the Salem Orb-e Talent competition and the decision was reversed and that Abstract Mindstate were the winners. They didn't give us the details as to why they came to this decision, and we didn't ask any questions because we already knew why. I was even more upset at this point because all of the hype and attention we should have received in New York was taken from us. We got our plaque in the mail—not at the Hammerstein Ballroom in front of Russell Simmons and the celebrity guests. Jonathan Mannion's schedule wouldn't allow him to come to Chicago and do our photoshoot, being that it was weeks past the expected time frame, so he had to be replaced by another photographer and none of the music publications wanted to run the story because it was old news by the time everything was officially switched to read "Abstract Mindstate were the winners." I was really upset about the press because it took about a month for all of the changes to take place, and it's understood that print media's goal is to be on or ahead of the news, not behind, so we lost in that respect. In the end, we did receive the forty-eight hours of studio time and a few good promotional pictures but Abstract Mindstate was never recognized on a national level, in the press as the winners. This could have been the final nail in the coffin for a very long and confusing run in the music industry. But I'm a dreamer with unbelievable drive, so **I REFUSE TO QUIT!**

Salem Orb-E event promo shot

Greg "Olskool Ice-Gre" Lewis

P.O Box 43088
Chicago, IL 60643

312 635.7345
Ice_majors@hotmail.com

Abstract Mindstate the Misfitz Of Dialogue

Objective To show the world that there are emcees who still have a love and respect for the art form.

Experience

1999

- National winners of the Salem ORB•e/Def Jam Records nation wide talent search (NY, NY.)
- Attended Rap Sheet newspaper 6th annual hip hop conference (Atlanta).
- Midwest regional winners of the Salem ORB•e/Def Jam nation wide talent search (Chicago.)
- EP featured on Big Nastee's debut album on Mercury Records (Born Ready Remix.)
- EP featured as one of the six forces of nature on the upcoming Chicago All-Star mix tape vol II.
- Headlined twice at Jazz & Java coffee house in Chicago.
- Special guest performance at the Coffee House (Jackson, MS.)
- Featured in Rap Sheet Magazine: Representing section (Progress Report) February issue.
- Independently released *The Last Demo: The EP* and second single "Shook" b/w "Get yo Groove On."
- Release Party for The Last Demo: The EP Hosted by radio personality Spank Boogie of WGCI (Chicago.)
- Special Guest performers for the Raw Deal Seminar (Macon, GA)
- Featured as 107.5 WGCI's "Home Jam" artist "Get Yo Groove On." –The Bad Boyz radio show
- Featured artist on the "Backstage Pass Seminar" a showcase hosted by Silver Lining Entertainment.
- Song featured on the soundtrack as well as performed at the premiere party for the independent film "Backstabbers".

1998

- Featured as 107.5 WGCI's "Home Jam" artist " Misfitz In This." – The Bad Boyz radio show
- Voted *About 2 Blow* – Rap Pages Magazine October issue.
- Auditioned for MTV's "The Cut." (Los Angeles)
- Guest appeared on the Chicago All-Star Sprite Mix tape.
- Special Guest for Kool DJ Red Alert's anniversary party in NYC.
- Listening Party I (Chicago) "Misfitz in This" recording artist Common and 3-2-1 records/Zero Hour Entertainment were in attendance. Sponsored by MOET Chandon
- Offered single recording contract for "Misfitz in This" by 3-2-1 records/Zero Hour Ent.
- Performing artist for the 15th annual African-American Festival of the Arts(Chicago)
- Listening party II (Los Angeles) "Misfitz in This LA Style" sponsored by Rap Pages Magazine
- Featured Artist in Rap Sheet Magazine's "Representing" section -July issue
- Attended Rap Sheet Newspaper's 5th Annual Hip-Hop conference(Atlanta). Highly recognized in both demo listening sessions.

Abstract Mindstate Accomplishment Sheet

TITTILATING THURSDAYS
With
BLAKK INKK ENTERTAINMENT
Presents

ABSTRACT MINDSTATE

The Misfitz of Dialogue

At
Jazz N' Java
3428 S King Drive
Open Mic 7-8 pm   Showtime 8:15 Sharp

CD's Available for Purchase

Early Arrival Recommended $5 Cover

August 05, 1999

Jazz N' Java Coffee House Flier

The Last Demo: The EP release party flier

Shook Flier

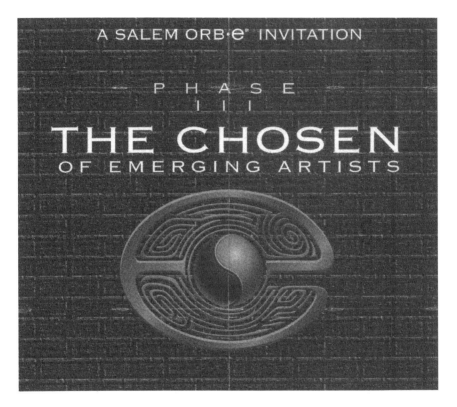

The Salem ORB-E Flier

The Last Demo Flier

Abstract Mindstate @ The Return to the ELBO ROOM

MARKETING GROUP

Chicago, IL 60610 PHONE 312.482.███ FAX 312.482.███

November 9, 1999

Lee Majors / Abstract Mind State

Chicago, IL 60616

Dear Mr. Majors:

On behalf of Salem we would like to congratulate you again on being selected to participate in "The Chosen" portion of the Salem ORB-e Program. This event will take place on November 18, 1999. You will showcase your talents with other emerging artists from New York, Boston, Philadelphia, Richmond, Chicago and Baltimore. The following is detailed information regarding Salem's ORB-e "The Chosen" event:

Date:	Thursday, November 18, 1999
Time:	8 pm to 3 am
Location:	Hammerstein Ballroom

NY, NY

Enclosed please find the travel and hotel itinerary. It is imperative that you follow the instructions detailed in this letter.

Thursday, November 18, 1999

8:00 am	: Chosen talent arrives at train Station
9:30 – 12 Noon	: Chosen talent arrives at New York LGA Airport
12 Noon	: Board bus to hotel
12:30 pm	: Talent check-in Best Western International Hotel
3:30 pm	: Meeting in hotel lobby
3:45 pm	: Travel to Hammerstein Ballroom
4:30 pm	: Check-in for rehearsal at Hammerstein Ballroom

Please allow for extra time when traveling to the airport in your city in case there are unexpected delays such as traffic, long lines at the airport, baggage check-in, etc. There will be a KBA representative at the New York LGA Airport to greet you (they will be holding a sign that says, "KBA, 'The Chosen'").

It is absolutely important that you follow the time schedule above, because if you are late, you will not be able to perform.

www.kbamarketing.com

Salem Orb-E Congratulations Letter

Rap Sheet Badge from
their last and final conference ever

January 4, 2000

Congratulations Abstract Mind State:

Salem ORB-e industry leaders have chosen you as the most talented emerging artists in Music.

ORB-e 1999 is over, but this is just the beginning for you. As the Chosen one for Music you will be awarded a five day demo master session at a recording studio. Def Jam will choose the recording studio based on the location of your home, or you may use D&D Studios in New York City. Studio time includes an engineer for production of one master DAT. The rest is entertainment history...

Contact cheryl fox spencer of Spencer Becker Media by phone at 212-625-█████ or by fax at 212-625-█████ for complete details on how to redeem your award before February 17, 2000.

You're off to a great start! Thanks for being part of ORB-e. We hope your experience in all three phases has been exciting and fulfilling, and proves to be the first step towards realizing your dreams. As your career progresses, we hope you remember your ORB-e experience and encourage other emerging artists to participate in the ORB-e program.

Sincerely,

Ronda Plummer
Ronda Plummer
Vice President
SALEM

Salem Orb-E Congratulations Letter - Winners

1st place Plaque my group received as the winners of the music category in the Salem Orb-e Nationwide Talent Competition

Abstract Mindstate Sticker

CHAPTER 18

Taking it to the Next Level

The following year, my investor and I were working so closely together I decided we should become partners. In the beginning she was a little hesitant because she felt she didn't understand the music business as thorough as I did. But I explained to her that the music business is 90% business and her understanding of business in general is what will make our partnership work. I also explained to her that she would learn the music side of the business over time because she will be actively working in it. Once she agreed we began the quest for an investor who could provide us with a substantial amount. It wasn't long before she brought a guy to the table for me to close. And within a few hours I negotiated and secured an investment for eighty-five thousand dollars receiving forty thousand dollars up front. At that point we made our partnership official by incorporating our entertainment company.

We both loved the original names of our companies so instead of coming up with a new name we merged the two to form 4 The Soul-Reciprocity Inc. The first order of business was to record an Abstract Mindstate album. I knew we needed the bulk of our investment for marketing and promotions, so the forty-eight hours of studio time we won from the Salem event came in handy. The rules of the event stated that the winners would record in a state-of-the-art recording facility. Since we weren't from New York, they transferred our time to a facility equivalent to the one in New York. We wound up recording at the Chicago Recording Company (CRC) as a result. We'd never recorded at CRC, but we were aware that it was the place where superstars like Toni Braxton and Michael Jackson recorded.

When we arrived, we were greeted with the respect of a major label artist. We were also introduced to the staff as well as the guy who runs the facility who gave us a tour. Our tour ended in the main room where we were set to record. There we were introduced to a guy named Jeff Lane who was appointed as our engineer for the duration of the recording process. The first question Jeff asked was how many songs we planned to record, and I'll never forget his expression when I told him an entire album. He thought it was unrealistic that I had such lofty goals of recording an album within the amount of time granted to us.

What Jeff didn't know was Abstract Mindstate's work ethic and how organized we were. I would negotiate with producers I had respect or an established relationship with, we would choose the track, write the song and learn our verse before going into a session. We were very tight, and I would often record my verse in one take. E.P and I averaged at least two songs every three hours. Mind you, we were recording on two-inch tape because Pro Tools didn't exist at the time, so I had the producer come in an hour before us to lay the track. Jeff couldn't believe how fast we recorded and corrected vocals. If the verse didn't have enough energy, or we said a lyric wrong, E.P and I wasted no time fixing it and moved on to the next song. We finished the recording process with several hours left to mix. Of course, we didn't have enough free studio time left over for the entire mixing process, but we mixed as much as we could with what was left.

Early into the mixing process, our city's main radio station, WGCI, was about to host their annual music seminar. I had the attitude that we were going to be a part of every contest and performance opportunity until the world was singing our song. I sent our press kit to the station and we were chosen to audition for the coveted Home Jam Artist of the Year spot. I figured if we could outperform twenty-three acts and make it to the finals of a nationwide competition, we should be able to make it to the finals in our own city. Chicago has some of the best talent in the world, so we didn't go into this thinking it was going to be easy, but we knew live performance was where we shined, so our chances of placing were great. The auditions were held at the same club we had advanced in the first phase of the Salem event and the panel of judges included George Daniels, former program director of WGCI; Elroy Smith, former music director of WGCI; and a couple of other individuals whose names slip my mind.

Before we gave the soundman the cue to start the track, we introduced ourselves, told them the name of the song we were about to perform and gave a brief description of what the song was about. We then told them to start the track and we went into the live show that made us the talk of the town. As we performed, I could see the judges smiling, whispering and nodding their heads not once taking their eyes off of us. When the track stopped the judges gave us a hearty round of applause as if we had just finished a concert performance. They then gathered themselves and said we would receive a call if we made it. They then told us "good luck" and thanked us for coming out. I walked over to the soundman, got our show CD and we left as if it was just another day at the office.

Once we were outside, we briefly talked about the judges' reactions, gave each other props on a strong performance, cracked a few jokes and left it alone. Since we were downtown, I decided to do a little music shopping at one of the nearby record stores. Not even a good hour into my music search, our manager Lee received a call. It was a representative from the WGCI Music Seminar congratulating us on making it. Lee told them, "Thanks, we had a feeling we would." In a surprised tone the woman on the phone said, "Y'all did?" Lee replied, "Yeah." He went on to explain how hard the group practices live performances. The woman said we'll receive a follow-up call in a few days with more details.

A few hours later we received a call from former WGCI radio personality Mike Love congratulating us on becoming Home Jam Artists of The Year. At that moment we became confused. We thought we were in the finals; we didn't know we were the overall winners and were crowned Home Jam Artist of the Year from that audition. That's why Lee told the women we knew we made it because we thought we made it to the finals. Mike Love told us the information he received at the station said we were the winners, so he advised us to check with the contact person who called us. The next morning Lee contacted the woman who called and asked for clarity on the situation. She said, "You guys won. You are the Home Jam Artists of the Year." At that point Lee began to explain why he came off so sure, and she laughed and said she thought we were just confident and that was OK because we had to be that way to make it in the business. When Lee hung up and told us our win was official, we screamed, hugged and cheered in excitement. Now that we knew we won for a fact we shared the news with our friends and family.

It was summer in Chi and anyone who has ever visited the town knows summers in Chicago are filled with music events and festivals. One of the coolest connections happened in the summer of 2000. A good buddy of mine named Coodie was doing promotions for both *The Source Magazine* and Sprite. He used to drive the promotional vehicles and would show up at every event that took place in and around the city. Coodie was a big supporter of Abstract Mindstate, plus we featured him on a few skits on our album. He asked if he could have an advance copy of our record to play exclusively in *The Source* truck to help promote our music. Although we weren't totally done with the album, we thought it was a great idea and gave him a copy.

A few days later I stopped by a spot called Krew Sports to drop off a few pieces of my group's wax for a DJ who was playing in the store. The owners were fans of my group's music so one of them told me to stop by their new Stony Island location because the urban clothing line Mecca would be doing a photoshoot for *The Source Magazine* at their grand opening. When I arrived the next day, all of the usual faces in the Chicago music scene were there. Coodie had the truck parked outside in the middle of the avenue blasting the Abstract Mindstate album at levels I had only heard in the studio. As set up for the photoshoot came to a close, out came the up-and-coming almost famous producer Kanye West. He was far from a superstar rapper but had production credits on a few hot records at the time. He played a principal role in the photoshoot.

As I leaned against the store watching everything from across the street, I could see Kanye's head bobbing to the music blasting. In between songs he kept asking Coodie, "Who is this?" After each song Coodie would say Abstract Mindstate. After the entire album played throughout the course of the photoshoot, I saw him ask Coodie again. But this time when Coodie said our name he pointed to me. At that moment Kanye began to make his way towards me. I watched as he got closer and, in true Chicago style, Kanye said, "Man, y'all got some fire. How come you never worked with me?" I replied, "Because we know who you are and we can't afford you." And he replied, "How you know I won't work it out for a dope nigga from the Chi?" I said, "Well act like it," and he said, "Take my number." I didn't know where this was going at the moment, but I knew from the vibe of our conversation we would work together. That moment came sooner than I expected.

An opportunity for the group to be featured on the soundtrack to the HBO series *Oz* was presented and I felt this was the perfect time to work with Kanye. To increase our chances of creating exactly what they were looking for we recorded two songs. The first was the Kanye West-produced "Pain" which was a soulful mid-tempo joint that was very emotional. The other was an aggressive joint called "26th & California (Lockdown)." When I submitted the songs to Eric B—not to be confused with the legendary DJ Eric B of Eric B & Rakim—who was the A&R of Avatar Records, he thought both songs were great! Eric B was interested in signing us and his plan was to use the soundtrack as a vehicle to introduce our music to the president of the label as well as a national fanbase.

Several things were going on for my group this particular summer. When we performed at the 19th annual WGCI Music Seminar in 2000 we were surprised with a special gift presented to us by a Sony/Columbia Records executive by the name of Cynthia Johnson. On top of being presented with a check for five-thousand dollars, as Home Jam Artists of the Year, Cynthia awarded us ten hours of free studio time courtesy of Tone and Poke of Trackmasters Productions (who had a deal with Sony), and we were advanced to the finals of their Natural Talent competition. A week or so later we received a call from a representative of KBA marketing, the company that RJ Reynolds hired to handle the Salem Event. The representative said the company wanted to fly us in for a special guest performance as last year's winners. Everything seemed to be going beautifully!

The investment and contest winnings allowed us to finish mixing and mastering the album. Not only were we able to pay for the completion of the music side of things but I was able to make sure all of the graphic work and promotional material associated with the record was done. We were on a high and it seemed as if all of my dreams were about to come true when things suddenly took a turn for the worse.

My business partner and I had given our investor a ninety-day grace period to make good on the remaining forty-five thousand of the eighty-five thousand dollar agreed investment. When the time came for us to collect the remaining funds, the investor was nowhere to be found. I didn't understand what was going on, but we chased this man for six to eight weeks straight and never made contact with him. It was as if he had suddenly disappeared. At this point we were forced to put it in the hands of our attorney. After several attempts our attorney eventually made contact with his attorney, who in turn expressed that our investor was a victim of fraud and all of his accounts were temporarily frozen. He faxed proof of this to our attorney who sent a copy to me and we waited a few months for this to clear up. After several weeks our attorney tried to make contact with him again but this time, he was unsuccessful. A letter was then sent threatening a breach of contract if he didn't comply within a certain amount of time.

Of course, we never heard anything from the investor or his attorney, so the contract was breached, and all obligations associated with the original agreement were null and void. We later found out the investor was behind the criminal acts that caused fraud on his accounts and he was sent to federal prison which is why we could not make contact with him. Everything started spiraling downward from that point. I never received the remainder of the investment, so we were stuck with a completely finished album without the proper marketing and promotion dollars behind it.

I then got a call from Eric B at Avatar records telling me he was very sorry, but our song wasn't going to make the cut for the soundtrack to *Oz*. He said if it were up to him he would leave us on but it turns out that the series is a hit with several national acts and they've submitted so many songs for the soundtrack, that the original idea of using new and unsigned artists got thrown out the window by the president of the label. At this point we started to feel desperate and anxious because we had done everything as a group to build our fanbase and create a name for ourselves, and I had done everything as a businessman to guide the project and secure the proper funding and opportunities but somehow it all went left. I hustled intensely over the next few months to find a new investor, but nothing transpired. Before I knew it, it was 2001 and the only thing that changed for me was the year.

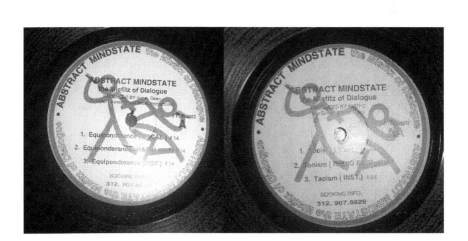

Equiponderance & Taoism 12 inch

Showtime @ Liquid Flier - Abstract Mindstate

Abstract Mindstate opening for Digital Underground

05/03/2000 03:30 3122259399 ARTHUR LEWIS PAGE 01

Date: May 1, 2000

To: Michelle Bussie
Abstract Mindstate

From: Kymberli Rose

Re: WGCI Music Seminar Information

Okay guys, the big day is quickly approaching. To make sure that is flows smoothly, please take note of the following information:

SOUND CHECK
Your sound check schedule is attached. Please make sure that you are on time. You will only have 15 minutes.

TICKETS
Your tickets are enclosed. Any additional tickets must be purchased through Ticket Master.

ATTIRE
Come dressed to impress.

MAKE-UP
Only the main performing artists will see our make-up artist (this excludes dances and background singers). You will be scheduled for make up immediately following sound check.

If you should have any questions, please give me a call.

332 South Michigan Avenue • Suite 600 • Chicago, IL 60604 • (312) 427-4800
www.wgci.com

WCGI Music Seminar Intinerary

Former PD of WGCI and former J Records exec Cynthia Johnson congratulates Abstract Mindstate on our win as Home Jam Artists of the year

Abstract Mindstate performing "Shook" on the main stage @ WGCI Music Seminar

CHAPTER 19

Things Fall Apart

In the midst of the chaos an interesting situation presented itself. I met a guy online through the social site Blackplanet.com who had been following the group's moves for a few years. This guy was from Chicago, but living in Atlanta, and had his own record label with national distribution through 404 Music Group. He and I emailed back-and-forth for a few days, which evolved into long phone conversations over the next couple of months. He told me he had a business partner, but it was obvious he was the business mind because all of my contact was with him. He said from what he saw he thought we were already signed. Once it was clear to him we weren't, he said he would love to put our record out. He wanted the first release to be a solid record from a hot group and we were the ideal act to kick things off for his new situation. I then explained to him how we were looking to establish ourselves on an independent because I knew the major labels wouldn't know how to market Abstract Mindstate. It was clear we were on the same page. He verbally extended an offer for us to put our record out through his label and their distributor.

I told him to give me a couple days to talk to my people and I'll get back to him. Shortly after, I had a low budget conference call (using three-way calling twice) and I shared the information with my team. We decided to take advantage of the opportunity. The next time the guy and I spoke, I told him we were with it and the process of paperwork began. We hired a lawyer to look at the contract and we negotiated until we came to an agreement. Since we didn't get to use the Kanye West-produced "Pain" for the *Oz* soundtrack, we added it to the album and handed the completed project over to our new label. Everything was going smooth until we signed the deal and sent them back the paperwork. We received a release date for the album but now that the deal was signed, the main guy, who I always spoke with, became a little cockier and more aggressive.

We got into several arguments before the release of the project because he had a problem with my knowledge and resourcefulness on the business side. Anytime I would try to use my connections for the greater good of the project his ego would get in the way and he would say things like, "You need to just be an artist and let me be the label." I never understood his attitude; everything I presented was going to put more money in his pocket at the end of the day. It got to the point where he and I almost got into a physical altercation. That moment is when my team and I chose to play it smart. We decided not to say anything else and let him and his ego run things so we could at least get the record out. We felt that once the record was out, our artistry would be the focus and we wouldn't have to deal with him much anyway. The funny thing is the label didn't pay for anything because we had everything done before we met them, so they really got over.

The album was released in June of 2001 and I set up, paid for and executed the release party myself. I was barely speaking with the cat at the label because my team and I decided it would be best to let Lee Majors do all of the talking. The release party was a success and the label guys were there to see the results of what I orchestrated with my team. After the performance the guy I spoke with the most approached me and said, "Y'all did y'all thing. This party is dope." He was playing humble and I could tell it was an act. But what could I do other than play along?

The next day, the record hit stores nationwide without any radio, cable or print advertisement. We were curious as to what happened because we were told all of these things would take place. We tried to contact the label several times, but our calls were unsuccessful. Weeks went by with no contact then a break came in the situation. We received a call from the distributor who left a message on Lee's voicemail. Lee gave me the number and I called back. We might have made a three-way call—I can't remember—but I do remember speaking to a woman at 404 Music Group named Laurie.

I began asking questions right away and she said they hadn't heard from the guys since the record was released and until our conversation, they thought we were a part of their scheme. Laurie confirmed that marketing and promotion dollars were advanced for the project, but they hadn't seen or heard from the guys since the transaction. Once it was clear that we both got bamboozled, she tried to work with us directly and offered a pressing and distribution deal. I tried to negotiate a regular deal, but they weren't willing to put up more money until they recouped their losses. I understood their position, and the terms were pretty fair, but we just didn't have the marketing and promotion dollars to support a P&D deal even if they continued to press and distribute it.

I was back where I started. As a company, I was unable to fulfill the financial obligations it would take to push our record, so we were forced to turn down the opportunity. Not only did this happen but Tone & Poke became unhappy with their deal at Sony/Columbia and left the label. Although we received our ten hours of studio time, we never got flown to New York City to perform in their Natural Talent Competition because it was part of their Sony deal and that dissolved when they left. RJ Reynolds did fly us back to New York as special guests' performers for their Salem Event, but, as they put it, "There was some sort of miscommunication" that resulted in us not being able to perform. We were very upset because we took time out of our very busy schedule to fly to New York thinking we would perform and be recognized as "last year's winners" but neither the performance nor the recognition happened. We were just there for the day hanging out—which didn't benefit our career.

Things start to really spiral out of control for me at this point. I was unemployed because I quit my job to pursue music and run my company full-time. My group was cheated out of the win at the Salem event. Our investor turned out to be a white-collar criminal who went to prison for fraud. The same company who cheated us out of a win in '99 lied to us about performing as special guests the following year. What seemed like a solid soundtrack opportunity and possible deal went left. I signed an indie record deal in haste and got burned by a thirsty egomaniac who stole the marketing money from the distributor. My group's debut album came out nationwide but died because of zero promotion. I'm months be-hind on my rent because of false promises made by our "so called" label. Not to mention one of the business deals I closed in 2000 went terribly wrong. Ok, I'm going to backtrack a bit and explain that situation.

I went out on a limb and secured an investment for a good buddy that I had been tight with since my freshman year of high school. He sold me on how he was ready to start his clothing line and how much he needed me to be the business behind it. My man is excellent with designing and sewing clothes and I was fully aware of his talent, clients and the various pieces he had made over the years, so it made sense. We spent a nice piece of the investment on t-shirts and hats to use as a vehicle to establish his brand and get his name out. The remainder of the money was supposed to be used to purchase a large amount of fabric for the couture line, which was the overall goal, but this never happened. I went as far as getting his branded tees and hats in every popular urban fashion outlet in Chicago and it sold very well. When it came time for him to do the part only he could do, he suddenly got cold feet and didn't handle his business. He also spent the remainder of the investment and stop returning calls from the investor who eventually was forced to reach out to me since I was the person who closed the deal.

Anyway, back to the original story. My aunt owns the building I was living in and she was fed up with waiting on her rent payments. A series of unfortunate events had me looking like the typical family member who thinks he can get over because it's family. Anyone that knows me knows that's not how I operate but due to the circumstances of the situation I looked exactly like "that guy." My car had a few minor problems that eventually led to engine problems ultimately resulting in the death of Yoki (the name I gave my Honda Civic). I asked my aunt for one more month to find a job, which she granted, but three potential employment situations fell through so I had no choice but to let go of my apartment and move in with another aunt who told me I could stay with her until I got back on my feet. This was a very dark, devastating and embarrassing time for me, and I had all of the ingredients to make a suicide sandwich. The easy way out would have been for me to just lower my shoulders, grab hold to that sandwich and take a big bite, but I'm just too damn in love with life. So even though I could, **I REFUSE TO QUIT!**

ABSTRACT MINDSTATE

the Misfitz of Dialogue

ALL
Management
Contact: Lee Majors
p: 312.907.████
f: 773.373.████

Debut album promotional poster

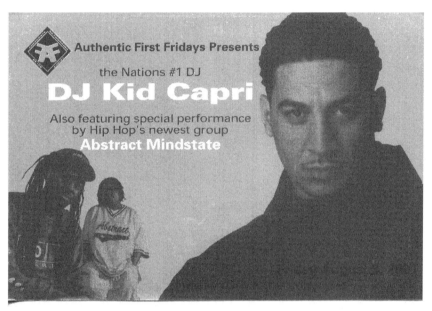

First Friday Performance Flier

Record Store Grand Opening - Abstract Mindstate

Abstract Mindstate Sticker

We Paid Let Us In VIP Pass

My groups nationwide debut album that
went terribly wrong

CHAPTER 20

Changes: Friend or Foe?

My album was in stores nationwide. It could be found in every record store in Chicago and the surrounding suburbs, but here I was
without a car, a place of my own, a job or a good record deal. The
people around me start acting very strange. The last days of having
my apartment was one of the worst periods of my life. I noticed that
a few of my very close friends and family members started to get
distant. It's weird because one friend, who I let stay with me for over
a year once, wouldn't take my calls. The same went for my cousin,
who was more like a brother, who stopped communicating with
me all together, even if I called him. I learned a lot about the people
who were around me and the type of energy money and success
attracts even on a small scale. Things were moving really fast for
me at the time and there was potential for an incredible outcome,
but the team that I thought was impenetrable turned out to be the
weakest under pressure.

I had been working tirelessly thinking it was all about "us" and "we"
and it turned out everyone around me was thinking "I" and "me." I
didn't figure it all out until it was too late. I'm now about to crash at
my Aunt Sandra's house with little to no contact with several of the
individuals I considered my immediate circle. I started going really

hard on my job hustle so I could sustain myself and get back on my feet. A woman I befriended during better days hooked me up with her mom, who was the principal of a charter school and a middle college. Since I had my degree, she told me to apply for a teaching certificate and, in a matter of days, I was working as a substitute teacher for both schools.

It was weird being back in a nine to five corporate hustle, but it was necessary, so I took it in stride. I never had an ego and getting caught up in the pride thing was never me, so I did what I had to do with my head up. I did do a lot of thinking during this period because I spent a lot of time alone. The person who showed me the most support during this period was my man Hollywood and my aunt Sandra who opened her house up to me without a second thought. I was a little embarrassed having to stay there, but she made it clear to me that I had nothing to be ashamed about. She told me that everyone needs help sometimes and that she was fortunate enough to have enough space so it's not a problem. If I went into detail about how incredible my aunt Sandra is, I would need an entire chapter, so I'll save those details for another book. Let's just say I was able to be comfortable while I worked to get back on my feet.

By the time spring 2002 rolled around I toyed with the idea of moving to New York to shop a new deal for Abstract Mindstate. I asked myself a few questions: where was Hip Hop born? Where does it get the most love? Where are all of the record labels? What city has radio stations with playlists that are 90% Hip Hop? The answer to all of my questions was New York City. I wanted to give it a shot, but I needed to check it out first. A couple of my people had already moved there for similar reasons, including one woman, in particular, who most knew simply as my sister. She and I grew up together, and we were best friends since fourth grade. I called and shared my thoughts with her. She encouraged me to do it. She told me I should give myself thirty days to really check it out and said I was welcome to stay with her. This was exactly what I needed so I planned it out and made it happen. I had no idea what was in store for me, but I was ready and equipped to take it all on.

I put together twenty Abstract Mindstate press kits, got business cards made and packed about two and a half weeks of clothes. Within weeks, I was on a plane to give the Big Apple a month-long test run. As I sat back in my plane seat, thinking about the infinite possibilities this trip had to offer, I decided it would be a good idea to document each day I'm there to see what I accomplished at the end of the thirty days. My mind was all over the place; I was in such a vivid daydream that I missed at least an hour-and-a-half of my two-hour flight from Midway to LaGuardia Airport. For those who have never been to New York City let me tell you. You can literally feel the energy when you land. If you ever wanted anything in life that required a little hustle, this is the place to put your hustle to the test.

Once I got my luggage, I followed the subway directions given to me by my "sister." I was headed to her job at Jive Records. I always looked at working for a major record label as a dream job. The funny thing is I helped her secure that position by allowing her to use my entertainment company on her resume as a previous place of employment because she had no record label experience. Needless to say I was the first person they called when checking her references. My first day in New York was cool. My "sister" showed me how to catch the train to her place in Brooklyn from Manhattan. She walked me all around the neighborhood showing me the little shops, bodegas and restaurants and she pointed out the residences of a few known actors and actresses. She stayed in a section of Brooklyn called Clinton Hills. The neighborhood reminded me a lot of the Hyde Park area of Chicago.

Things really kicked into to high gear the second day I was in town when I reconnected with my very good friend Coodie. He told me that Kanye knew I was in town and that he wanted me to come by his apartment in Newark, NJ. Every day was unbelievable, especially for a guy who dreamed of getting close to the situations I was around during this period. Matter of fact, I won't try to explain what I did each day, I'll just put the actual sheets from my spiral notebook at the end of this chapter so you can see for yourself.

Even after an amazing thirty days in New York I was still unsure if I would be able to move there. I was willing to make it happen, but I realized two things: the cost of living was extremely high, especially compared to Chicago. And you don't get much space unless you can afford a few thousand for rent. My "sister" was persistent about me returning to New York. When I told her my main concerns she said: "Look, things are about to change. I'm about to move into a bigger place. It's a bi-level one bedroom and the bottom area can be your room and I'll take the bedroom upstairs. There's a regular size bathroom and a small kitchen area with a little space off to the side big enough for a futon so we'll have a place for company to sit." It all sounded good, but I told her I wouldn't have the money it would take for me to take care of myself right away. I needed time. She said, "You got a job your second day here and you have crazy connections. Plus, you have business to follow up on at most of the record labels here, so you need to come back." She reminded me of all of the positive things that happened in that thirty days and told me I was made for New York. After fifteen to twenty minutes of trying to convince me she said, "You don't have to worry about anything your first few months. I know from experience that it's going to take you two or three months to get on your feet and I can handle it. All you need is your clothes and you; I got the rest. Just come back and make your dreams come true, and I'll hold it down until you get on your feet." At that moment I said "OK."

I felt as if God was letting me know (through her) that I needed to be there, so I had to take a chance. If I said no after that I would be giving into fear. And fear is the one thing I never have when it comes to my dreams. The things she said hit home because they were true and anybody that knows me know I finish whatever I start. And I had a lot of unfinished business in New York. Now I'm back in Chicago with plans of returning to New York in a month or so. I started saving all of my money because I needed to take every cent I had if I was really going to make a move. About two weeks into my return home, I received a call from my "sister" saying she may lose the apartment that we were supposed to move in to. She had to pay the first months' rent to the person she would be sub-leasing the place from and her next pay period was more than a week away. She told me she had a couple of unexpected bills that had to be paid and it cut into the money she planned to use for rent. Although I wasn't moving for another month, I told her I had a little something saved up. It wasn't much but enough to cover what was needed. She told me a specific date she would give it back which happened to be three days after my move-in date so in my head it was all good. There was also a clear understanding that my savings was all the money I had, and I would need it to get me through the first few weeks in New York. When I sent her the cash, I was led to believe we were on the same page. It seemed as if she was acting in the best interest of the situation, so I did what I felt was right.

A month later I moved back to Brooklyn. But this time we were staying in Prospect Heights on a street called Bergen between Washington and Underhill. I thought nothing of it when she didn't have the money three days later and asked if she could pay me back on her next paycheck in two weeks. The reason behind this (as she put it) was by the time I moved in it was time to pay rent again and she was still a little behind. I said no problem because I still had a little bit of cash, plus I was working another promotion that Coodie hooked me up with. I would be getting paid from that in less than two weeks, so I didn't trip. An interesting thing occurred during this time.

I started spending a lot of time in studio sessions with Kanye as he recorded tracks for several of Hip Hop's hottest acts. I helped him get through a few sessions by effectively communicating his ideas to the individuals he was working with. At the time, he wasn't that good at translating the ideas in his head into words because his mind was constantly moving forward so I took up the slack. He somehow took notice of my skill and made me an offer. He told me he was going to be the biggest thing in Hip Hop, but he needed a team. He said he could use an assistant as well as someone to help him with the business duties of his production company. This was an offer I wasn't expecting but couldn't refuse. We worked out the logistics and I became his personal assistant/head of business affairs. I was still doing my own thing with my group, so I needed to put together a few more Abstract Mindstate press kits for meetings and mailings. I told my "sister" what I needed to do since this was her payday weekend and the day I was supposed to get the money back she owed me. She and I made plans to go to Circuit City to get blank CDs; an office store; and a paint store because she wanted to paint the small lounge area outside of her room.

That weekend we went to a mall like area not far from our place that had all of the stores we needed. We talked the whole time we were shopping so I didn't notice she was paying for all of my items with her debit card instead of just giving me the money she promised to pay back. I told her about the offer Kanye made me—which was a position she often said she wanted to do for him—and that

I accepted it. She acted as if she was happy for me as we went in one store for the CDs and another for two pocket folders. At that moment I remembered I needed a pack of socks and boxers so I asked if she could just withdraw the remainder of the money and let me buy the rest of the things myself because I needed to get a couple personal pieces.

That's when all hell broke loose. She started by asking, "What money?" This was extremely odd; she had to know what money I was referring to being that she asked if she could pay me on her next check twice. Before I went into detail, I simply asked, "What were you giving me three days after I moved here that I've been waiting to get for two pay periods?" She said she thought the money was for my half of the rent and instantly got an attitude with me. I asked if she forgot our talk about giving me a couple of months to get on my feet and she lost it. In the middle of the street she began screaming and hollering, "I'll give you your damn money back" as if I was asking for something that wasn't promised to me. It was as if she was in a drama class the way she exaggerated her character. I felt that her actions were very unnecessary being that we never had an all-out screamfest and were the best of friends since fourth grade. I asked her to calm down and talk to me because she and I don't get down like that, but she refused to calm down.

She stomped her way to an ATM, simultaneously cursing me out. But the amount she was supposed to give me wasn't available (I believe she knew it wasn't). She then said, in a pouty tone, "My check hasn't cleared yet, but I'm going to give you all of your money when it does!" I told her she was taking this way too serious and that she needed to calm down and talk to me in a normal tone. However, at this point she refused to speak to me. Things got pretty ridiculous, and I wasn't expecting her to act a fool a month and some change into my stay. Over the next few weeks things were very strange in the apartment. Not only was she not speaking to me but she started coming home very late every day so I would be asleep. And she left for work before I had to be up, so we didn't see each other for at least two to three weeks. During this period, I was working various promotions with Coodie to supplement my income, so I was cool.

By September a mutual friend of ours (who she dated on and off) got a position at Violator Management and asked if he could crash at the house until he found an apartment. He told her he would pay the rent as long as he was there and that was right up her alley, so she agreed. She tried to act as if she didn't need or want the help but that was all part of the game she played. He knew but he played along with it. A few weeks into his position he approached me about assisting him in the office at Violator. He told me he would pay my portion of the rent in exchange for my assisting him. This was a good deal, being that my gig with Coodie was coming to an end, because it was a summer promotion. As we approached the bottom of September, I began assisting my man at the offices of Violator Management. After a few weeks of work, he took care of my portion of the October rent. The timing of this hustle was perfect because it allowed me to hold my own even though my "sister" told me she had my back. I still couldn't believe she tripped like that over money she promised to repay. Regardless, I was happy to get past the drama so I could focus on my goals.

Just as things were starting to feel normal, I spoke to my stepfather who surprised me with an awkward comment, "I heard you are out there living off of your sister in New York." I asked where he got that information from, and he told me he spoke with her mother who told him she was taking care of me because I refused to work. I was very upset by this because it was a flat out lie. Not to mention my stepfather and I weren't on the best of terms at the time, so hearing that from him didn't make the situation any better. I called my mother and asked if she'd heard anything and she began telling me that my "sister" called her saying the same thing except she added that I thought I was too good to wait tables (something she did when she first moved to NY). She also said I fell in love and that's all I cared about.

I was furious at this point and asked my mother why she didn't tell me anything. She said she knew there was more to it because she knows me, so she chose to stay out of it and let us work it out ourselves. I hung up with my mother and called my "sister" at work and asked her what was going on. She replied, "What are you talking about?" And I asked, "Why does my family and yours think you're taking care of me because I won't work when I've been working since, I got here?" She tried to downplay it by saying "I have no idea." But after I told her I spoke to my stepfather, who got the information from her mother, and my own mother (who said the same thing) she started getting defensive telling me not to call her at work with drama. I then asked her, "What did my social life have to do with our living situation and why did she feel the need to discuss my personal life with my mother when I'm a grown man?" She lost it at that point and started screaming, cursing me out. She then hung up on me. I called back and she went right back to cursing so I hung up on her. She then called me back and told me if I don't leave her place, she would call the police on me. At that point I knew our friendship was over.

My girlfriend at the time came by and when I told her what happened she began moving my things into her car and insisted that I stay with her. I spent the last three weeks of October living with her in the Bronx before she and I packed her car with our things and moved back to Chicago. I'll never forget that day because it was Halloween, and the first time I heard the terrible news that Jam

Master Jay of the legendary rap group Run-DMC was killed. This was only eight days after the accident that almost took the life of my very good friend Kanye, who had just hired me as his personal assistant and head of business affairs for his production company days before the incident. Things were totally out of whack and it would have been easy to take everything that happened as a sign that the music business was not for me. But ambition forces me back up every time I get knocked down, so **I REFUSE TO QUIT!**

Olive-Harvey College

CITY COLLEGES OF CHICAGO

FACULTY / STAFF

Signature

232

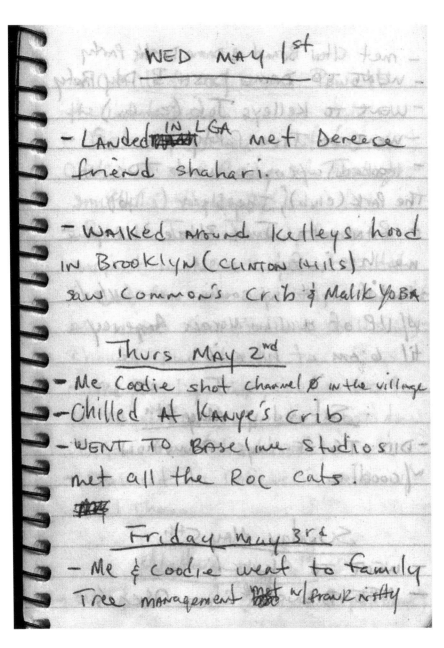

WED MAY 1st

- Landed ~~IN USA~~ IN LGA met Dereece friend shahari.

- Walked around Kelleys hood in Brooklyn (CLINTON HILLS) saw common's crib & Malik YOBA

Thurs May 2nd
- Me Coodie shot channel 0 in the village
- Chilled At Kanye's crib
- WENT TO Baseline studios met all the Roc cats!
~~thru~~

Friday May 3rd
- Me & coodie went to family Tree management ~~met~~ w/ frank nitty

My 30 day trial in NYC

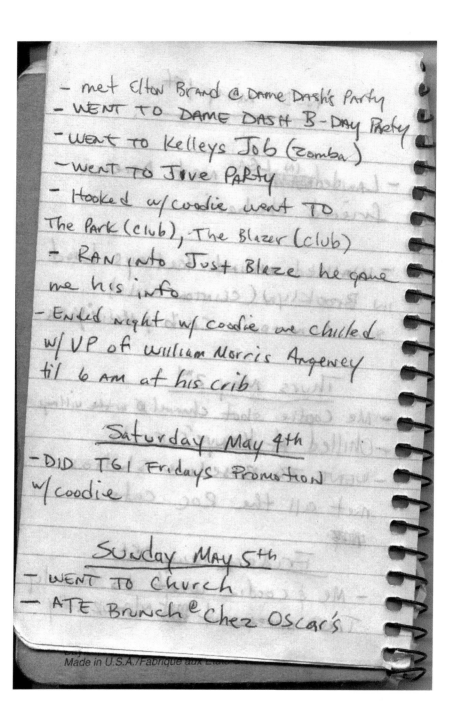

- met Elton Brand @ Dame Dash's Party
- WENT TO DAME DASH B-DAY Party
- WENT TO Kelleys Job (Zomba)
- WENT TO Jive Party
- Hooked w/ coodie went TO The Park (club), The Blazer (club)
- RAN into Just Blaze he gave me his info
- Ended night w/ coodie we chilled w/ VP of William Morris Angency til 6 AM at his crib

Saturday May 4th
- DID TGI Fridays Promotion w/ coodie

Sunday MAY 5th
- WENT TO Church
- ATE Brunch @ Chez Oscar's

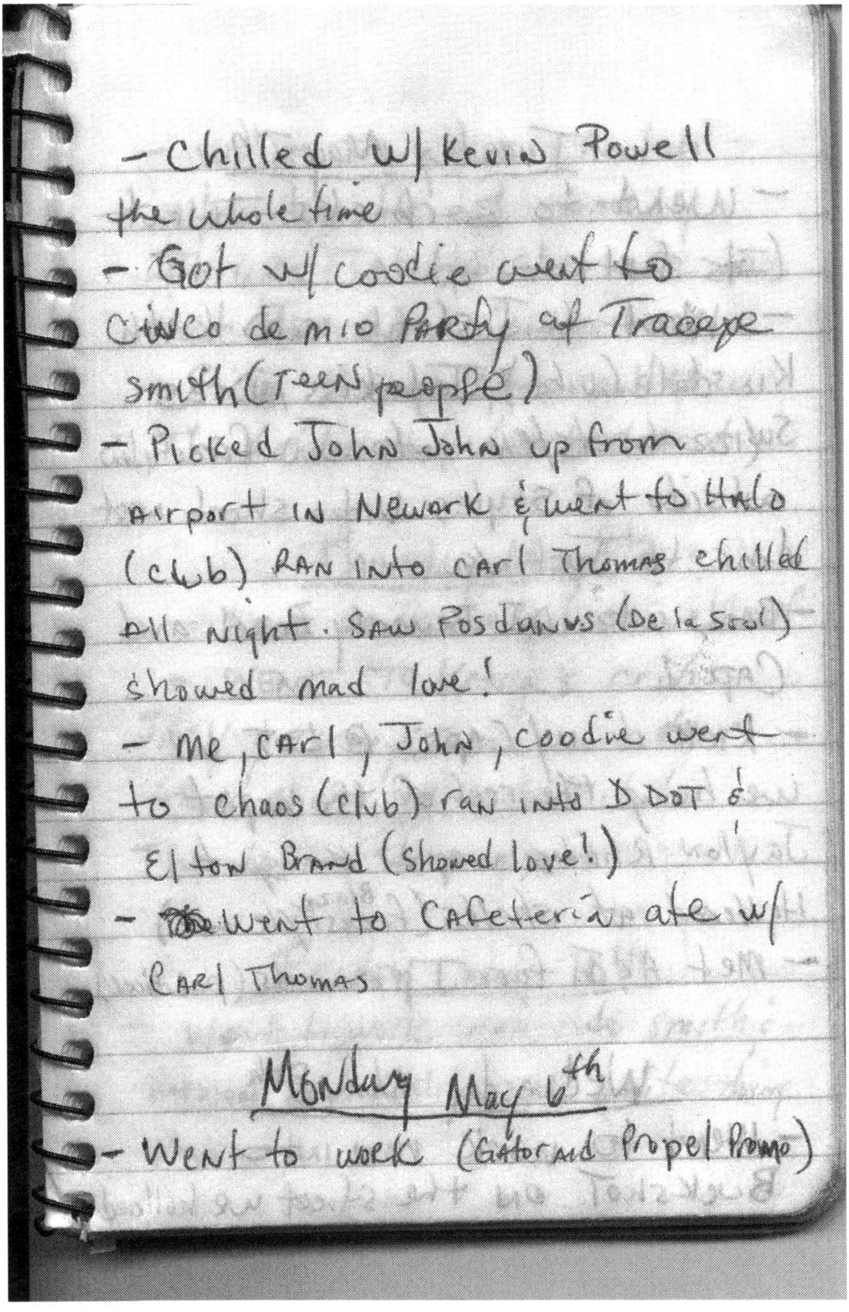

- Chilled w/ Kevin Powell
the whole time -
- Got w/ coodie went to
Cinco de mio Party at Tracaye-
smith (Teen people)
- Picked John John up from
Airport in Newark & went to Halo
(club) RAN into Carl Thomas chilled
All night. Saw Posdanus (De la soul)
showed mad love!
- Me, Carl, John, coodie went
to chaos (club) ran into D DOT &
Elton Brand (showed love!)
- went to Cafeteria ate w/
Carl Thomas

Monday May 6th
- Went to work (Gatorad Propel Promo)

235

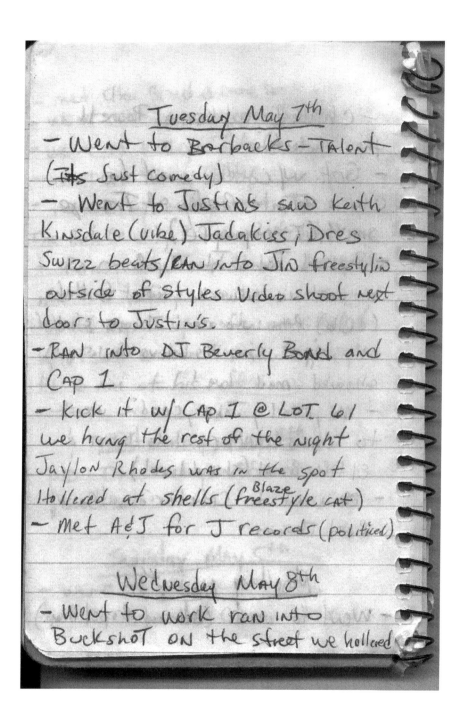

<u>Tuesday May 7th</u>
- Went to Barbacks - Talent
(Its just comedy)
- Went to Justins saw Keith
Kinsdale (vibe) Jadakiss, Dres
Swizz beats/RAN into Jin freestylin
outside of styles video shoot next
door to Justin's.
- RAN into DJ Beverly Bond and
Cap 1
- Kick it w/ Cap 1 @ Lot 61
we hung the rest of the night.
Jaylon Rhodes was in the spot
Hollered at shells (freestyle cat) Blaze
- Met A&J for J records (political)

<u>Wednesday May 8th</u>
- Went to work ran into
Buckshot on the street we hollered

236

- WENT TO CLUB cheetah -
w/coodie He did comedy
It WAS "TAlents" showcase
Met Joe Clair (cool AS hell)
- Slide through spot called
The Coffee shop (BAr/restaurant)

Thursday May 9th
- DIDNT work we got rained out
- WENT TO KANye's crib
JIry & Torrey Tarue came over
from phili we kicked it to
The Coffee shop again

Friday MAy 10th
- Went to work RAN INTO smith &
wesson and Talib Kweli while doing
Promo

— Hooked up with Traceye & kelley
   we went to Talib Kweli concert
 met Kanye there DID THE Backstage
 thing. Chilled with Wood Harrison (actor)
MOS DEF, Bootcamp click, Rah Digga, Craig G,
Kelis, Beverly Bond, Young Zee

— Me & Traceye went to "Franks" in BK
 I met PENNY who came up from Boston
 we chilled

                Saturday May 11th
— Me & coodie went to roof top
party w/ kurt, PENNY came later
we went to KANYE's
— WENT TO slither (club) it was
   jumping

238

Sunday May 12th
- Went to Queens shot footage and chilled w/ consequence
- Rode the bus to the Wiz
- Went to laundry Mat w/Kelley

Monday May 13th
- Promo got rained out
- Went to The Apartment (club) & saw Rosie Perez & John Ritter inside. Bobito was DJ'n (Dope music!)

Tuesday May 14th
- Did Promo (Propel)
- Went to Rockafella saw Meth we talked
- Went to Baseline (Roc Studio)
- We to Talib Kweli Show in NJ w/ Kanye

—chilled w/ Kweli & Dead Prez
Backstage (super cool)

<u>Wednesday May 15th</u>
- DID Promo (water)
- Caught train to Raukus
  gave A&R my CD
- Kanye picked up me & Coodie
  had JB in car we went to
  MTV w/ Yazmin (Producer)
- Walked around time Square
- Me & Coodie caught train
  home

<u>Thursday May 16th</u>
- woke up too late for work
- went to Meechi's party @
  SX 137 (club)

Friday May 17th
- DID PROMO (work)
- WENT TO kelleys Job her friend showed me around Brooklyn heights
- TOOK TRAIN BACK TO CLINTON HILLS
- Hung out around the house

Saturday May 18th
- WASHED CLOTHES
- Hooked w/ Larvetta went TO Dope House PARTY saw michi, Renee etc (Dope)

Sunday May 19th
- WENT TO EAT & to the movie's
-

Monday May 20th
- DID Promo (work)
- WENT uptown (upper eastside)
Spanish Harlem
- WENT TO APT (club) saw
Crazy legs, kool Herc, ? Love
(chilled & talk w/ em) vibed w/ Bobbito

Tuesday May 21st
- Talked w/ kera
- WENT TO WORK (Promo)
- Kera went w/ us to work
Picked up Andy C from Train
went uptown
- WENT TO Flow (club) Bev Bond,
TEK (s;w), OUSMAN, Cipha sounds, Cons §
Rhyme Fest, Kanye, Kelly, coodie

Wednesday May 22nd

- Went uptown took meeting w/ Radios
- ~~went to Quad studios w/~~
Kanye to track song for Trina
met Def Jam cats took info
- Meet Mos Def's manager (Howie)
- stop thru D.J CLUE Session (Right Track)

Thursday May 23rd

- Went to Chelsea Piers MTV2
was shooting all the memorial day shows
Kanye was interviewed by Cuddish
- Met w/ Sapna for lunch (Ent Attorney/
Publishing)
- Went to Club SX/37 (Bomb!)
- Laughed it up w/ D.J CLUE &
Cuddish while @ Chelsea Piers
- Andy C D.J @ SX137

243

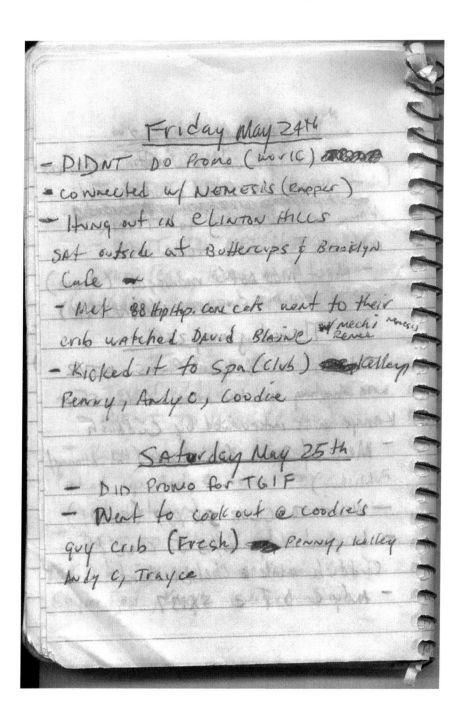

Friday May 24th

- DIDNT DO Promo (movie) ~~crossed out~~
- connected w/ NEMESIS (rapper)
- Hung out in CLINTON HILLS
sat outside at Buttercups & Brooklyn
Cafe
- Met 88 Hip Hop core cats went to their
crib watched David Blaine W/ Mechi, Mussy, Renee
- Kicked it to Spa (club) ~~Kelley~~
Penny, Andy C, Coodie

Saturday May 25th

- DID Promo for TGIF
- Went to cookout @ coodie's
guy crib (Fresh) ~~Penny, Kelley~~
Andy C, Trayce

<u>Sunday May 26th</u>

- DID Promo (TGIF)
- chilled at Kelleys - her, Andy c
PENNY
-

<u>Monday May 27th</u>
- DID Promo (TGIF)
- Went to BBQ @ Lori's (fromchi)
Laruetta, Renee, Kim, Andy C, Coodie
- Went to Apt (club) Andy c, Kelley
Coodie
- Saw crazy leggs Again, Curious
George hollered at Bobbito gave him
Andy C MIX CD

<u>Tuesday May 28th</u>
- HUNG OUT IN the HOOD

<u>Wednesday May 29th</u>
- WENT UPTOWN TO PICK UP
Beat CD from Kanye's man -
- Walked around SoHo w/ Andy C
- chilled w/ Ali from rice
& shine vibe out listening
to music
- met spike rebel

<u>Thursday May 30th</u>
- Went to Carol's Daughter
w/ Kera
- met w/ Jez Blink listening
to her music
- Andy C left

<u>Friday May 31st</u>
- Vibed w/ spike rebel early
7:00am for an hour on porch

246

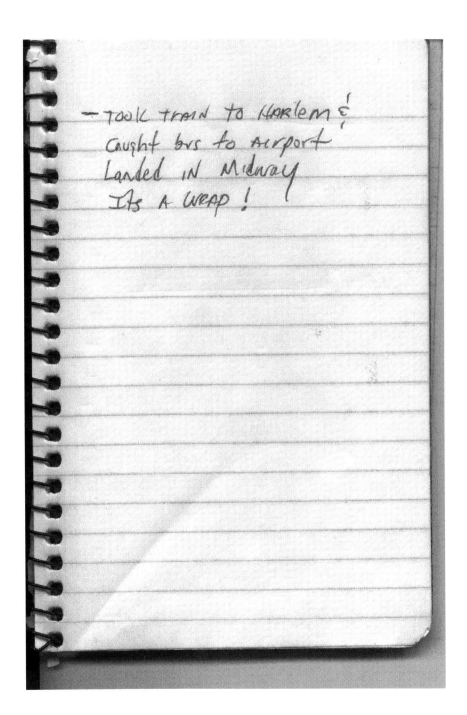

— Took train to Harlem &
Caught bus to Airport
Landed in Midway
Its a Wrap!

Abstract Mindstate performs at Chicago UN-Plugged event

CHAPTER 21

The College Graduate Joins Forces with the College Dropout

Now I'm back at my Aunt Sandra's crib in Chicago in disbelief thinking about all that happened. At that moment I realized I hadn't spoken to Kanye since the accident and gave him a call. When he answered the phone, I could hear his mouth was wired so I asked how he was feeling and if he was able to talk. Before I could get clarity, or a full understanding of his condition, he excitedly started telling me about a song he wrote that details everything he went through in the car accident. He began rapping the verses for me and said, "I call this joint 'Through the Wire' because I'm going to record it while my mouth is still wired shut." Then he went on to tell me he wants to sample Chaka Khan's song "Through the Fire," because he felt like the song captures the essence of what he was trying to say. After he explained everything I asked if he needed me out there in LA. His exact words were, "You would come out here?" I said, "Yes!" I told him I believed in him and I was down to continue the plan of helping him become a rap superstar. I also shared with him that I lived in LA for almost a year after I graduated college, so I was familiar with the territory. He told me I could stay in the hotel with him and asked when I would be able to come. I said, "Tomorrow!" We both laughed (although I was serious) and he put me on a plane to Los Angeles the following Friday, which was only two or three days later.

When I landed in Los Angeles, and made it to the hotel, it was like a dream because we were residents of The W in Westwood. The look and feel of the hotel, as well as the neighborhood it's in, was super fresh. Since the surgery didn't allow him to get on a plane for several months, we worked every day. In LA, I did everything from help find him a good oral surgeon and urologist to keeping all aspects of his life organized to setting up times for musicians to come by and record in the makeshift studio he set up in our hotel room. This was during the construction of The College Dropout, so we were very busy. He wasn't an official artist with a budget at the time, but he was the label's star producer, so they took care of him. We stayed in The W Hotel for seven months and continued to travel back and forth between coasts once his wires were removed. The majority of the production that became The College Dropout was laid out while we were on the West Coast.

When we eventually moved back to the East Coast, I really went to work. As his live-in assistant I was in charge of making sure all aspects of his personal life were in order such as condo repair, paying utilities, automobile servicing, laundry and dry cleaning, shipping and receiving, internet maintenance, medical and house-hold needs. I was also the contact person for family and friends. As head of business affairs, I handled all of the business surrounding Kanye West the producer and artist, such as taking meetings with Roc-A-Fella and Def Jam executives, facilitating all DJ activity, man-aging his calendar and travel arrangements and studio assistance. I traveled with him everywhere and I was his point of contact for all business. I did a few major creative things for him as well, such as put together his first press kit. I wrote his bio that went in the kit, found the photographer, set up a photoshoot and helped make the decision on the photo that became his first promo shot. When Rockafella made it official that he was an artist, Def Jam used the press kit I created for some time before creating its own.

During this time, I befriended Kanye's cousin Devon, aka Devo Springsteen. He was also Kanye's assistant and although Devo didn't travel or live with him, he had his share of responsibilities. Like his cousin, Devo is a producer. One day he played some of his production and I liked it so much he made me a CD with several of his tracks. I began listening to it regularly and was moved to write. This led to us recording an album worth of songs over the next month, or so, whenever we had down time. The business surround-ing Kanye didn't leave a lot of free time, so we seized the available moments. John Legend was Devo's close friend and roommate, so I asked him to sing a couple of hooks for me which he did without a problem. We were all chasing the dream, and no one had a deal at the time so when an opportunity to be creative presented itself you best believe it was welcomed by all of us. This was the period when John and Kanye began building their creative relationship so whenever John came to Kanye's crib to record, I would go to Devo and John's crib to record. I wasn't pursuing a solo deal; I was just using the art as therapy. Kanye was so fond of the work I had done he contributed two tracks and asked if he could feature the song, we recorded on his I'm Good mixtape. If you have a copy or familiar with the mixtape the song is titled "Brigade Level Formation."

After a year and a half of working with Kanye his dreams were finally becoming a reality. At the same time an investment opportunity presented itself to me. The opportunity allowed me to do another Abstract Mindstate album. In my mind this was the perfect time to give my all because my dawg was about to blow in a major way, and I figured if business was handled correctly, we would be at the top together. I told Kanye what was going down and let him know that I was going to take this chance. He wished me well and told me he had my back on any production or features I needed for the album. Without a second thought I packed my bags and moved back to Chicago. The cost to record the album was invested by E.P.'s best friend from high school who was a mortician. He was by her side a lot during this time because she had recently lost her brother to the streets; he was willing to do whatever it took to get her spirits out of the dumps and he knew doing her music was the only thing that could possibly lift her spirits.

The relationships and connections I had established through working with Kanye allowed me to pull off some amazing things. The album featured collaborations with some of the best producers and artists of the time: Kanye West, John Legend, Consequence, Malik Yusef and my guy David Banner. I also had a Common collaboration in the works. The production duties were handled by several producers but the most notable were Kanye, Devo Springsteen, Xtreme and 88-Keys. I dug deep into my artistic side and came up with some of the most creative concepts and hooks. The record was fun and personal, but evenly balanced because we both had a lot to get off of our chest. We had already earned the title in our city as "Chicago's hardest working rhyme duo" so I thought it would be a good idea to play off of that concept because we grinded as hard for this record as we did for the first. We recorded, mixed and mastered the album in Chicago, except for John Legend's vocals on a song titled "No Love Loss"— which we arranged a session for him to record after his show in St Louis—and Kanye's verse for "Welcome 2 Chicago," which was done in LA. The graphic design and layout for the cover art was complete and we were ready to go to press with our second album, *Still Paying*, which was supposed to be the sequel to the severely mishandled We Paid Let Us In.

Finally, all my hard work was about to pay off. It felt as if nothing could stop me this time. I had a project that major label artists didn't have the relationships to pull off even with a huge budget. The plan was to release the project independently, get the numbers needed to secure a major distribution deal and release it worldwide. Just as I was about to question why I couldn't reach my new investor; I received a call from E.P. telling me someone broke into his place and stole everything. He was one of those individuals who had bank accounts but also kept a stash in his house. The loss he experienced was so great it forced him to pull out as our investor. Instantly, all money associated with the project came to a halt. The album was finished and ready to ship out to be pressed but, once again, I found myself in a situation where there wasn't a penny for marketing and promotions. This was a very sad day, and I felt as if the whole world was against me at this point. How did I go from having an investor who was willing to sacrifice whatever was necessary to make the dream a reality one day, to having no idea how I was going to make it the next? This was the last straw in a never-ending sequence of "almost" opportunities. I should have hung up my hat and quietly walked off into the sunset, but my passion and desire burn far beyond failure, so **I REFUSE TO QUIT!**

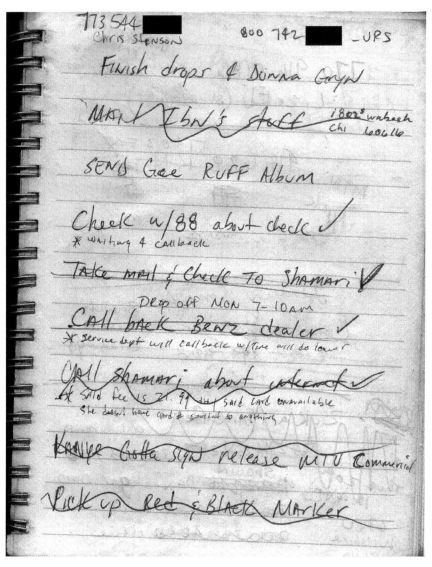

Actual notes from my days as personal assistant to Kanye West

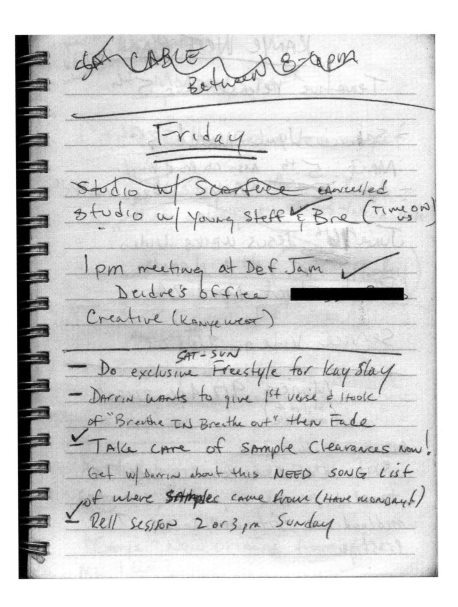

GET CABLE Between 8-9pm

<u>Friday</u>

Studio w/ Scarface cancelled
Studio w/ Young Steff & Bre (TIME ON us)

1pm meeting at Def Jam ✓
  Deidre's office ▬▬▬
Creative (Kanye west)

SAT-SUN
— Do exclusive Freestyle for Kay Slay
— Darrin wants to give 1st verse & Hook
  of "Breathe In Breathe out" then Fade
✓ Take care of sample Clearances Now!
  Get w/ Darrin about this NEED SONG List
✓ of where samples came from (HAVE MONDAY!)
✓ Rell session 2 or 3 pm Sunday

KANYe WeST PLAN
Tenative release Aug 5th

- Service VyNL MarRch 3rd
~~MAY~~ 5th Also CD Pro & Vinyl
- ~~April 21st~~ Service "Jesus WAlks"

June ~~16th~~ "Jesus wAlks Video"

Photo shoot April 24

Service Video 26th & 27th

MoNIcA ▬▬▬▬▬
(Stylest 4)
(MTV Battle)

DirectioNs To BeNz dealer
exit 18 W Route 80W TO Route 17 N
travel to you pass Huge mall (2 exits)
midland ave exit will be oN 17S
Prestige

Kevin
wireless ████████████
wherchouse

MONDAY 24th

Cradle 2 the Grave red carpet

~~Tuesday 25th~~
~~11 am sharp !~~ — meeting w/ Nicole Smith !

MARCH 5th (Def Poetry)

— 2 30 - 3pm Rehearsal
w/ STAN

— Taping 6pm (2 min)
Courtney six will call for car service
arrangements

———————————————

Kanye & coodie Flights to Chi

around 2pm
after

        Thurs 11am
Kanye ^ New Orleans from chi
Me 1 way

CHAPTER 22

Keeping it Moving

I always have several music related things going on at once, so it doesn't allow me much time to wallow in self-pity when one falls apart. Remember the girlfriend I told you about who I stayed with in the Bronx before moving back to Chicago? Well, she was actively pursuing a career as a singer and dancer, which was how she ended up in New York in the first place. She wasn't interested in the business side of music, so I started managing her career by default. For years everyone knew me as an MC who lived for real Hip Hop, but only a chosen few knew I was a talented R&B songwriter. For some strange reason I kept it to myself, revealing it only when I found myself close to an artist who I knew was serious about singing. I have actually been an R&B songwriter as long as I've been an MC so it's my other love. Anyway, during the time my investment went bad I was helping my girlfriend organize her one woman showcase in Chicago. At the event I ran into Mary Datcher, an individual I've known for some time who is a mover and shaker in the Chicago music scene. She watched the show attentively, making complimentary remarks every now and then. I let her know I wrote the song she was listening to and she said, "I didn't know you were a songwriter," in a very surprised tone. I simply said, "I have been writing for as long as I've been rapping." She then asked if I knew

Frayne Lewis, the son of Jazz legend Ramsey Lewis. I told her I met him years ago, but he wasn't anyone I knew personally. She told me he did a deal with EMI and they were about to record an R&B album and needed writers. She asked if it would be OK if she turned him on to me and I said, "Sure, give him my info."

A few days later, I was on the phone with Frayne setting up a time to come by and meet with him. He had a very nice office/studio set up in the downtown area of Chicago. His studio was on the second floor of a building that shared space with a jingle house. We small talked for a second then got right down to business. He told me he heard great things about my songwriting and that he wanted to give me a couple of tracks to see what I would come up with. He explained to me that he was offered a solo deal with EMI but decided to put together a group that consisted of his brother and a female vocalist. Together, they called themselves Frayne. I told him "cool" and that I would call in a couple of days with something to hear.

Exactly two days later, I called and told him I wrote five songs. He couldn't believe I wrote in such a short period of time. He then asked if I could come to the office. When I arrived, we went into the studio where he played the music and I sang the songs. Now, in no way am I a singer. As a matter of fact, I have an awful singing voice. But as a writer and arranger I have to sing the songs so the real singer or producer can learn the arrangement. To his surprise he loved them all and wanted me to meet the group so they could hear the songs. When I met the group, they were cool. They explained to me that they had writers block, so I was greatly appreciated. They dug the songs (some more than others) and I started working regularly with the female vocalist in the group. We went over my songs for several days until she was comfortable with the arrangements then I left it in their hands. A few months later EMI released the album, and, to my surprise, only one of my songs were used. But, hey, that's the business so I didn't sweat it. I felt blessed to have my first placement after years of songwriting. To be honest that situation inspired me to get back on my artist grind, so I decided to move back to LA and shop *Still Paying*, the unreleased Abstract Mindstate album. I figured it couldn't be too hard with our level of talent and production, coupled with the all-star supporting cast pulled together for the project.

Not long after my return to LA, I met a brother by the name of Trent, who was in the business of brokering record deals for artists. We were introduced to one another at a house party in Ladera Heights. Our conversation was rooted in music so in a matter of minutes we were stepping outside to sit in his car so he could hear my material. After I played him the Abstract Mindstate album, he went crazy and said, "There's no way I can't get a deal for a product like this." He couldn't believe we were unsigned, and he was amazed at the caliber of talent on the project. From that day on Trent aggressively shopped the record. During this period, I met another guy by the name of Ken Rose. Ken is a middle age gentleman who was unlike any guy I've ever met in my entire life. We often tell people we're biological brothers, even though he's white and I'm black. I shared that information so you could understand the level of our brotherhood.

We met in the skybox of an arena football game at Staples Center. Our conversation started all because of the Abstract Mindstate logo emblazoned on the front of the tee shirt I was wearing. When I walked through the skybox door, he saw it and immediately started pointing, saying, "That's the circle." My reply was, "Yes, it is." I then explained to him that the circle in our logo represents 360 degrees of Hip Hop, the cipher that completes my group. He began to explain what it meant to him and it turned out to be a project called "the circle" that unites all cultures and races through music. Our conversation about music in general became so interesting and intense that we left the skybox to go to his car so he could hear my music. I carried CDs everywhere, so I was always prepared for moments like this. I played him a few songs, breaking down the meaning behind each, and he was totally taken aback. So much so that I left the music with him as well as a copy of the solo material I recorded with Devo just to get his feedback. There was something about Ken that I couldn't put my finger on, but I knew this wasn't the last time he and I was going to see each other. Over the next few months, Trent and I took several meetings regarding Abstract Mindstate. And although every meeting went well it always turned out to be more talk than action.

As I stated earlier, I always have two or three irons in the fire. While I was taking meetings for Abstract Mindstate with Trent, I was also working hard to secure another investment to put the project out myself. Remember the investment I closed for my high school buddy to get his clothing line started? Well, I went back to the brother who fronted the money for that. His name is Rafi, he has been a buddy of mine since high school who has his own trucking and transportation company. He respected my business sense but more than that he honored my desire and passion. After I laid everything out for him, and emailed my business plan, he agreed to go all in with me. He said he didn't have the amount I needed in liquid at the moment, but he had some serious capitol coming. In the meantime, he said he was going to add me to his account and give me an American Express Business Platinum Card in my name. After that he simply said, "Make your dreams come true." I was pretty much in tears on the phone at that moment. The feeling was truly surreal. We made arrangements to have a dinner meeting in Chicago so we could make the transaction.

I happened to be at a studio in the Valley with Kanye while he was working on Common's album Be when all of this took place. I spoke with Common earlier that evening about collaborating with us on a song for the album (which he agreed to do) so I thought I would share the good news with him. He smiled and told me "congratulations" and that I deserved it because I've been, "working hard for a long time." Common is one of the few artists who have made it that I not only consider a friend but a very good person so hearing that meant a lot to me. A little less than a week later I was on a plane to Chicago to make the transaction with Rafi, my new investor.

When the plane landed in Midway Airport, I felt accomplished. I had just gotten a solid "yes" from Common to collaborate with us on the album, and I secured a new investor who was giving me an American Express Business Platinum card to take care of business. That night, Rafi picked me up and took me downtown to Ruth's Chris Steak House for a wonderful meal. I still remember my order to this day: stuffed chicken breast, garlic mashed potatoes and vegetables. At the time I was drinking white wine, so I had a couple of glasses of Pinot Grigio and I believe he had a red or maybe it was cognac. Doesn't really matter. The point is we had an excellent dinner and great conversation. Although we are old buddies from high school there was so much about him I didn't know.

I won't share any personal information about my man, but I will say this: like myself, he is a dreamer who is successful; he's unafraid to take a chance; and he believes in circulating the black dollar. As we sat and talked, giving our food a moment to digest, he asked if I cared for dessert. I didn't have room for anything else, but I began to wonder why the credit card hadn't come up and if he received it yet or had he changed his mind? Just as anxiety was starting to build, he pulled out an envelope, put it on the table and slid it across to me and said, "There you go, my man. I already know you're

I Refuse to Quit! The Autobiography of A Dreamer

gonna do the right thing." I slowly grabbed the envelope, opened it even slower and smiled as I read my name in black print across the bottom. At that moment I knew it was meant for me to finish what I started. I was all smiles on the ride home and my man seemed to be just as happy because he felt that he was making a wise choice by investing in me. The funny thing is I didn't go out and celebrate after our dinner. He dropped me off at my aunt Sandra's—where I was staying while in town—and I shared the news with my family. I literally thanked God a thousand times that night.

The next day I got right to work and started organizing myself so I could effectively execute the plan now that the money was in place. A few days later I was back on a plane to Los Angeles. I wasn't using the card as much as you would expect because there were so many things that had to be paid for in cash. Rafi would deposit funds into my business account periodically to take care of the small cash-based needs of the business at hand. Before I could get any real use out of the American Express, he ran into a problem. Like I said, he has a trucking and transportation company and through it he provides his drivers with cell phones. For several years he had all of his phones on a fixed plan that he was comfortable with and had no intentions on ever changing. One day he decided to upgrade all of his driver's phones but the company that gave him the upgrade also took it upon themselves to change his rate plan without his knowledge or consent. He wasn't aware of this until he received the bill that followed a month after the phone upgrade and noticed it was double what he normally pays.

Not one to get excited, he called the company and asked why his bill was eleven hundred dollars when he's been paying five hundred for several years. They told him it was because of his up-grade but he explained that he upgraded his phones not the plan. The company checked his account, realized it was their mistake, admitted fault and told him the correct amount will be reflected on his next bill. When he received the next bill, it was twenty-five hundred dollars, so he called again a little more upset but still calm and explained the situation. The representative said they see the notes and admitted fault again and promised the change would be reflected on the next bill. When the next bill rolled around it was thirty-five hundred dollars and this time, he was furious. He called and spoke to a manager, asked what was going on and explained the situation. The manager then told him he was right but unfortunately the phone usage is his company's debt, so he has to pay it. At this point he felt mishandled and disrespected so he told the representative he refused to pay anything more than the five hundred dollars he normally pays. So, he wrote a check and mailed it to the company.

A few weeks later he received a letter from the company demanding payment in full with his check enclosed. They didn't accept the money. He refused to pay anything more than what he would normally pay since the mistake was made by the cell phone company. Not long after this incident, the cell phone company reported the delinquent balance to his credit report. Now I don't know if everyone is familiar with American Express Business Platinum Cards, but they have no limit and with all American Express cards you have to pay the balance in full each month. To have one means you're transacting business at a level equivalent to the privileges that come with having the card. Paying the monthly balance wasn't a problem but paying the cell phone company more money than he should owe was. Well, once the thirty-five-hundred-dollar delinquent balance hit his credit, American Express discontinued his privileges. Can you guess what happened to the American Express card he gave me when they discontinued his privileges?

You guessed it. My privileges were discontinued as well. There went the money again to market *Still Paying*, my groups second album. I'm sure you can feel how upset my stomach was at this point. The crazy thing about it was the entire mishap was neither mine nor Rafi's fault. This was simply one of those strange unexplainable occurrences that happen when you're at the top of your game. I gotta tell you, I was ready to jump out of a plane without a parachute, headfirst, arms folded with a frown because this was unbelievable to me. After having my spirits lifted so high, being smashed to the ground was enough to make the strongest-of-the-strong throw their arms up and just walk away. But in a twisted psychological way, the obstacles that were constantly placed in my path made me want it that much more, so **I REFUSE TO QUIT!**

When I initially approached Rafi, I also reached out to one of my very close college buddies named Twan who also attended the same high school as me. He and I knew one another in high school but our friendship became a brotherhood at Jackson State University. I reached back out to him and shared what happened with Rafi, he told me he would be able to invest if a real estate deal he had in the works closed. Unfortunately, the deal didn't close so I didn't get the full amount I needed. But he did put up enough for me to press the wax for our single "Welcome 2 Chicago" featuring Kanye West. Desperation was so high that my partner in rhyme E.P. approached my cousin—who I had no interest in asking—about contributing two-thousand dollars to the project. He eventually came through with the money, but it was a stressful transaction which is why I didn't approach him myself from the beginning.

By the time he made good on his promise, Twan's money had already taken care of the wax, so my cousin's money was used for the rental car and road trip. What road trip you ask? Well, I setup and executed a low budget West Coast radio run with a Def Jam rep that I befriended while hanging out with Kanye when he was a guest on *Jimmy Kimmel Live!*. It's funny because there were rumors in Chicago about our friendship after I split to do my thing, but Kanye and I continued having a close relationship and hung out regularly upon my return to LA. Everyone in the inner circle knows when you hang out with the homey, you're liable to meet anyone.

Anyway, the Def Jam rep worked in the Los Angeles office. His name was Pat and he was a good dude. He liked my groups music but even more than that, he saw and respected my hustle, so we did business. When he and I hit the road, we visited radio stations in San Diego, Sacramento, Oakland, San Francisco and Las Vegas. This guy had solid relationships everywhere we went; it was truly a positive experience. I never thought I would be working radio promotions for my own record. I've always been a business-driven artist who really understands the business of music, so I was down to do whatever it took, even if I had to do it myself. My reply to fellow artists in Chi who'd approach and ask how Abstract Mindstate accomplished so much would be "don't have any pride." To this day, I don't believe they really knew exactly what I meant when I said it but that was my way of saying, "If you put limitations on your hustle, you'll get limited results." I'm a go hard or don't go at all type of person. Ask my real friends—they'll tell you.

Bottom line is the single started to get a buzz as well as mix-show adds, mixtape love and a few write ups so I can proudly say my West Coast rental car promotional run worked. A short time after the buzz of the record started dying down, the mixtape movement started getting outrageous. It wasn't just a New York thing anymore, like it had been for many years, but it started becoming a tool to introduce new acts as well as introduce old artists to a new audience. I saw the relevance in this and decided it was time for Abstract Mindstate to break into the mixtape game. I took it upon myself to consult with a few hot Chicago DJs, who advised me that we should rap over the instrumentals of a few popular singles. This would allow them to put us in the mix without having a problem at the station. We didn't want to rap over any popular instrumentals, but I knew we had to play the game if we wanted the spins.

I approached E.P. with the idea and told her I had a concept for a mix-tape series called Chicago's Hardest Working that borrowed from the name bestowed upon us by Mr. George Daniels. We picked four popular instrumentals we thought were dope and the rest were original songs specifically created for the mixtape. I reached out to all of the producers we usually worked with and they submitted tracks for us to choose from. We recorded the entire mixtape at an in-home studio called The Soul Kitchen owned by our good friend and producer at the time named Rashid Hadee. We also added a few R&B songs we were featured on to show diversity. All-in-all, it was a good effort and the project received a moderate amount of press. The purpose of the project was to keep our name relevant and our music alive while I figure out a way to secure marketing dollars for our album.

It was during this time that I decided to launch www.4TheSoul-Reciprocity.com. Doing business as a company and as an artist became much easier with the launch of the site. The thing is, I didn't have any real separation with the dual roles I played until then. Through the company site I was able to highlight everything I was doing on the business side and artistic side with a much smoother flow. I was now able to showcase the other acts the company represented and highlight everything they had going on as well. The site was great, and it provided a great deal of exposure to the brand as well as all of our associated artists, so its purpose was served.

This was the first single from the unreleased album Still Paying that featured Kanye West

Actual credit card that was supplied by my investor

Abstract Mindstate Performs at The Chicago Hip Hop Awards

I wrote and arranged the song entitled
"Ooh Wee" (Track 7). This was my 1st song placement

Seagram's Gin and 4 the Soul-Reciprocity Inc. invites you and a guest to the VIP
listening party for Chicago's "hardest working" rhyme duo

Abstract Mindstate

For their highly anticipated album

"Still Paying"

Come listen and hear why producers such as Kanye West, 88 Keys, Spike & Jamal, Xtreme,
Absolut and artist such as David Banner, Consequence and Kamikaze all contributed to this project.

Tuesday, September 23rd, 2003

Seagram's
Extra Dry
Gin

@ D'Vine (1950 W North Ave)

(near the corner of Milwaukee & North Ave)

6:30 – 10 pm

Complimentary food and Seagram's Gin drinks. Arrive early, compacity is an issue.
Press Kit, interviews and wax will be available on location.

Abstract Mindstate's "Still Paying" Album Listening Party Flier

With my very good buddy Antuane

CHAPTER 23

A Rose Grew from the Concrete

In the midst of everything that was going on, I received a phone call from Ken Rose. At least three months had gone by since my outing at the Staples Center—where he and I met—so his voice was the last I was expecting to hear. In a very serious tone, he told me he's been listening to my music non-stop since we met. He loves my voice and the way I'm in key with the music. He told me the subject matter was great and that he would like to sit down with me again. I was caught off guard by the passion in his response, so I did the only thing I could do in a situation like this and that was humbly thank him. When we got together, he explained that he was more interested in my solo work than the work I had done with Abstract Mindstate. He stressed that he never gets involved with artists but there was something special about me and the world needed to hear my art. He then asked if I had representation because he felt he could secure me a deal. I let him know I didn't have management and told him I had been shopping my group's music for several years myself.

A very short time later we worked out a situation and he started representing me as a solo artist. We built such a solid business and personal relationship I was finally able to let go and let him man the ship that was my solo career. I spent so many years representing my group that I forgot what it was like to have someone else handle the business. It was a very welcomed and much needed change because I had grown tired of trying to win over record company executives who had burnt ears.

A couple of months later Ken and I were in negotiations for our first deal with a guy who seemed to have the exact situation we were looking for. He was a Haitian rapper with an independent label that had major distribution. He happened to be looking for the right act to release through his distribution situation and met Ken. I have to admit, this guy came off like a serious businessman. He was very articulate, professional, thorough and to the point. He was an artist and businessman like myself and I respected that. It also helped that I'd seen his ads in magazines for years and ran into him a few months earlier in an LA studio when Kanye was working with a Def Jam recording artist named N.O.R.E. This guy had a flashiness about him that seemed regal—like he could have been a Haitian prince. Everyone in the Hollywood scene, from actors to music-industry types, greeted him with open arms so he walked into high profile events without a problem. Ken and I attended a few events with him and watched as he worked the room.

Several meetings and a few outings later we took him as the real deal. After a couple of months of interaction, we began drafting up paperwork and discussing marketing ideas for my release. I lived between LA and Chicago, so I spent just as much time at home as I did in Los Angeles. I went home in between the business that was taking place with my solo career and recorded the second Abstract Mindstate mixtape: Chicago's Hardest Working Vol.2 (Project Soul).

Although I had a solo deal in the works, I never stopped recording with my partner as a group. Let's not forget, I also had someone shopping the group a deal, so I was trying to cover all bases. Anyway, I finished recording our mixtape and came back to LA to finish the deal Ken and I had on the table. As we were approaching the final stages of paperwork things started to get funny. Our new contact became harder to reach and became busier than ever. We weren't hearing from him as much, but Ken continued to put forth effort. What was once a great deal of action turned into a whole lot of talk and, before I knew it, we were stuck with unfinished paperwork, a well thought out marketing plan, lofty ideas, and a bunch of false promises. I was in a total state of disbelief. Just as quick as the situation happened, it was over and there was nothing Ken or I could do about it. Actually, I could have screamed, jumped up and down, got mad at the world, became depressed and gave up on the dream. But my determination doesn't leave much room for tantrums and self-pity, so **I REFUSE TO QUIT!**

Not long after the solo situation took a turn for the worst, Trent came to me with a potential situation for Abstract Mindstate. Some guys from his old neighborhood had a distribution deal with TVT Records and they were looking for a hot act to be their first release. He met with them initially then set up another meeting so they could meet me. When I came over and played them the material from the *Still Paying* album they were amazed at the quality of the product. Like Trent, they couldn't believe we had so many big names attached to the project but didn't have a deal. I must have met with those guys five or six times and each time more plans were made. Trent's guy who ran the label actually called one of the owners of TVT and put him on speaker phone so I could hear for myself that his situation was real. Everything he said was proven in that conversation but when it came time to move to the next level, nothing happened. I never knew what went down or why, but I do know we didn't do a deal.

During this period, I met more guys who talked a good game than I met the entire time in the business. I kept myself busy by taking advantage of any recording opportunity that presented itself, such as a collaborative effort I composed with a Latin Jazz musician named Freddie Ravel, in which we fused Hip Hop and Flamenco music to create a song/genre called Flip Hop. We performed the song at venues and festivals all over California and got an amazing response from all ages and ethnicities. He and I were supposed to create a full album worth of material merging the Latin and Hip Hop genres but, for reasons beyond me, that project never took flight. This was truly a great idea that could have taken both of our careers to new highs. But, as the old saying goes, "It takes two to tango."

As I said before, I split my time between Chicago and the West Coast and opportunity presented itself at home. My partner in rhyme E.P. has a cousin named Duron who is a former all-pro basketball player that now works in social services. He is the biggest Abstract Mindstate supporter I've ever met. Duron is one of those rare guys who actually listens to the lyrics and not just the beat and the hook. We spoke often because he is a very positive brother who is always interested in the progress of the group. One day he told me he had a guy he wanted me to meet. He said the guy is a very successful real estate investor who he told all about me. He followed that by saying he wants to sit and talk about the possibility of investing. I was obviously very excited about the prospect of securing the much-needed finances to finally release the Still Paying project. I revised and tightened up my marketing plan, put together a press kit on the group and caught a flight to Chicago.

When I arrived, I headed straight for my aunts' crib, dropped my bags and let Duron know I was in town. A few hours later he picked me up and we headed to the south suburbs to the meeting that was going to change everything. Duron was as excited as me because he really wanted to see our album released. As we approached the neighborhood of my potential investor, I found myself staring at the really nice homes adjacent to the street we were riding on. Suddenly we took a left into a well-manicured subdivision of million-dollar homes and stopped in front of one of the residences. Duron looked at me and said, "You know he built this subdivision." in a tone that let me know the level of business I was dealing with. I took a deep breath, shook my head in amazement and got out of the car. As we approached the door, I quickly thought about everything I was going to say. I was a little nervous, but prepared, so I put on my game face as I watched Duron ring the bell.

When the door opened a regular looking gentleman, who was very polite welcomed us in and offered us a seat in his front room. It's funny because he fit the description of the multi-millionaires, I read about in a book called *The Millionaire Next Door*. Anyway, he and I shook hands and got right down to business. I began breaking down Abstract Mindstate and then segued into our marketing plan. I gave him a copy, as well as Duron who sat quietly in a chair watching me explain my plan with boardroom swagger. Somewhere in between my corporate style pitch and detailed rundown of my marketing plan he gave one of his sons our cd. He told him to listen to it because he needs to know what he thinks of the music. He went on to explain that he didn't know anything about Hip Hop, but he does know good investments, so he'll leave the evaluation of the music up to his sons.

After a series of questions that were followed by thorough answers, we wrapped up the meeting. He had given me at least two hours of his time without rushing me out so it was definitely time to leave. He told me he was going to give one copy of my marketing plan to his financial advisor and another copy to his lawyer and that I'll hear from him in a couple of days. He expressed interest and complimented me on having a very well-organized plan but made it clear that he doesn't move unless his financial advisor gives him the green light. He told me to give him a few days and that we could meet again later in the week. I left his very new and nicely manicured home looking forward to our next meeting. Some odd days later he and I got together to discuss his decision. He sat me down and told me his sons thought our music was great and stressed that was a big plus, so I felt good about where the conversation was going. Then he said, "But my financial advisor said this is too much of a risk." He went on to explain that his financial advisor had been with him since the beginning and he trusts his advice, so he had to pass. I asked how he felt, and he told me he liked what I presented and would have went with it if his advisor saw fit. But, more than anything, he said he was impressed by me. I tried to talk around his decision a few times but when I realized he was set I shook his hand, thanked him for the time and told him he would see me again. "I'm looking forward to it," he replied.

Not securing an investment was a letdown but I was OK, only because my man Trent had another situation in the works that could potentially secure my group a deal. Trent had an old friend by the name of Sherman who worked at Ziffren Law. This company represents some of the biggest names in music and entertainment. Sherman presented a package on Abstract Mindstate to an attorney named David Byrnes. He thought we were great. He heard the material, recognized the talent, saw the production credit and features and felt he wouldn't have a problem securing us a deal. A meeting was set up for us to meet Mr. Byrnes in person. We had an extensive, in-depth conversation. I let him know all about our history as well as answered several questions he asked. At the end of the meeting he let us know that he was going to move forward and try to secure us a situation.

We left his offices in Century City and went across the street to Houston's and discussed the future and how excited we were to be represented by such a major entertainment firm. Sherman contacted me a few weeks later saying Mr. Byrnes has been so overwhelmed with one of his clients that he hasn't had time to do anything regarding Abstract Mindstate. A few more weeks passed, and I was told he decided not to take us on as a client at the time because his current client doesn't leave him with much time to concentrate on new business. As fast as we were in, we were out. I was sick! I didn't understand how an attorney with so much experience didn't see the value in holding on to a group like ours. There wasn't anything I could do it at this point other than be upset or sad. I dealt with both emotions, but I will tell you what I didn't do. I didn't let it stop or slow me down because **I REFUSE TO QUIT!**

During this time, I began working as music director and co-producer of a huge music event for the city of New Orleans. This was a year after Hurricane Katrina and the event was spearheaded by Ken Rose and his partner Chik. The event was going to be massive, and I was in charge of securing talent as well as performing myself. I was in touch with a guy by the name of Ernest Collins who was the head of arts and entertainment for the city of New Orleans. I also had the privilege of meeting and hanging out with the mayor at the time Ray Nagin. He liked my music and felt I was very talented. If there was an opportunity for someone with clout or connections to hear my music Ken took full advantage of it. He and the mayor were hanging out like old buddies so Mayor Ray Nagin listening to Olskool Ice-Gre was inevitable. Unfortunately, after hundreds of thousands of dollars spent, extensive amounts of travel and count-less organizational meetings the event didn't happen. This wasn't by any fault of Ken or his partner Chik—who both lost thousands of dollars. Let's just say the advertising dollars depended upon a certain amount of celebrity support and every celebrity was waiting to see what the other was going to do before they committed so the whole thing went down the drain.

Somewhere in the mix of all of this Ken connected with an old friend of his by name of Budd Carr, who is heralded in the industry as a legendary music supervisor. Ken played my solo material for Budd on one of his business trips to LA and he was so blown away he had Ken call me so he could tell me himself. He said he was going to put in a call to one of the music industry's top music executives and ask him to give us a meeting. The guy he was referring to was none other than Big Jon Platt formerly of EMI Music Publishing. The funny thing about this was that I was in the studio with him in a session with Kanye a week before our meeting. We were having an extensive conversation about Kanye's record Late Registration which was being played for him at the time. As Ken and I waited outside the doors of his Santa Monica office, I wondered if he would remember me from a week ago. Just as I was getting deeper into my thoughts his secretary called Ken's name and said, "Big John will see you now."

When we entered the office, he immediately shook our hand and let me know he remembered me. To me this was a good start, but I played it cool and let Ken do the talking, only speaking when asked a direct question or a question only I knew the answer to. Judging from the head nods, occasional smiles and positive frowns it seemed as if Big John really liked my solo work. A meeting with an executive of his caliber is usually over in fifteen minutes. But Big John gave us at least a full uninterrupted hour of his time. When the music and conversation was over, he told us he liked it and asked if he could have a copy to live with for a little while. Ken gave him a full press kit. We left the meeting feeling very good because everything went well, and his reactions let us know he was impressed.

Weeks went by and we didn't hear from Big John. A few more weeks coupled with a few unanswered calls and still no Big John. We didn't understand. Everything about our meeting said he loved it but after several days without a single reply we had to accept the cold hard truth—he must not have been as interested as we thought.

Once again, I didn't have time to sulk because I was traveling to Atlanta with Ken to finalize pending business, he had with Usher's mom Jonetta Patton. The trip was in the midst of us organizing the New Orleans event (as a matter of fact, I believe Usher was supposed to be involved in that as well). I don't remember the full play by play but what I do remember is Ken negotiating an American Express sponsorship deal for J Pat Management. As I sat in the office taking notes as we discussed the various ideas surrounding the sponsorship deal, Ken alluded to the fact that I was also an incredible artist (his words, not mine.) Jonetta Patton immediately took interest and asked if we had any of my music for her to hear. Ken told her he did but that it was back at the hotel. He said we could go get it when we were finished with our meeting. The meeting ended and we hustled back to the hotel, which was only minutes away, and came right back. I sat back and let Ken sell me because I learned from past experience not to try and sell myself.

When the music began, she instantly liked what she heard and asked if I was interested in a writing opportunity. I replied, "Yes," then she said she liked my style and wanted me to collaborate with her son James who was an up-and-coming producer and aspiring rapper. She then gave the CD to her assistant Terrence and he took it to the studio connected to the J Pat management offices and played it for at least thirty minutes. He grooved to every song that came on, listening intently. He told us Jonnetta really liked my material and was serious about the writing opportunity. As Ken and I were leaving the offices a car pulled up in the parking lot. It was James. When Terrence introduced us James said, "Olskool, so you're the guy my Mom wants me to work with?" I replied, "Yes." He said, "Cool. I'm looking forward to it because I'm ready to get busy on my record." Terrence co-signed me by telling James I was a dope lyricist and my CD was banging. I was amazed because his mom obviously called him and told him about me while we were gone or in the studio. Either way it was a very good look for me.

Ken and I talked about the infinite possibilities of working with Usher's family half the plane ride back to LA. It seemed like every time a situation went bad another situation presented itself and I was open for any and all opportunities. A few weeks went by and we didn't hear anything from Jonnetta. Ken called a few times but never got a reply in regard to my writing situation. A few more weeks went by and eventually it faded away like most of the bright ideas thrown my way by established music industry executives. I would be lying if I said I wasn't extremely excited and optimistic about the opportunity but unfortunately it never manifested. During this period, I had a massive music event where I was the music director fall apart; an hour-long meeting with one of the most established men in music publishing—set up by one of the biggest music supervisors in the business—go nowhere; and the mother of one of music's brightest stars offer me a chance to write with her youngest son dissolve into thin air. I still didn't lose hope, and I never lost my focus. **I REFUSE TO QUIT!**

Love Song & Necessity 12inch

At Critics Choice Awards (New Orleans Event Fundraiser)

CHAPTER 24

Executive Decisions

As if everything I mentioned wasn't enough, I shut my company website down with the intentions of upgrading. But, due to financial reasons, it never happened. Around the same time Trizonna McClendon, a female vocalist who was signed to my entertainment company, mailed me a CD of a few songs she was working on while living in New York. I was so impressed and caught off guard by the quality of the material, I told her it was time to get an album out. A few days later I called my man Rafi who gave me the Amex and put the money up for my buddy's clothing line for the potential investment. By this time, the problems that put things on hold before had long gotten cleared up and he agreed to finance the project. As soon as we finalized all of the particulars, I booked a flight to Chicago to begin recording her debut album, Overtones and Innuendos.

Not only was the album executive produced by me, and released independently through my company 4 The Soul-Reciprocity Inc., but I also wrote a few songs, oversaw the mixing and mastering, produced a little and took on the role of A&R. Trizonna is a hell of a songwriter and she and her producer from New York pretty much set the tone that sold me on this project. I spent the next two years of my life as an executive and artist manager, navigating and directing all aspects of the company business as well as her singing career. With the help of my team, Trizonna's talent and her unwavering drive we had a wonderful run with the album. I created and executed tours, listening sessions and release parties. I got the record in Best Buy and Wal-Mart—with no distribution—secured a licensing deal with Japan and the UK for the album and hustled an impressive amount of press. Even garnered a couple of independent music award nominations for Best New Artist in Detroit and Chicago. We walked away with a win in Chicago so that was cool. In the midst of my role as an executive, I found time to record the final project for my group Abstract Mindstate, titled Chicago's Hardest Working Vol.3: The Celebration. I consider it our swan song because it was our last project as a group.

As the end of the year approached, I ran into another stumbling block. My investor was hit with divorce papers from his wife—who he'd been separated from for years—and things were about to get ugly. The divorce proceedings began and him being able to continue investing in the project became more and more of a problem. It got to the point that he was forced to pull out to avoid it affecting my business. This was a terrible time to suddenly not have funding because the momentum of Trizonna's record was great and things were moving forward in a positive direction. As I hoped for things to get better with my man, I continued working the project. To get a few things off my chest I used the little personal time I had to record my first solo mixtape, The Gregarious Mixtape.

I find that I do my best writing when I have a lot to think about, so I used this moment to be creative and turn my thoughts to art instead of letting these unfortunate situations—that are beyond my control—get me down. No one outside of my team knew we no longer had funding for Trizonna's project because press and live shows kept everything current and alive. This gave me time to come up with another plan. I worked the project through the Thanksgiving holiday. Christmas was approaching and I decided to go back to LA and spend the holiday with my mom since all of our family is in Chicago and she was in LA alone (I try to spend the holidays with her when she can't make it back to Chicago; I know you're thinking, for a guy with limited funds I sure travel a lot).

During this particular stay I spoke with my very good friend Armers and he told me about a book written by Donald Trump and Robert Kiyosaki titled *Why We Want You to Be Rich*. He advised that I read this book because it changed his way of thinking. Let me give you guys a little history: Armers was Abstract Mindstate's manager when we were college students at Jackson State University. We have done several ventures together and, to this day, we inspire each other. He always recommends reading material to me. I have given him a few titles over the years but the number of books he's recommended to me out-weigh the number of books I've recommended to him by a long shot. Also, keep in mind that this was before Donald Trump became the most hated man in America. Anyway, I read the book and got just as jacked as he told me I would get. I then took it upon myself to read *Rich Dad, Poor Dad* because Robert Kiyosaki referenced it several times throughout the book.

When I shared that information with Armers he told me to check out Reallionaire by a young brother named Farrah Gray. After I read Reallionaire something inside of me changed. I felt stronger and more motivated than ever because of the newfound knowledge I acquired. I had an overwhelming desire to achieve the level of financial freedom I felt I deserved. Regardless of our age difference, it was clear Farrah and I share the same qualities in regard to drive. Plus, he's from Chicago, so I connected with the information he shared on a personal level and it sparked a flame in my entrepreneur spirit. I felt so inspired I gave my good buddy Duron a call and asked him to track down the millionaire real estate guy he introduced me to a year ago. I told him I needed to sit down with him again. But this time I was sure I would get the investment I needed. It took Duron a couple of days, but he called back with the new number and I made the call.

I hadn't spoken to him in a year. But as soon as I said my name, he knew exactly who I was and gave me a warm reception. We small talked for a brief moment then I got right to the point and asked if he had a moment to sit down with me again because I wanted to present another potential investment to him. He agreed to meet with me. We set a date and time and I booked a flight back to Chicago. This trip back home was unlike any of my many trips to Chicago from Los Angeles. I knew without a doubt I was going to get the investment I was seeking. My clarity and confidence were beyond words; "no" wasn't an option.

When I made it to his home, he greeted me like an old friend. We sat at the table and briefly updated each other on the latest things taking place in our lives. He asked what I had for him. I pulled out a copy of Trizonna McClendon's cd and simply said "this." I began to breakdown what I had been doing since we last met and showed him the results of all of the hard work that was put into Trizonna's project. I showed him a press kit full of positive write-ups on the record, a purchase order from Best Buy and Wal-Mart, the paperwork for the licensing deal with Japan, proof of past performances and the list of stores and online sites that sold the product. He was extremely impressed. I was showing him physical evidence of what would have been done with his money if he had invested the first time. I explained to him that everything was solid and moving forward but I needed the necessary marketing and promotion dollars to make the record a success. Giving him a professional high-quality

CD with all of the trimmings showed him my seriousness, professionalism, dedication, drive, passion, experience, knowledge and overall leadership skills. He was so blown away he just laughed and said, "You're a smart young man Greg." At that moment I knew I accomplished what I failed to do the last time we sat down in his living room table to talk business. I sold him on me, not my product.

The funny thing about business is it's more about the person behind the business than the actual business itself. Whatever the situation may be, a person who is about to spend or invest money has to feel a sense of security in the person behind the product. And in this case that person was me. He then said to me, "You know the routine. I'm gonna have to present this to my financial advisor and attorney just like before because that's how it goes." I told him I understood, and I looked him straight in his eyes and asked, "Are we going to do business?" He said, "Well, you know I have to…" and I cut him off. "I'm not concerned with your financial guy or your lawyer because they are not dreamers like we are," I said. "That's why they work for you because they like sure things. We know nothing is a sure thing. That's why we take chances." At that moment he chuckled and shook his head with an impressive grin and replied, "Yes, Greg, we're going to do business." I then said, "I can get up from this table, walk out the door and ride home knowing I'm going to get the investment amount I have written in the business plan?" This time he simply replied "yes" with a smile. This had to be one of the most accomplished moments of my life! I felt like I won the championship and got voted MVP of the game. The thing that excited me most was seeing the results of my newfound financial education work so effectively in such a short time. As Ice Cube said in his most popular song: "today was a good day."

A week or so after our verbal agreement my investor to be ran into a problem with a land development project he had in the works. A million-dollar subdivision project turned into a one million six hun-dred-thousand-dollar situation after his workers ran into problems with pipes underground. It cost him an extra six hundred thousand dollars to dig up and remove all of the piping that was found un-derground. This figure is important because it was a half of a million dollars more than he expected to spend in order to complete the job. Our deal was contingent upon the completion of this project so the paperwork that I was told I would receive in a few weeks turned into a few months.

Those few months turned into a few more months and, before I knew it, we were approaching the end of the year and no business was done between us. The funny thing was that it wasn't his fault and he was being honest and upfront with me the entire time. We had numerous phone calls where he gave me the play-by-play of what was taking place and where he was in the project. I knew as a businessman myself he didn't have to be so open with his information, but he wanted me to know so I wouldn't think he was stringing me along. It was great to deal with an honest, straight up person even if things weren't going the way I would have liked. He eventually finished the project, but the real estate market had gone bad by then and it became even harder to sell. In the past, he had built and sold without a problem. But the market changed. My investment was tied to the sale of the project and when the market went bad, so did my chances of receiving the verbally agreed six figure investment. Unfortunately, things never turned around, so my potential investor took a very serious loss. In corporate America, this is when you find guys wearing suit and ties on the roof of the building, standing on the edge ready to leap to their death. For me, death is not an option. I feel I have too much to offer the living so even under the worst of circumstances, **I REFUSE TO QUIT!**

A new year ushered itself in and I was still working Trizonna's project. We shot a video for her single towards the end of the previous year and I received a phone call from the head of programming at BETJ telling me he loved her video and that they wanted to add it to their rotation. This was the type of news I needed. I never slowed down or lost momentum when it came to working any and all angles to keep the record moving. This was despite the fact that I had no more money to finance the marketing and promotions. Not long after receiving the good news about the video being added to BETJ, I received an email from an executive at a UK-based label called Freestyle Records expressing interest in licensing Trizonna's self-titled single for a compilation called Future Soul. It was as if I was being rewarded for not letting anything stop me.

The funny thing about me: it doesn't take a monumental occurrence for me to feel grateful. I recognize my blessings on all levels. I constantly thank God. Besides, I strongly believe positive movement attracts positivity which is why I avoid negativity at all costs. My focus was building my brand, 4 The Soul-Reciprocity Inc., and keeping the project alive so I remained optimistic. I came up with a few creative ideas to keep the focus on my artist and the business as well as introduce other aspects of the company. One of the ideas that went over pretty smooth was a download-only mixtape put together by 4 The Soul-Reciprocity Inc.'s DJ Cvicious titled The Indie Soul/R&B Suite. The goal was to further expose the very talented artists in the Indie Soul movement we had become a part of and made an impact within. I also wanted to introduce our DJ and highlight Trizonna's second single. Around the same time, we also released the last Abstract Mindstate project, Chicago's Hardest Working Vol.3: Project Soul and my solo project The Gregarious Mixtape. Creative marketing and connections pushed these projects without any financial support, and they received a respectable amount of exposure.

My very good friend and music manager Ken Rose never stopped searching for a situation for me as a solo artist and his persistence landed us in yet another situation. Through business outside of music, he met a venture capitalist by the name of Randall. Although he and Ken were meeting for business totally unrelated to anything I could benefit from, it's always Ken's style to find out more about the person he's taking a meeting with. It turned out that Randall's business hand extended outside of the investment world right into ours. His other title was Vice President of Finance for The Machine Productions, a California-based multimedia entertainment company that functions as a record label amongst other things. Ken told him all about me and my various music related talents. He then let him hear my music. Randy loved what he heard and agreed to take a meeting with Ken and myself.

A few days later I found myself sitting in a swanky seafood restaurant on Rodeo Drive ordering a Caesar salad discussing the possible future of me recording under The Machine Productions. Randy and his assistant were very fond of my work. He said I was the type of artist that needed to have product in the marketplace. He told me he was in the middle of a finance deal that should close in three weeks and when it's was done, he wants to sign me to the label. Our meeting was pretty straightforward and to the point which is my favorite way to do business. After a few questions and concerns, he asked if we would join him for a cigar and cocktail at his favorite cigar bar a few blocks away. I chose not to but Ken enjoys a stogy and a sip every now and then, so he agreed to partake.

Three weeks later Ken and I both received a call from Randy's assistant asking what a good time for us would be to meet regarding the deal. Once a day and time was established Ken and I cleared the line so we could speak amongst ourselves. I said to him Randy's investment deal must have gone through being that we got a call from his assistant not more than a day or two from the time I was expecting to hear from him. Ken said, "We'll see." We did some small talk for a few minutes before we both got back to our individual hustles. Because of the many let-downs, anticipation doesn't come often in my world. But I felt as if this situation could be a good opportunity for me. As we approached our planned meeting date the most unexpected of occurrences happened. A very close family friend of Ken's died, and he and his wife had to step in and take care of the arrangements.

For obvious reasons, we postponed the meeting while Ken spent the next week helping to organize the funeral arrangements for his friend. A week or so later everything went back to normal. Ken reached out to Randall's assistant to reschedule the meeting. Once again, we all agreed on a date and time and looked forward to meeting in the next couple of days. As we approached the new meeting date tragedy struck again. Randy's grandmother became deathly ill, so he had to catch a last-minute flight to Detroit the same day as the meeting. Fortunately, his grandmother lived, but unfortunately—and very unexpectedly—his father passed away. Because of this, he was forced to stay in Detroit for a few weeks to get all of the odds and ends squared away. I felt really strange during this time. It seemed as if death was hunting my business.

Things finally went back to normal and Ken and I met Randy and his assistant at the same Beverly Hills restaurant to discuss my deal. It turned out the deal he was waiting on a few weeks prior did go through, but he had another situation on the table with one of the soft drink giants. I asked if we were going to start the paperwork on my deal—since the other deal went through—and he told us it would be even better if we waited two more days to allow his new deal to materialize because it would really work in my favor. When you've gone through as much as I have in the music business another few days can't hurt. Ken and I waited a few days, but we didn't get a call. A week passed and Ken reached out to find out what was going on, but we couldn't make contact. A second week went by and it began to feel like we were heading into very familiar territory. I remained optimistic, keeping in mind that I was dealing with a serious investment guy who had just experienced a significant loss.

It's strange but I've met such a wide variety of personalities in the business, but I have yet to figure out—regardless of race, financial status, religion or area or expertise—why people who are associated with the entertainment industry don't call you back. Whether an individual is a full-time entertainment guy or a part time hustler, not calling back is a constant. Unfortunately, we never heard from Randy again and I can only imagine what could have caused things to end so unfinished. But in this game, you have to let the chips fall where they may, or you'll end up in an insane asylum. Regardless of how irritating and unbelievable these recurring acts were to me; I've built up a resistance that has made me immune to it, so **I REFUSE TO QUIT!**

The Gregarious Mixtape

Overtones & Innuendos
Japanese Import

This 12inch single was part of the UK licensing deal secured
with Freestyle Records in the UK

Trizonna McClendon's "Overtones & Innuendos"

Sunshine & Lemonade CD single

CHAPTER 25

The Epiphany

This was the point at which I spoke to my girlfriend at the time and shared a few stories about my series of "almost." She advised me to start writing this book. Although I expressed everything in a slightly joking manner, she knew I was serious. I reached back out to the millionaire real estate guy who agreed to invest to see if things had gotten better and they hadn't. He advised me to stay in close contact with him. He promised he would make good on the investment as soon as the market turned around. In the meantime, I took on a few entertainment consulting gigs and oversaw a couple of outside projects to supplement income. Things got so slow at one point I decided I needed to get a job. Not just a regular job but something in entertainment that would allow me to make the money I deserved. I couldn't help but think how far I had gotten away from my degree at this point.

Here I am a college graduate who couldn't use my degree because I hadn't worked in corporate America in years. At this point, I got online and browsed all of the job sites looking really hard. In the midst of my hustle I was introduced to a company whose purpose is staffing for entertainment jobs. I filled out the online form and a representative contacted me for a meeting. This was a positive step for me. A lot was changing in my life and I needed job security. I met with the company and they were very impressed with my experience. The woman stated that I was overqualified for any of the positions the agency could bring my way. But if I didn't have a problem taking an entry level position with senior level experience, she would put my resume out. I explained to her that I didn't mind. I was looking for stability even if it meant starting at the bottom and working my way up. She was obviously impressed because she told me she would start trying to place me immediately. I hadn't been on anything close to a job interview in years and just the thought of corporate structure—even in an entertainment job—made me queasy.

In the meantime, I continued browsing the various staffing sites, sending my resume to all of the entertainment related positions I felt fit my qualifications. Weeks went by and I never heard anything from the agency, so I took it upon myself to send an email to my contact. She replied saying she hadn't forgotten about me, but the job market was slow at the moment. Just as I was starting to feel a little pressure about my situation Ken gave me a call with the oddest out-of-the-blue situation. He said he received a call from a music associate of his who desperately needed to find an unsigned Hip Hop artist whose vibe was somewhere "between Common and Kanye West." This information sounded like a joke to me because it was almost too perfect. Ken assured me it wasn't a joke and told me those were the exact words that were used to describe the artist his guy was looking for.

It turned out that Ken's guy brokered a deal and in the final phase, the artist's management got greedy and started making outlandish requests to the label. This screwed up the deal. Since the deal was done and the terms were already set and in place, Ken's guy needed to replace the artist in order to finalize the deal. The terms of the deal were given to us and from what was said it seemed like a good situation. The best part about it was that it was a worldwide situation with a major record label. But, here's the twist. The label is based in the UK. As strange as this may sound to the uninformed, I didn't have a problem with that. I always felt my music would be the vehicle that afforded me the opportunity to see the world, so I was down with it.

As promising as the deal seemed, I had been here many times before, so this was just another day at the office. A short time before the deal presented itself, I approached Kanye about becoming A&R of his G.O.O.D. Music label. I've always been close to him and his business so I pretty much knew where I would be most valuable even if he didn't realize it. Kanye is a very creative guy with a musical vision like no other, but he's also a guy who has so much on his plate he needs to be in two or three different places at once. After hanging out in the studio during the early recording of his album *808s* and *Heartbreak*, it became clear to me where I was needed. I watched him as he gave one of his newly signed artists Big Sean direction in the middle of his own recording session. At this moment a light bulb went off in my head.

I had been thinking about stepping in to help with the direction of his artists ever since I heard the material GLC was working a year or two prior. The only problem then was the timing. I knew it wasn't the right time for me to step back into the fold, so I waited. I always felt as if Kanye and I would work again in a business capacity. I just didn't know when or what I would be doing. It's a touchy thing with us because we are such good friends that neither of us want to be in a situation that would compromise our friendship. In that spirit, business choices are made carefully. I remember telling GLC he and his project was the original inspiration behind me realizing my new position with Kanye. But my thoughts weren't moved to action until that day in the studio during the 808s and Heartbreak sessions. As I watched him try to explain what he needed from Big Sean, while directing the studio engineer on his own project and approving artwork and designs for his clothing line Pastelle, I knew it was time for me to step up and let him know I was interested in positioning myself with him again.

I gave him a call the next day and told him I wanted to talk to him about something. He asked me to come to the studio so we could build and that's where the process began. After a few days of tossing around ideas and opinions centered around *808s* and *Heartbreak*, I asked if I could be A&R. He was very receptive to my proposal. So much so that he immediately presented the idea to Don C and Gee Roberson. Right away Don C said, "I think that's a great move." Kanye then advised that we leave the control room to further discuss the situation. It was pretty clear everything was a go; we just needed to work out the logistics. After a few weeks of back-and-forth with Don C, they figured out how to make everything work, and I received a call from the homey telling me he approved everything.

At that point my position was official, and in true Kanye fashion he left the business talk alone and asked if I could come to the studio and help him with more ideas so he can put the finishing touches on *808s* and *Heartbreak*. In the midst of securing the new position with my man, the deal Ken had in the works with the UK label started moving fast. Ken said the label was going crazy over my work—so much so that another major label in the UK had expressed interest. There was a potential bidding war over me. I dreamed of being in a position like this. But after years of letdowns, I wasn't as excited as I could have been. One of my biggest concerns was walking away from my man after he had just given me the position I was born to do. Nothing is promised when dealing with record deal situations, but I still had to think about it in case it happened. I was barely settled into my new position with G.O.O.D. Music and I was already stressing. The ironic thing about the record deal situation was how it presented itself when getting a deal was the last thing on my mind. Ken never stopped looking and working to secure a situation for me. Like I said, he feels the world needs to hear my art and I'm grateful to have a cat like him in my corner.

The day after our business was finalized, Kanye left the country to finish the European leg of his Glow in the Dark tour. The following weekend was my homecoming at Jackson State University, and I was looking forward to attending it. I arranged my trip so I would be able to make a stop in Detroit to get a few days of work in with Big Sean. The plan was to put him in the studio with my man Young RJ who is a producer protégé' of J Dilla. Instead of flying to Mississippi from Los Angeles, I decided to fly to Chicago and ride with my guy Twan to Jackson and back. Then, I would fly to Detroit and back to Los Angeles from there. Everything was well thought out so it would work for me in a business and personal sense. So, this was a good plan.

Homecoming was everything I thought it would be and more and we returned safely without a hitch. I made it to Chicago at about 3 a.m. on a Monday with plans of catching an afternoon flight to Detroit. I woke up at about 9 a.m. and reached out to Big Sean but couldn't make contact with him. I called several times throughout the day, but I was never able to get him on the line. He and I spoke prior to this and made plans for me to come there so I spent the rest of the day trying to make contact. While in Chicago I spoke to a few of my guys and they all wanted to know how long I would be in town. I told them one day if I get in touch with the artist I'm trying to reach. One of the guys, who is a part of my 4TSR team, said he and a few of the homeys wanted to do something to celebrate me getting my new position. At first, I was hesitant because I don't do parties. Plus, I didn't want to put the carriage before the horse, so to speak. But when it was explained that they were talking about a small toast in my honor with a few close friends and associates I was down with it. My guy is a graphic designer, so he put together an email flyer and sent it out as an invite.

Everything seemed OK until I received an email from Kanye who was sent the flier by mistake. Well he misinterpreted the small toast as a huge party because of how the invite looked. I wasn't involved in the organizing of the toast, so I wasn't really thinking anything of it until then. Because of our huge time difference, and the fact that I saw the email a day later, I was unable to reach him by phone to explain. The tone of his email was as if I'd broken protocol and orchestrated a huge event in my honor without his knowledge, which he felt was totally out of character for me. He was pretty let down by my actions. I realized I wasn't going to be able to reach him to clear things up so, to avoid further confusion, I had my man cancel the toast and I got back to Los Angeles to handle business. It took another few days to finally reach Kanye but once we spoke everything was cool and I moved forward.

I spoke to Big Sean as well and it turned out he had a very bad cold and was under the weather when I was trying to reach him so that was clarified as well. By this time things started to slow down a little with the record deal. Ken wasn't hearing from the guy who was brokering the deal for us with the UK label. He reached out to him and the guy assured him everything was still in the works, but I had heard that line many times in the past, most commonly right before a deal fades away. Out-of-the-blue I received a call from my man Sherman asking me if I was interested in revisiting Abstract Mindstate. Confused and caught off guard I asked what he meant. He told me he never stopped playing our music and there was a new guy at Ziffren Law who he let hear the music. He thought it was incredible and he wanted to take it over to a guy named Tubby at Interscope Records. I told him I'd put the group thing behind me, but I would be willing to revisit Abstract Mindstate if the situation was right. He said he would keep me posted as things progressed. I received a call from Sherman about three days later. He told me that our product was "being walked into Interscope Records as we spoke." I calmly said, "OK," thanked him and hung up.

Less than a week after receiving the call from Sherman, my man Trent called asking if I had any music on my hands. I told him, "Yes, my solo project." He said he met a guy who was behind some of the most successful artists in Japan and he had serious connections with the labels out there and he wanted to turn him on to my music. Now, if you remember from the earlier chapter, I met Sherman through Trent, so it was wild that they were both presenting potential situations. Since Trent was the main person shopping Abstract Mindstate a deal on the West Coast I asked if he wanted his guy to have my solo project or the group. He said it was up to me. He just wanted to give him some quality Hip Hop and he knew he could get that from me. I then told Trent I would prefer to give him my solo stuff and he said cool. We made arrangements for him to pick up the product.

Now I have to play the waiting game—my favorite part of the business (yeah, right!). Life is a trip: you never know what lies ahead unless you follow your heart. This world was built by people just like yourself and the only difference between them and you is that they weren't afraid to take a chance. I honestly cannot predict the fate of my new position with Kanye and his label; neither can I determine the outcome of the major label deal Ken has in the works with the UK label; nor can I say Interscope Records will do anything with Abstract Mindstate; and, lastly, I have no idea what may come with

Trent presenting my solo work to his label connection in Japan. But I have to step out on faith and take that chance.

I've learned through my never-ending hustle and never-willing-to-die optimism that anything is possible if you believe. I realized a long time ago that I'm a hard nut to crack, too thick of a drink to shake. Everyone isn't built as tough. But, at the end of the day, opportunity doesn't discriminate. There are people who will take on many roles in your life so choose your associations wisely because relationships are the determining factor in helping you reach your goals. I can humbly and honestly say I do not know all of the answers nor can I foresee or predict the outcome of my situation so I definitely cannot determine yours. What I do know is that there are several people in our lives, including friends and family members, who will tear us down and overload us with negativity. Regardless, I encourage you to stay inspired. I'm not a cocky or arrogant person but I'll say this with a confidence like none you've ever heard before: regardless of the many obstacles that have been placed in my path, the jealously and unwarranted hate I have experienced, the bad energy and shady acts I have encountered and the ugly and bitter spirits I have faced, **I REFUSE TO QUIT!**

Release Party Flier (Los Angeles)

Sophomore Album

Release Party Flier (New York)

Release Party Flier (Chicago)

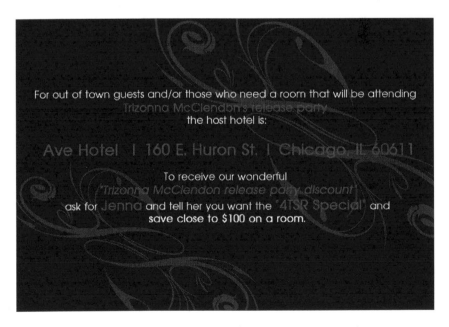

Release Party Flier (Chicago–Back)

The Refresh

My road to becoming a published author was solidified in 2009 when I self-published the original version of *I Refuse to Quit! The Autobiography of a Dreamer*. That was ten years ago. In an effort to make sure my journey is fully understood and appreciated, allow me to share the details of why it took me ten years to re-release this book. As I stated in the previous chapter, I'd secured the role of A&R at G.O.O.D. Music. But what I didn't plan for was how busy I'd be in that position. The release of the book and my new job happened at the same time. Although the book came out, I didn't take the time to acquire the necessary services to promote it. Outside of a book signing in Marina Del Rey, California — where I lived — there wasn't much more in terms of promotion.

Being A&R at a label was something I always dreamed of so when I got the job, I gave it my all. I traveled city to city playing a part in everything G.O.O.D. Music related and, quite honestly, I had the time of my life. My love for the music and the opportunities that were presented took precedence to point that I didn't give my book any thought. I was assigned to Big Sean for God's sake! The talent level of that brother even back then was beyond explanation. So outside of the amazing moments I experienced working with him, I traveled to various cities assisting with artists and label-related events and activities, attended video shoots, sat in on music video edits, contributed to the creative process during studio sessions and acted as a liaison between artists and outside business. I did just about anything that comes along with being part of a team headed by a high-profile recording artist with a very successful record label.

Two years went by without me realizing it. Everything was moving at light speed and seemed to be going great until I received an official letter letting me know my employment would be ending. I spoke with Don C and he gave me more insight. I was told that substantial investments were made on the fashion side of things and business management advised cutbacks in overhead needed to be made immediately. I was given a six-month payroll grace period by request of Kanye to allow me time to get myself prepared for the transition. In true go-getter spirit, I immediately start working on other projects while the energy was high from all that I was already doing.

Several months prior to my position ending, Trizonna McClendon and I began working on her sophomore album. Her project was the only outside music I worked on while I was A&R. As a matter of fact, I'll never forget taking the finished product with me to Hawaii when we went there to record Good Ass Job which later became My Beautiful Dark Twisted Fantasy. Kanye knew all about her and how long we had been working. He actually asked me to let him hear the finished product so by default it became the soundtrack to our rides in the car service the entire day. Since I no longer had to balance my time between Trizonna and my G.O.O.D. Music duties I went all out on her project. I wrote and directed the video for her first single. We had a pretty good run with the album. But after a year and a half, the lack of marketing dollars decreased our momentum and eventually things came to a halt.

About a month or so before shooting the video for Trizonna's single, I'd decided to take on management for a white male pop artist who I had known for some time. He had been very persistent in pursuing me for representation so after turning him down a few times, I decided to take him on as a client. This guy was a talented singer and we had history. He was a driver for the car service we'd use during our residency in The W Hotel in Westwood, California. Kanye and I liked him because he was closer to our age so given the time spent, I trusted and believed in him. I started investing lots of time and energy into him since he had a relationship with a guy named Matt Nelson that allowed us to record in a really nice facility on a tab. I wrote nine of the eleven songs that became his album and brought in DJ Self Born to handle the music production duties, since I managed him as well.

After spending several months working on his project, things went up a notch. He told me his girlfriend had a lead on a potential investor for us. The only catch was I needed to present a business plan. Writing business plans and investment proposals were common practice for me so that wasn't an issue. A short time after receiving this information I spoke to the guy, got the paperwork together, set up a meeting and ultimately closed the deal. Once the funds were available our studio tab was the first thing I paid. Matt later revealed to me that he took a chance on us solely because of my energy, business acumen and background. Our mix sessions were very focused and fun but we were on a tab so all of our sessions started very late and often times would end at 4 a.m. I didn't want to release official singles into the market from his project without building interest first. Since he was a new artist, with no previous releases, I came up with a very creative mixtape concept and the plan was to use the mixtape to create a buzz before dropping an official single.

Things started out amazing, but it wasn't long before all of the busy days and late nights invested into him proved to be a complete waste of my time. I blame myself because I created a monster by using investment money to take care of his rent, bills and personal needs. We treated the marketing budget like it was an artist advance and I didn't realize how much personal spending was done until the budget was depleted. I immediately tried to correct this error by advising him to find an alternative way of taking care of his personal things. This is when he completely lost all sense of reality and flipped into full diva mode. Until that moment, I had never dealt with ego and entitlement in regard to him. Our relationship went really bad really fast. The outcome was a year and a half of extremely creative work being flushed down the toilet and a six-figure investment being reduced to play money.

The project wasn't the only thing that went down the drain. My life followed not too far behind. I'd invested so much of myself that I lost it all: time, money, my apartment and pretty much my mind. I didn't want to leave L.A. And, even if I did, going back to Chicago wasn't an option. All of my resources and relationships were on the West Coast so I did the only thing I could do and that was shake off the shame and embarrassment and ask my mom if I could crash at her place until I got back on my feet. A few months before I was forced to let go of my place, I took on another client. This time it was a close family friend of a friend who I helped secure a song placement on an independent movie soundtrack. I had no intention of managing this aspiring rapper. I was simply doing a favor for a friend who is more like a sister to me. Once the business of that was finalized, the artist stayed in touch with me. He and the guy featured on the song for the soundtrack decided to become a group so he asked if I would represent them. I was laying low but had time since I took a step back after my life had fallen apart.

I decided to give the guys a chance. I signed them to a management deal and we immediately got to work. Both guys were recent graduates of a studio engineering program at the Los Angeles Recording School. The cool part is that they were given a laptop with Pro Tools installed upon graduation. This allowed us to record most of the material ourselves. During the early stages of their project the guys had a falling out, but I continued working with the rapper I met through my play sister's friend. He and I got a lot done: a couple of mixtapes, another movie soundtrack placement, songs for an official release, several live performances, a couple of on-air interviews and solidified situations with individuals that could have been very instrumental in helping kick off his career. Unfortunately, the more real things began to look, the more problems I began having with this guy's mother.

People who don't understand the business of music often get caught in the hype and excitement too fast. This was a classic case of that. The music and entertainment business are one of those fantasy professions where a lot is said, promised and offered but the reality is nothing is real until it's real. Let's just say, because of her overzealousness, she kept crossing the line, got too involved and disrespected me and the role I played in her son's life. Let's be clear: this artist wasn't a young child. He was over twenty-one years old and knew everything his mother was doing but never once tried to stop it. There's a big difference between hunger and thirst and at this point I began to see the thirst. To alleviate the anger, stress, disrespect and backdoor business practices I was experiencing, I made an executive decision. Terminate the management agreement, accept my losses and simply walk away.

In this business bad situations sometime lead to a good one with another artist. Case in point is the business relationship I built with a Filipino female vocalist named GG Smith. I met her simply as a featured vocalist and thought nothing more at the time. Once I heard her voice, I told the rapper whose song she was on we definitely have to help her once we get his career off the ground. GG was an extremely laid back, mature, fun, funny and super talented artist. Not only did she have a great voice, but she was trained in ballet, Polynesian, Tahitian, Hip Hop, Belly, Go-Go and Pole dancing. Her love for Pop, Hip Hop, Jazz, R&B, Latin, Dance, Electro, House and World Music made working on her music addictive. I was able to experiment with various writing and music production styles and she effortlessly sang my songs and nailed the arrangements. I brought a variety of producers to the table for her project and GG was up for the challenge. All genres were welcomed as long as she was feeling the track. We got a lot accomplished during our time working together. To showcase the range of her musical taste I came up with a mixtape idea called Jukebox. The concept was based on an actual jukebox, which allowed GG to sing a variety of her favorite songs. The mixtape included four original songs accompanied by music videos (I directed) that can still be seen on the Honest Management Youtube channel to this day.

GG was what I refer to as the perfect artist. What that means is she was very easy to work with, never complained or made a big deal out of anything, always on time, very stylish, ready to work and nonchalantly optimistic. The only problems GG and I had, were with potential investors. Every single investor that came to the table was a man and all of them had ulterior motives, like wanting to date, sleep with or marry GG. Like me, all she cared about was getting the work done. GG is a very attractive girl, but she and I had a big brother/ little sister relationship that was rooted strictly in business. We had many nights of laughter about the guys who would sell themselves as serious music investors but were really trying to use their money as a front to get the booty or a date. GG was never impressed by these guys or their money. Often time she'd tell me she wouldn't mind going on a date, but none were her type.

To make a long story short, she and I never secured the necessary funding to properly release and market her music. Although we released the mixtape, as well as the aforementioned videos, without financial backing, we knew it would be a waste to release the seven song EP we had created. Let's see here: the project with the male pop artist cost me my apartment and finances; I had to release the rapper as soon as momentum was starting to build; my most promising artist was at a standstill because of lies and ulterior motives by horny potential investors; and I was executing all of these projects while in a depressed state, sleeping on a futon at my mom's house. Even at what I felt was my worst, **I REFUSE TO QUIT!**

I decided to take a break from music and focus on myself as well as getting back on my feet. As much as I didn't want to work a nine to five corporate job, I knew it was what I needed to do. I immediately started circulating my resume and registering with staffing agencies. In the midst of this process my man Carl turned me on to a temp agency he would use when work in the film world would slow down and he needed to supplement income between gigs. During this period, I worked as a switchboard operator at one of the world's largest advertising agency and worked another job in accounts payable at a Toyota dealership. My bro Trent also turned me on to a sales position at Terminix. I bounced from job to job until I secured an inside sales position with a company that executed state to state moves for residential and businesses customers. Inside Sales is a job that requires an excessive amount of phone communication which is normal for the life I live. I did pretty well in this position. I stayed at the company for a year and just as I was starting to get my life back in order, I received a call that changed everything. A young professional woman whom I considered a very good friend presented an opportunity that was worth me giving some serious thought. She had recently been offered a high-profile position in the Chicago Public School system and, in her words, she "couldn't do it without me." The position she offered — although in education — was creative. The skills, resources and relationships I have in music and entertainment were exactly what was needed to fulfill the duties.

I didn't want to leave LA but I'm a loyal person and my friend stressed how bad she needed me, so I told her I was in. The position didn't begin until almost a year later, so I had several months to pre-pare. Well, that was instantly cut short when she called two weeks later informing me that so much needed to be done, she needed me now! I tied up a few loose ends and a week later I was on a plane heading home to restart my life in Chicago. Unfortunately, for me, it was the dead of winter. A day, or so, after I landed the city was hit with a snowstorm. As if the weather wasn't cold enough, I had to deal with the even colder new attitude that surprisingly devel-oped within my friend in her new position. I'll spare you the details of what will forever be remembered as one of the worst decisions of my life and simply say six weeks later I was on a plane back to Los Angeles. I didn't feel good vibes about the abruptness of my move, but I downplayed it. I have a saying that goes "first mind God, second mind you" and I say it to people all the time. Well, this was a time I really needed to take heed of my own saying.

Upon my return, I immediately began searching for work. The com-pany I left to relocate to Chicago was willing to rehire me, but I strongly felt the need to keep moving forward. I quickly secured a couple of positions, but neither was favorable. I found myself on the hunt again. Getting my daily workout has been a constant in my life so one particular morning, after leaving the gym and checking my phone, I saw a missed call. Close friends know my day gets started before 6 a.m. PST so it wasn't a surprise to get in the car, grab my phone and see I already had a missed called. I'll answer them but I normally don't concern myself with calling back unfamiliar numbers. I figure if it's important they will call back. But there was a strong energy pushing me to call this particular number back. The surprise came when I heard the voice on the other end of the line. It was my bro Kanye.

He and I hadn't seen or spoken to one another in five years. In typical real friend fashion, we laughed, reminisced and caught up on the latest in each other's lives. The conversation ended with plans of getting together later that afternoon. Every day for six months straight we spent what was equivalent to a full workday together. Out of the blue on one particular day he leaned over and said, "I want you to A&R my new album." Pleasantly pleased, and caught completely off guard, I kindly accepted the offer. This unexpected blessing allowed me to put an end to the "regular job" search headache and get back to where I belong and that's being a creative.

Immediately I was back at my post as an A&R at G.O.O.D Music and the games began. So much has been accomplished over the past few years with my brother that it would take another book for me to share it all. Unfortunately, in some cases for him but fortunately for my history in music and entertainment as well as the legitimacy of this story, most of it has been highlighted in the news and on social media so you have an idea. In closing I'll say this: regardless of how blessed and confident I am, I can honestly admit I have no idea what the future holds for me and the variety of projects I have in the works with Honest Management and my new company G2 Productions, with my partner DJ Self Born. I also don't know how the world will receive the brand new Abstract Mindstate project produced exclusively by my bro Kanye West. I definitely can't predict exactly how many lives this book and the speaking engagements that follow will globally impact once the vibes are out in the universe for like minds and spirits to absorb. But there is one thing I do know: Regardless of hold ups, setbacks, heartbreak, losses, turmoil, unwanted negative energy or depression, I wholeheartedly promise, with every fiber of my being, **I REFUSE TO QUIT!**

1st single off Mixtape

Mixtape Cover

Mixtape Tracklist

3rd single off Mixtape

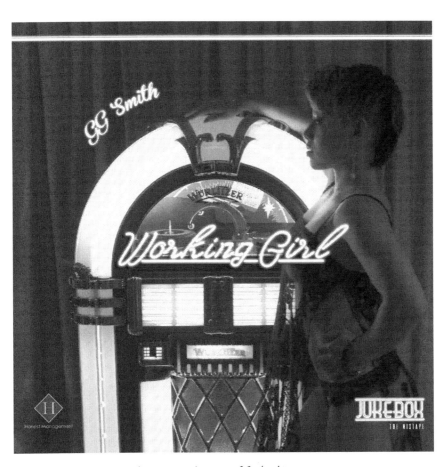

2nd single off Mixtape

Made in the USA
Columbia, SC
09 November 2021